# SITE PLANNING

# SITE PLANNING

James E. Russell

**RESTON PUBLISHING COMPANY, INC.**
A Prentice-Hall Company
Reston, Virginia

**Library of Congress Cataloging in Publication Data**

Russell, James E. (James Emmerson)
  Site planning.

  1. Building sites.   2. Construction industry.
I. Title.
TH153.R87     1984          690          84–4809
ISBN 0–8359–6998–3

© 1984 by Reston Publishing Company, Inc.
*A Prentice-Hall Company*
Reston, Virginia 22090

10  9  8  7  6  5  4  3  2  1

PRINTED IN THE UNITED STATES OF AMERICA

# CONTENTS

## GRADING, EARTHWORK, AND CONSTRUCTION LAYOUT 4

## DRAINAGE 5

## LANDSCAPING AIDS FOR GRADE CHANGES 6

## THE SEWAGE DISPOSAL SYSTEM 7

## PLANTING PLAN, SURFACE PREPARATION, AND EQUIPMENT 8

## LAND CLEARING 9

## GRAPHICS AND MODELS 10

## COST 11

# PREFACE

Years ago, a progressive general manager of the development firm I worked for called a meeting of his subordinates. The manager brought an architect, a landscape architect, a real estate broker, a financial expert, and a general contractor all together under one roof—a relatively new and not especially accepted idea at the time. The architects were in charge of design; the broker and financial expert in charge of marketing; and the general contractor was in charge of production. I was a young project manager assigned to the production department.

After the obligatory humorous anecdotes and an update on the status of various projects and other company business, the general manager got to the real meat of the meeting: a lecture on teamwork. It was a young company that had grown rapidly and the tension between the staffers of the various professions was palpable. The designers thought the market people were crass and tacky; the market people thought the designers were trying to dream up impossible monuments to themselves that could not be sold; both the designers and the market people referred to the production (construction) staffers as "dirty shoes"; and the production staff thought it was the only department that did any "real" work. It was not an environment of mutual respect and cooperation.

The firm was building speculative tract and multifamily housing and all the projects were slow coming off the board, behind schedule in the field, and the completed projects were selling slowly. Even from my lowly station, I could see that something had to be done, but I did not know what. I knew there was no lack of talent in the company and I could not understand the lack of cooperation.

Stepping to the blackboard, the general manager drew three large circles, all the same size, and let each of them overlap. In the center of one he wrote *design*; in another, *marketing*; and in the third circle, *production*. These major disciplines represented by the circles, he said, had to be considered equally important if the company were to succeed. The overlapping areas, he continued, represented what each staff must know about the other. He then outlined a plan, effective immediately, whereby each staff person would be exposed to the work of the other departments.

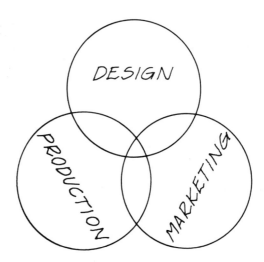

Soon, design people found themselves scheduling concrete pours. Sales people donned work boots and trekked through the mud with the "dirty shoes." Field people changed from jeans to slacks, put on ties, and leased apartments. This game continued for weeks. Everyone complained. And everyone learned. For me, and many others, it was an invaluable experience. When the experiment ended, so did the infighting and bickering and professional snobbery. Whether the new cooperation came from fear of having to return to jobs they hated or whether it came from a new respect of allied professions, it came, nevertheless.

I have long since forgotten the general manager's name. But his example of the three circles stayed with me. Although I made no attempt to formally lay this book out in terms of design, marketing, and production, I *did* write the book from the viewpoint that successful sites represent careful consideration of these three elements.

Thus, I hope that students and professionals in the fields of planning, architecture, landscape architecture, civil engineering, building construction, marketing, and others involved or interested in the broad field of site planning and development, will find the book helpful and interesting.

The techniques and ideas presented in this book come from countless sources and are, of course, heavily influenced by my own experience in over 20 years of building and development. It would, therefore, be difficult or impossible to identify any particular source, other than those mentioned elsewhere. However, I would be remiss if I did not mention the help given me over many months by Gene Barta and Charlie Goforth of Barta & Goforth, Inc., Planning Consultants, Memphis, Tennessee. To Gene and Gary I give much credit for this book but no blame for any errors or shortcomings it may have. Thanks also go to Greg Towles at Caterpillar Tractor Co., Peoria, Illinois, for his help with the land clearing machinery shown in the text.

I hope that those who read the book go on to do something kind for the planet—it needs all the help it can get.

*James E. Russell*

# SITE ANALYSIS 1

We define segments of land with artificial boundaries and call them *sites* for simplicity. Often, victims of this simplicity, we have thought of sites as independent of the area that surrounds them, as simply bases on which to set a building or wall. We know now that these sites are complex, living segments that interrelate with an even more complex whole. But we can never learn enough about these segments or how they relate to the whole to be able to predict what the ultimate impact of our disturbance of them will be. The purpose of site analysis, then—because we have no choice but to disturb the land if we are to live—is to gain enough information about our sites and how they relate to the land that surrounds them at least to plan our activities with intelligence and sensitivity and avoid undesirable effects that we *can* predict. This is the job of the site planner.

When and how the site planner enters the site planning process is unpredictable. The site planner may be presented with a site and be asked to determine how it should be developed; most site planners would welcome such an entry. Or the site planner may be presented with a program and be asked to find an appropriate site on which to implement that program; that too is a welcome entry. Another case is where the site planner is given a survey of a site that has already been acquired, given a program, and asked to fit the program to the site. There are other situations, as numerous as clients. In any case, the site planner's analysis begins with the site itself.

The site planner must gather enough information about the site from which to make decisions that will result in the best relationship of the development whole to the site and to adjacent sites.

Site analysis begins with firsthand, visual inspections of the site. Inspections are needed throughout the site planning process. Ground reconnaissance is necessary, and it may be necessary to fly over the site. A topographical map of the existing site should be taken on the inspection trips to help gain a feel for the site. The site planner should take notes during the inspections, as narrative descriptions and explanations later become part of the formal site analysis; initially the narrative descriptions help the site planner fix the site features in mind. Photos, both eye-level and bird's-eye, are helpful in recalling site features when the planner is back in the office.

Site data gathering begins before design starts and continues all the way through to the completed project. But data gathering is expensive and time-consuming. Therefore, it must be pursued with the same efficiency and planning as the design process itself. A field inspection of the site, noting its topography, gives the site planner an indication of drainage; outcroppings give an idea of what the subsurface may be like; site vegetation is an indicator of soil type. Test pits, a minor expense, give ground water and soil information. In addition to such simple tests and observations, a site planner may call on other inexpensive sources of information: the experience of local builders; government agencies such as the Department of Housing and Urban Development, the U.S. Army Corps of Engineers, and agricultural extension centers; local planing commissions; and geological maps.

With experience a site planner can glean much preliminary information from the site in a short time and at little cost, determining a broad range of activities that the site could appropriately accommodate. Some of the information is studied in a negative light: Poor soil (observed in the test pits), for example, often makes some types of developments economically impossible; too many steep slopes also eliminate or restrict many types of development. If too many negative factors are discovered initially, data gathering on that site will of course cease at once. Thus, the site planner gathers data as needed but does not "gamble" money and time by betting too far ahead on what data *may* be needed.

A site planner initially studies such site factors as the following:

- Site topography and drainage
- All natural elements such as wooded areas, rock outcroppings, streams, and lakes
- All human-made objects such as buildings, drives, masonry walls, wells, and ponds
- Location of water, sewer, gas, electric, and telephone lines
- Solar orientation
- Climate and microclimates

If the site planner determines that development is feasible, data gathering continues, expands, and becomes more precise as design proceeds. Such data bring design alternatives and problems to light; as design develops, more detailed data are required. Thus, data, or knowledge of the site, influence design, and the design process brings about the need for still more data. As the process continues, the site planner records the key information graphically, numerically, and narratively.

As site analysis continues, the factors that influence the site are analyzed more intensely. These factors are both general and specific (such as climate and microclimate) and physical and intangible (such as drainage conditions and site image); they include studies of the anticipated eventual users of the site.

Where are the city business districts? government agencies? industrial and manufacturing areas? warehouse and distribution centers? any other significant employment centers? Where are the service facilities, such as hospitals and shopping? other service facilities? (See Figure 1–1.)

| Local Services which require consideration in the design of a site include | Size | Shape | Color | Scale | Location | Utility Connection | Ground Area | Paving | Appearance | Visibility | Accessibility | Graphics | Structure | Screen | Cost | Local Regulations | Material Selection |
|---|---|---|---|---|---|---|---|---|---|---|---|---|---|---|---|---|---|
| Street Construction & Maintenance | X | | | X | X | | X | X | X | X | X | | | | X | X | X |
| Sidewalk Construction & Maintenance | X | | | X | X | | X | X | X | X | X | | | | X | X | X |
| Street Planting & Maintenance | X | X | X | X | X | | X | | X | X | X | | | X | X | X | X |
| Street Lighting Maintenance | | | | | X | | | | | X | X | | | | X | X | |
| Trash, Garbage, & Ash Removal | | | | | X | | | X | | X | | | | X | X | X | |
| Snow Removal | | | | | X | | X | | | X | | | | | X | X | |
| Fire Protection | | | | | X | X | | | | X | X | | | | X | X | |
| Police Protection | | | | | X | | | | | X | X | | | | X | X | |
| Ambulance Service | | | | | X | | | | | X | | | | | X | X | |
| Water Service | X | | | | X | X | | | | X | X | | | | X | X | X |
| Gas Service | X | | | | X | X | | | | X | X | | | | X | X | X |
| Electric Service | X | | | | X | X | | | X | X | X | | | X | X | X | X |
| Sewer Service | X | | | | X | X | | | | X | X | | X | | X | X | X |
| Mail Delivery | | | | | X | | | | | X | | | | | | X | |
| Household Deliveries | | | | | X | | | X | | X | X | | | | X | | |
| Local Park, Playground, & Community Space & Maintenance | X | X | X | X | X | X | X | X | X | X | X | X | X | | X | X | X |
| Public Transportation Stops & Shelters | X | X | X | X | X | X | X | X | X | X | X | X | X | | X | X | X |
| Community Social & Family Services | X | X | X | X | X | X | X | | | X | X | X | | X | X | X | X |
| Street Furniture, Installation & Maintenance | | | | | | | | | | | | | | | | | |
| Traffic Signals | X | X | X | X | X | X | | | X | X | X | X | | | X | X | X |
| Police Call Boxes | X | X | X | X | X | X | | | X | X | X | X | | | X | X | X |
| Fire Alarm Boxes | X | X | X | X | X | X | | | X | X | X | X | | | X | X | X |
| Seating | X | X | X | X | X | | | | X | X | X | | | | X | X | X |
| Planting Tubs & Boxes | X | X | X | X | X | | | | X | | | | | | X | X | X |
| Hydrants | X | X | X | X | X | X | | | X | X | X | | | | X | X | X |
| Trash Receptacles | X | X | X | X | X | | | | X | X | X | | | X | X | X | X |
| Lighting Posts & Fixtures | X | X | X | X | X | X | | | X | X | | | | | X | X | X |
| Signs | X | X | X | X | X | X | | | X | X | | X | | | X | X | X |
| Railings, Parapets & Safety Barriers | X | X | X | X | X | | | | X | X | | | X | | X | X | X |
| Pedestrian Direction Facilities | X | X | X | X | X | X | | | X | X | X | X | | | X | X | X |
| Mail Collection Boxes | X | X | X | X | X | | | | X | X | X | X | | | X | X | X |

FIGURE 1–1. Design considerations for services
*Source:* FHA

Where are the major existing and proposed transportation facilities that link the site with the surrounding area? Is public transportation available? What are the vehicular speed limits for state highways, interstate highways, major roads, streets?

Where are the recreational facilities within range of the site? the convention centers, theaters, sports stadiums, parks, lakes, hunting areas, and other recreational areas?

Who will live on the site? What are their lives like? Where do they work? How old are they? How many children do they have? How much money do they make?

Is population in the general area increasing or diminishing? What are the population movement patterns? Why are people moving away or coming in?

Are there any strong feelings about the site in the surrounding community? What are these feelings? How did they come to be?

What are the present land usage and zoning around the site? What kind of street patterns exists near the site? Is other development planned that may influence the site? Are any requests for zoning changes being made?

What constraints and opportunities are offered by the natural physical qualities, climate, and form of the site? by existing buildings and other human-made objects?

What are the existing drainage patterns (surface and subsurface)? Where are the existing sanitary and storm drains? existing utilities?

These questions, and similar ones, must be answered in the site planner's quest for a harmonious land use plan. The analysis of all sites has certain factors and procedures in common. And yet each site planner weighs the factors a little differently and proceeds a little differently; with experience the site planner develops a particular methodology that is personally comfortable and that works. At this point let us consider a particular land use study in detail, a land use study performed by a practicing firm of planning consultants.

---

## Case Study: The Bob White Farm Community

---

(Courtesy of Barta & Goforth, Inc., Planning Consultants, Memphis, Tennessee)

## INTRODUCTION—SECTION 1

This report is a synthesis of interrelated studies, all directed toward the development of a land use concept for a 1,400-acre site located in DeSoto County, Mississippi. To ensure that a maximum of variables affecting the site were taken in consideration in planning land use for the site, the study area was outlined to include some 45 square miles. This area is referred to in this report as Southwood Village, within which the 1,400-acre site, Bob White Farm, is located. Of further significance is the fact that the Whitehaven Country Club will be relocated within Bob White Farm.

The Southwood Village area is relatively undeveloped. Specifically, development has not yet reached that point where the vicinity can be referred to as a community in the same sense as Whitehaven and Southaven, which have their geographic identities already fixed in the public mind. With this in consideration, a land use plan for the area was approached in a manner that would give this segment of DeSoto County an identity and set a future image appropriate for the quality development of a partially self-contained community with a population of 250,000 to 300,000— Southwood Village—which in turn would have at its nucleus the Bob White Farm community. Although a land use plan concept has been developed for the 1,400-acre Bob White Farm community, initial development and detailed plans involve only 756 acres, which will contain an eventual population of 8,200 persons.

The relocation of the Whitehaven Country Club within the Bob White Farm site has set the tone for development. It has been the major contributing factor to the land use concept and around which this report revolves and relates. Essentially it will provide an initial market by drawing its members from Memphis into the Southwood Village area.

Out-migration of families from urban centers to nearby rural towns has been projected nationwide and specifically for the areas surrounding the Memphis community. Data for the state of Tennessee denote evidence of this trend. This projection and data viewed in light of national growth policy advocating the establishment of satellite communities to relieve urban centers and achieve a balance between urban and rural growth patterns suggest that the development concept for Southwood Village–Bob White Farm community is timely.

## CONSIDERATIONS INFLUENCING APPROPRIATE USE— SECTION 2

The highest, best, and most logical use of the Bob White Farm property is influenced by several factors, ranging from the physical attributes of the property to the characteristics of potential inhabitants of the community. This phase of the overall general planning study was designed to identify and analyze both the general and specific attributes of these factors affecting land use for incorporation into a general plan.

Exhibits A through D (Figures 1–2 through 1–5) graphically represent information obtained in this phase of study. From these exhibits a

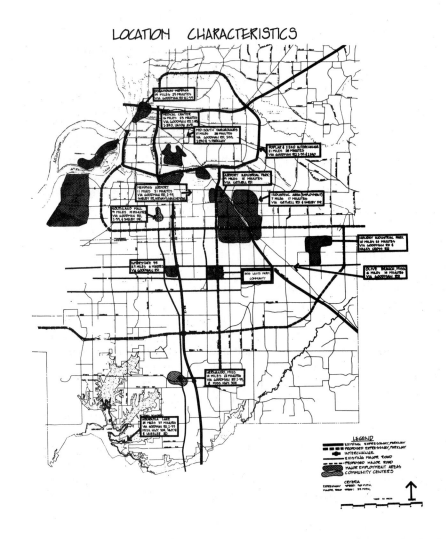

## BOB WHITE FARM COMMUNITY
### DESOTO COUNTY, MISSISSIPPI
## A PLANNED UNIT DEVELOPMENT
#### DEVELOPER
## WILKINSON & SNOWDEN CONSTRUCTION CO.

FIGURE 1–2. Exhibit A. The vicinity map locates the site within the surrounding community. The location characteristics map identifies factors that influence the proposed site use; among these factors are transportation facilities, employment centers, and recreational facilities.

# VICINITY MAP

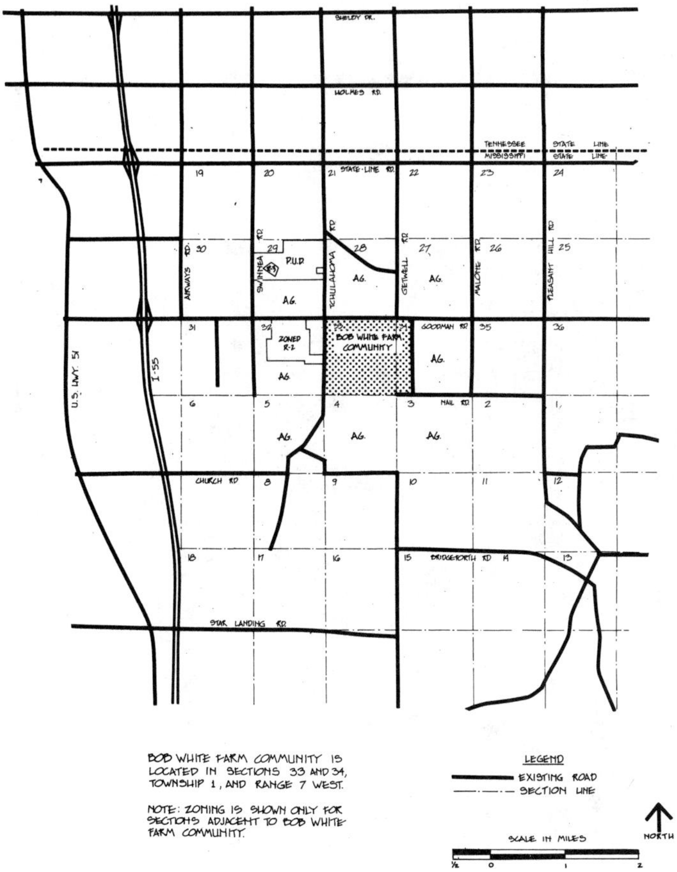
SHELBY DR.
HOLMES RD.
TENNESSEE STATE LINE
MISSISSIPPI STATE LINE
STATE LINE RD.
AIRWAYS RD.
SWINNEA RD.
TCHULAHOMA RD.
GETWELL RD.
MALONE RD.
PLEASANT HILL RD.
P.U.D.
AG.
ZONED R-2
BOB WHITE FARM COMMUNITY
GOODMAN RD.
MAIL RD.
CHURCH RD.
BRIDGEFORTH RD.
STAR LANDING RD.
U.S. HWY. 51
I-55
BOB WHITE FARM COMMUNITY IS LOCATED IN SECTIONS 33 AND 34, TOWNSHIP 1, AND RANGE 7 WEST.
NOTE: ZONING IS SHOWN ONLY FOR SECTIONS ADJACENT TO BOB WHITE FARM COMMUNITY.
LEGEND
EXISTING ROAD
SECTION LINE
SCALE IN MILES
½ 0 1 2
NORTH

## SHEET INDEX

| SHEET NO. | SHEET TITLE |
|---|---|
| 1 | TITLE SHEET |
| 2 | PRELIMINARY SITE PLAN |
| 3 | PHASING PLAN |

W. H. Porter - Consulting Engineer

John W. Frazier - Golf Course Architect

1–2B.

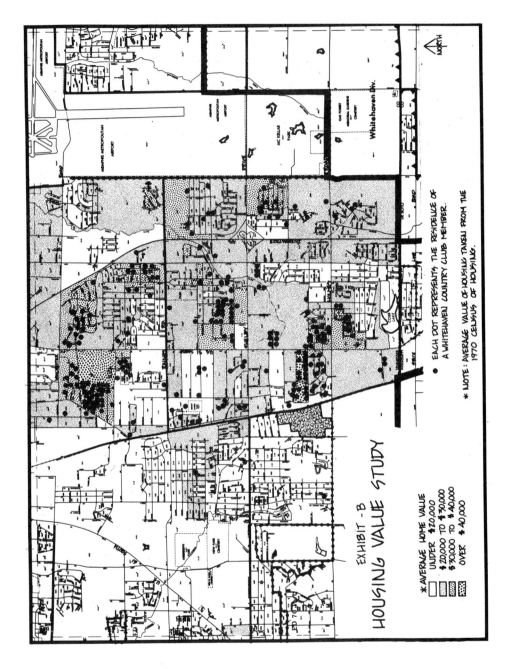

FIGURE 1–3. Exhibit B. A housing value study was done for a portion of the project's market. Using such data, the developer can decide on the advertising and sales approach.

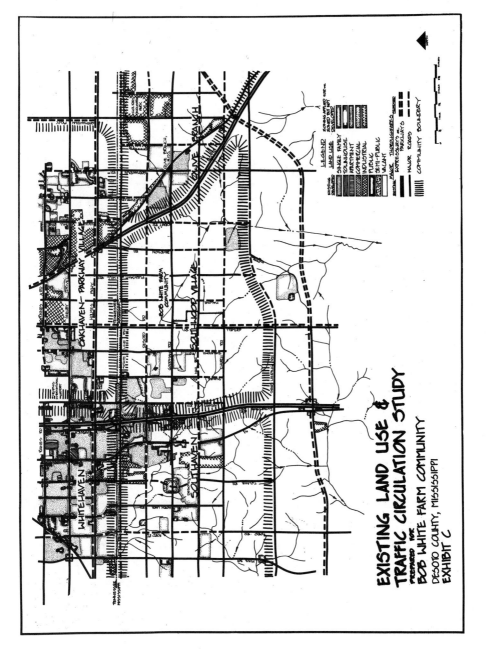

FIGURE 1–4. Exhibit C. This exhibit shows the proposed community boundaries, existing land use and zoning of the proposed community and of the surrounding area, and shows the existing traffic circulation system.

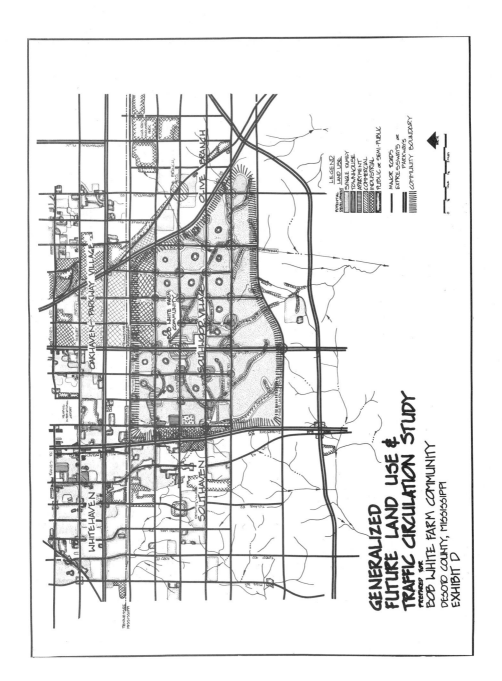

FIGURE 1–5. Exhibit D. Existing and future land use was studied and incorporated into a plan both for the proposed project and for the surrounding area.

perspective was gained to provide a sound base for making decisions regarding land use of the Bob White Farm property. The following narrative describes the purpose of the studies and the conclusions drawn from them.

## Site Location Characteristics

The successful development of the site predicated a consideration of its geographic relationship to Memphis, Shelby County, DeSoto County, and other major activity centers in addition to adequacy of transportation facilities. The marketing potential of the site is partially qualified by the proximity to areas of employment and recreation with ease of access. Accordingly the purpose of Exhibit A is to demonstrate attractiveness of this area relative to distance, driving time, and transportation facilities to various points within Memphis and DeSoto County.

The following facts are considered pertinent because residents of the Bob White Farm site and the Southwood Village area in all probability will work within or near one of these major employment areas. It is certain that residents will depend on Memphis to provide some types of services, for example, hospital facilities. Relative distances to these areas are necessary information for marketing.

### A. Major Employment Areas

The distance and driving time from the Bob White Farm area to the Memphis central business district is comparable to that of several residential areas within Memphis developed in the 1960s (for example, Parkway Village and Fox Meadows), the central business district being the location of state, county, and city office buildings and other major employment.

The Airport Industrial Park is a 12-minute, 5-mile drive from the Bob White Farm site. Expansion proposals for this park reflect its continued importance as a major employment area for the future. Also located in this general vicinity are the Schlitz Brewing Company, Ralston-Purina, American Can, and the RCA manufacturing facility now owned by General Motors.

Proximity to the Memphis International Airport offers the benefit of convenient access to air transportation facilities and the growing employment facilities surrounding the airport, which is 14 miles, 21 minutes from the site. Indicative of the multiple employment facilities in this area are the Nonconnah Corporate Center, Executive Park, and the Internal Revenue Service–Memphis Service Center.

Holiday Industrial Park is a 10-mile, 24-minute drive from the site. Located just across the Mississippi-Tennessee state line in Mississippi, it fronts on Hacks Cross Road and is 2.25 miles north of Highway 78 Relocated. Planned development is expected to encompass some 3,000 acres at completion.

The tax advantages and incentives offered in Mississippi to industry and manufacturing are drawing business to relocate in the state at an impressive rate. Generally the state exempts manufacturers moving to Mississippi from most taxes on business property including land, equipment, vehicles, and inventories for 10 years.

Several large-scale industrial warehouse and distribution centers are under development in close proximity to Bob White Farm. These centers are locating along the major road corridors, which run from Memphis-Shelby County areas across the Mississippi-Tennessee state line into Mississippi-DeSoto County. Most current of this type development is the Rocky Creek Industrial Park, which will cover 257 acres at the intersection of Goodman Road and Interstate 55.

This trend toward industrial and commercial expansion and development is projected to continue. With this growth a demand for residential development to serve these businesses is forecast.

As noted, the ease of reaching major areas of activity is a major marketing influence. A 6-minute, 2.5-mile drive from the Bob White Farm site brings residents to Interstate 55, which provides access to the interstate system around and throughout Shelby and DeSoto counties. The Poplar and I-240 interchange is easily reached. The Memphis Area Medical Center, Southland Mall, and other facilities are reached with ease.

### B. Major Transportation Facilities

Also indicated on Exhibit A are those routes used in computing the time-distance study from the Bob White Farm site to various destination points. Speed limits used in calculating the data were 50 mph on expressways and 25 mph on other major roads. The existing major transportation facilities serving the Bob White Farm site and Southwood Village are Interstate 55 and U.S. Highway 78 Relocated.

### C. Major Recreational Facilities

Memphis offers numerous recreational facilities that can be utilized by residents of Bob White Farm and Southwood Village. In particular are the recently dedicated Everett R. Cook Convention Center in the Memphis central business district, which will offer a regional facility for the arts, in addition to conventions; the new Memphis Little Theatre, which will be completed in January 1975; the Coliseum; and the Memphis Memorial Stadium.

Arkabutla Lake is a 24-mile, 37-minute drive from the site. The lake provides facilities for water sports, fishing, camping, and hunting.

# DEMOGRAPHIC TRENDS AND CHARACTERISTICS OF FUTURE AREA RESIDENTS

A series of special studies was undertaken to determine the relationship of site to population and to project population growth patterns for the area. In addition it was undertaken to project some characteristics of residents who might be attracted to the site. Analysis of the site's location in relation to existing population trends of the area reflected the following:

1. Distribution of population within the 45-square-mile area of study remains sparse. The 1970 census population count for this area was approximately 500.

2. Most of the growth and development activity relative to population in DeSoto County has taken place in and around the Southaven community. Southaven's population has increased from less than 2,500 in 1960 to 9,004 as of 1970.

3. Recent activity in residential construction has occurred in the extreme northwest quadrant of the study area, which is adjacent to the Southaven community.

Two demographic factors suggest support for development of Southwood Village–Bob White Farm as a satellite of the Memphis area (quasi-independent of Memphis). First to be considered is the report issued by the U.S. Bureau of the Census. The preliminary population statistics for 1973 indicate that the rural areas surrounding Memphis are drawing residents from the urban and suburban areas of Memphis.

This trend follows identical national residential mobility patterns. Second, and more significant, is the relocation of the Whitehaven Country Club to the Bob White Farm site. The approximately 300 families who hold membership in the existing club were seen as a highly probable market for a residential development built in coordination with the new club.

It was a known fact that the Whitehaven Country Club intended to change locations. To help determine the housing relationship between the members and the existing country club, the locations of members' homes were plotted on a base map of the city of Memphis (Exhibit B, Figure 1–3). After study it was discovered that

1. 84 percent of the membership lived in close proximity to one another—from within a few blocks to a maximum of 2.5 miles.

2. The homes were also within the same relative distance from the Whitehaven Country Club.

3. The homes of these 84 percent were clustered within neighborhoods where the value of the homes exceeded $40,000 (based on statistics from the U.S. Bureau of the Census Report*).

The members jointly agreed to relocate their country club, which suggested that they might be motivated to move to a new community close to or developed in coordination with the new club facilities.

To substantiate the level of effective buying power of the membership, a survey was made to determine occupation and incomes. As Table 1–1 shows, the greatest percentage of members hold management positions, own businesses, or are self-employed professionals such as physicians and attorneys.

From this survey, incomes of members are estimated to be $30,000 per year and up (based on Bureau of Labor statistics, 1972). It was difficult, of course, due to the nature of income data, to determine what incomes

Table 1–1

| OCCUPATION* | NUMBER OF MEMBERS |
|---|---|
| Farm | 2 |
| Management<br>Board members<br>Executives and officers<br>General managers | 107 |
| Miscellaneous | 11 |
| Owners of Businesses | 57 |
| Professionals (Self-Employed)<br>Architects<br>Attorneys<br>Engineers<br>Physicians | 27 |
| Sales | 23 |
| Retired or Widow<br>(No occupation given) | 16 |
| Information Not Available<br>(Majority of these members are out-of-town<br>residents) | 31 |
| | $N = \overline{274}$ |

*Occupation of head of household only

* These figures were roughly current with the date the land study was completed in August 1974. Housing costs have of course continued to rise.

might be for certain self-employed individuals. However, considering the size of the companies owned (personnel employed, and estimated dollar volume per year for the type of business), the estimate of income is conservative.

In summary, the families holding membership in the Whitehaven Country Club are economically capable of a move to a new community. And because of the characteristics of their existing community and its ties to the existing country club, we feel that a new community—Bob White Farm—developed in coordination with their new club facilities would be attractive to them.

# GENERAL CHARACTERISTICS OF AREA SURROUNDING SITE

## Boundaries

To arrive at a land use concept for Bob White Farm, it was necessary to consider the relationship of Bob White Farm to other developing areas within north DeSoto County and Shelby County. It was hoped that the general community boundaries selected would identify the site as distinct with possibly an independent commercial trade area.

Exhibit C (Figure 1–4) illustrates the community boundaries, which were set in the following manner: The boundary to the north of the Bob White Farm tract was extended to the Mississippi-Tennessee state line; the southern boundary was set as Star Landing Road, at which point a natural boundary was provided because the road runs generally along a ridgeline; as the east boundary, Highway 78 Relocated was used; and, to the west, Interstate 55.

In setting these boundary delineations some 45 square miles were encompassed. A projected population estimate for this area calculated at 10 persons per acre projects a population of 250,000 to 300,000 persons. The projected population of the 756-acre Bob White Farm community is 8,200. These projections, in addition to the rate of growth in surrounding areas, support the forecast for a commercial trade area in Southwood Village, supported primarily by Southwood Village, with the surrounding communities of Southaven, Olive Branch, and Whitehaven adding support. With development of such a trade area, facilities that are not now available would be provided for Mississippi and DeSoto County.

## Transportation

Existing streets as shown on Exhibit C follow a grid pattern system, which has been established under the Memphis Urban Area Transportation Study (MUATS) for this particular area within north DeSoto County.

Two major roads exist bordering Southwood Village. On the west is Interstate 55, which runs north-south and will be the main high-speed, high-capacity thoroughfare serving the Southwood area; to the east is U.S. Highway 78 Relocated, the major arterial highway, which will be another long-distance traffic way serving the area within and through the county and which is undergoing construction to increase capacity from two to four lanes. The major east-west thoroughfare providing access into and through the site is Goodman Road with a proposed 106-foot right-of-way according to the MUATS plan.

## Generalized Existing Land Uses and Zoning

A study of the existing land uses and zoned but undeveloped land within the 45-square-mile study area revealed that

1. The major land use is predominantly agricultural;
2. Single-family residential covers the next greatest area of land use, but this constitutes less than 6 percent of the total study area;
3. Other uses are insignificant in that they constitute less than 1 percent of land use and are so located that they do not pose any problems for devising a land use plan for the site; and
4. Information provided by the DeSoto County Planning Commission indicates zoning applied for and approved but not developed is for primarily residential land uses.

# GENERALIZED FUTURE LAND USE

The purpose of Exhibit D (Figure 1–5) was to incorporate existing land uses and estimated population density into a future land use concept for Southwood Village and from this guide to set the uses appropriate for the planning of future specific land uses in the Bob White Farm tract.

## Population

A population of 250,000 to 300,000 was projected for the 45-square-mile area in determining land uses and developing the site concept.

## Land Uses

It was determined that a regional shopping center at the geographic center of Southwood Village would serve the growing population in DeSoto County, in addition to providing a focal identity point. The regional center uses approximately 188 acres, based on allowance of 0.67 acres per 1,000 population.

Neighborhood shopping centers are planned for alternate intersections of major roads, which are approximately 1 mile apart. These centers are to serve as supportive, secondary shopping centers. Multifamily residential uses, such as apartments or townhouses, are planned at each of the major road intersections. Thus, the regional center and the subcenters alternating with residential multifamily development at alternating intersections will be high-density areas. The residential development will offer a variety of housing types and a range of prices.

Future industrial development has been planned along Interstate 55 in keeping with the existing, predominantly industrial character of this area.

## Open Spaces

Park and school sites located in relation to the neighborhood units help meet open space requirements.

From this phase of the study it was determined that Southwood Village could develop as an identifiable community containing a distinct commercial trade area. The suggested location of the major regional shopping center was at the geographic center of the 45-square-mile area, within the Bob White Farm tract, as shown on Exhibit D.

# FACTORS INFLUENCING DEVELOPMENT—SECTION 3

This phase of the study determined the factors that directly influenced development of the site and had to be considered in the development of a land use plan for Bob White Farm. The planned and existing uses of surrounding land and the physical characteristics of the site land were taken into consideration in the study. Exhibit E (Figure 1–6) illustrates these factors.

## Drainage

The area in which the Bob White Farm tract is located has two drainage districts formed by a predominant ridgeline running from north to south in the eastern segment of the property. The west two-thirds of the tract drains from this ridgeline toward Horn Lake Creek. The area to the east of this ridgeline drains toward the Cold Water River, which feeds the Sardis Reservoir.

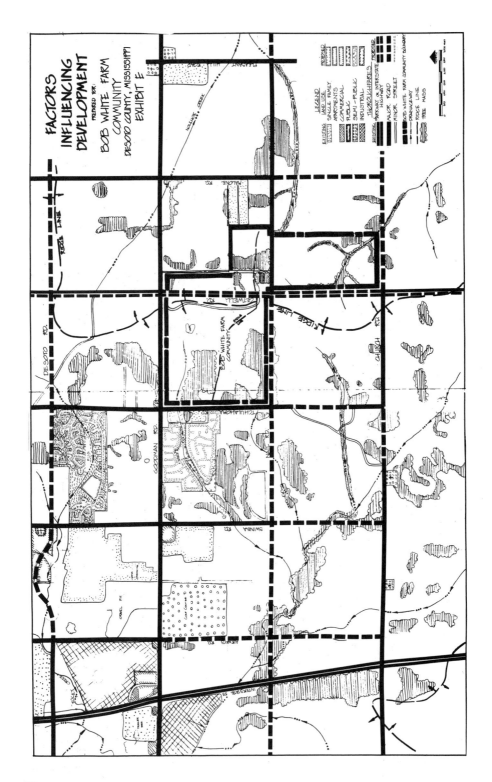

FIGURE 1–6. Exhibit E. Existing uses of surrounding land and the physical characteristics of the land directly influence the planning of projects.

## Existing and Proposed Land Uses

As shown on Exhibit E the predominant existing and planned land uses (other than agricultural) influencing the development plan for Bob White Farm are residential. There is a limited, existing residential area immediately adjacent to the site on the east and to the northwest. At this northwest site an extensive residential development is proposed. Further northwest a planned unit development (PUD) is proposed, and another residential development is under construction.

## GENERAL PLAN PROPOSALS—SECTION 4

Studies heretofore have been designed to establish a framework of possible general patterns of future development in the area surrounding the Bob White Farm site, taking into consideration all major variables that would influence development. Within this framework, and based on information obtained from these studies, basic planning decisions with respect to appropriate use and development were made for the Bob White Farm tract; these decisions included not only appropriate land uses but also use relationships. Exhibit F (Figure 1–7) illustrates the arrangements and types of land uses, utilizing Exhibit D as a guide.

## The General Plan Concept

Three criteria were set as guides to developing a functional land use plan:

1. To incorporate all known factors influencing development into the highest, best, and most logical land use plan for the property.
2. To create a land use plan that would protect the integrity of the community and the Whitehaven Country Club for the future.
3. To provide for diversified land uses, avoiding the community's dependence on too limited uses.

The Whitehaven Country Club provided the major factor for developing the concept. An open-space approach to development was chosen as the basic concept for the general plan of Bob White Farm community, the club's golf course lending itself to this approach and providing the focal point for development.

The neighborhood units were defined by the system of major traffic arteries; these arteries were generally spaced at 1-mile intervals. From these intervals a system of traffic service has been established, using a collector street system generally spaced at half mile intervals.

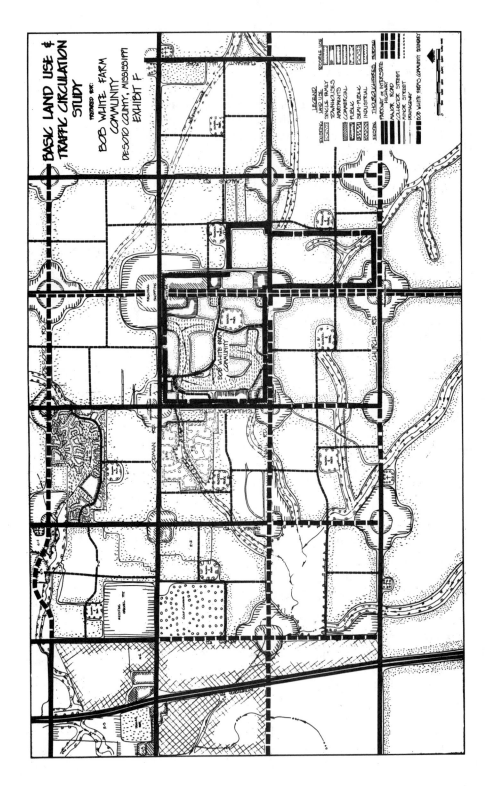

FIGURE 1–7. Exhibit F. This exhibit illustrates the arrangements and type of land uses, utilizing Exhibit D as a guide.

The pattern established for residential neighborhood units along the golf course fairways and relative to the street system has been influential in arriving at other specific land use proposals for the site. However, the most significant consideration at the concept level is the provision for utilizing divergent types of uses in the site while striving to maintain the quality atmosphere of the open space concept. This was achieved in a number of ways.

The primary method used to achieve and thus maintain this quality was careful location of land uses according to the typical density factors associated with each individual use. The locations for high-intensity use areas were placed around the perimeter of development, adjacent to major thoroughfares; intensity of use decreased moving from the perimeter toward the center of the development, which is the country club and golf course. The concept also provides for appropriate locations of schools and parks; these locations are at the intersections of proposed collector streets near the center of the neighborhoods.

Comparison studies were undertaken to decide placement of the golf course and residential development, relative to the topography of the site. Two alternatives were available, determined by the rise and fall topographic character of the site: location of the residential to be placed on ridgelines with the golf course placed in the somewhat lower areas formed by the fall and rise between ridges or the reverse. The former alternative proved more advantageous from an economic and aesthetic standpoint.

## PHYSIOGRAPHIC CHARACTERISTICS OF SITE—SECTION 5

The site possesses physical characteristics that can contribute to economic development as well as enhance the tract for community uses. These characteristics, illustrated in Exhibit G (Figure 1–8), were analyzed as a prime consideration in developing the general land use and the development concept.

In general the site is situated atop one of the major drainage divides of the region and is not subject to flooding. Lowlands along the main drainage courses are generally well drained and, being gently sloped, will support good turf and be well suited to golf course use.

The terrain of the site exhibits significantly different characteristics in its eastern and western portions. The eastern one-third to one-half of the site is characterized by a broad, flat ridgetop running north and south without a strongly defined drainage pattern; in this location the tract lends itself well to almost any use with a minimum of site work. The western portion of the site on the other hand is characterized by narrower ridgetops, gently to strongly sloping hillsides, and a well-defined drainage pattern.

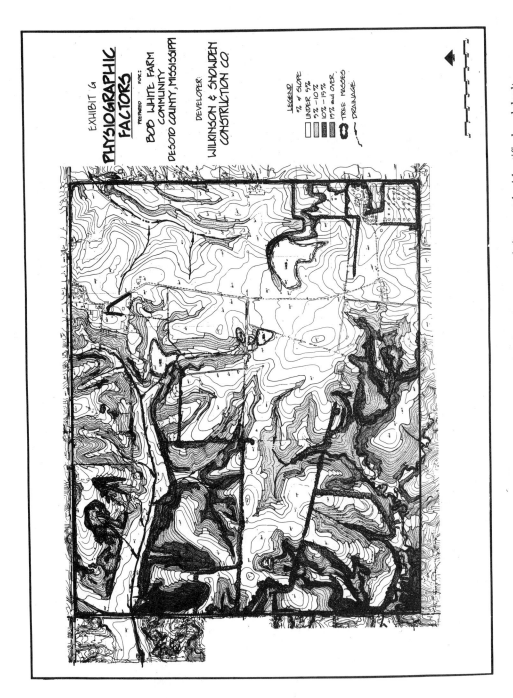

FIGURE 1–8. Exhibit G. The physical characteristics of a proposed site must be identified and dealt with such that the project can be built economically and still function well and be aesthetically pleasing.

The western portion offers an excellent opportunity for location of the golf course, large lot development, and more innovative planning approaches to residential uses.

For the vast majority of the site the slopes are 10 percent or less with only a few scattered areas of terrain having grades over 15 percent. The overall slope of the site to the west offers the opportunity for natural sewer flow in the direction of anticipated outfall lines. Approximately 25 percent of the site is wooded. Much of the land is either cultivated or being used as pasture.

In summary, the physiographic characteristics of the site are a definite advantage to developing with variety and economy.

## PRELIMINARY LAND USE PROPOSALS—SECTION 6

Using the basic land use and traffic circulation study (Exhibit F, Figure 1–7) as a guide, the generalized land use study (Exhibit H, Figure 1–9) was developed. Its purpose is to indicate the specific land uses for the initial development of approximately 756 acres of the Bob White Farm property.

In planning the Bob White Farm community, coordination of the proposed Whitehaven Country Club facilities and golf course with the surrounding community was a significant factor in the design process. The location of the golf course was based on the physiographic studies of the site, placing in the drainage ways of the tract. Exhibit H illustrates the proposed location of the club house and golf course relative to the topography. Also shown are the proposed uses for the entire community surrounding these facilities, planned in coordination with the facilities.

As stated in the general plan concept, the overall objective for planning is to ensure that each individual land use would contribute to the total environmental quality of the development. In keeping with this aim, the use of open space and greenways throughout the site was a necessary feature. Also, providing maximum visibility of the golf course contributes to a feeling of spaciousness.

Further, a feature referred to as a *greenway vista* was employed. The vista is a parcel of land left free of structures between the golf course fairway and the street. These vistas were placed along the minor and collector street systems at intermittent points, providing a view of the golf course fairway for through traffic and for the neighborhoods in which they were placed. The effect achieved by creating this visual pathway to the golf course fairway is best exemplified by comparison of the golf course fairway to a lake. As a lake creates a certain atmosphere, so will the fairway and the view that it provides, thus enhancing market attractiveness of the

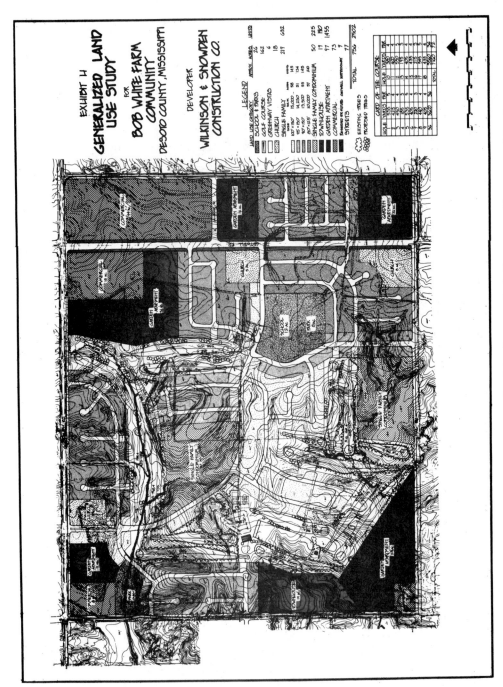

FIGURE 1–9. Exhibit H. The generalized land use study indicates specific proposed land uses, including a street plan.

26

development and therefore property values, adding assurance to the development's success and long-term quality. Also, the golf course fairway has been planned to have limited frontage on two of the major roads bordering the Bob White Farm tract.

An additional contribution to open space in the development has been made by a 6-acre park located contiguously with a greenbelt planned for the Tanglewood subdivision adjacent to the Bob White Farm tract.

A school with an adjacent park area has been located in the southeast quadrant of the site. The school is at the intersection of two collector streets, which will allow a smooth flow of vehicular traffic, safe for the high volume of pedestrian traffic.

Three church sites have been dispersed in the development: one site at the intersection of two major roads; two sites at the intersections of major and collector streets.

High-intensity commercial land use is located at the perimeter of the Bob White Farm development. The major commercial development within the site is located at the intersection of two major roads, Goodman and Getwell, at the center of the Southwood Village area; this acreage is a segment of the total proposed for the regional shopping center and the only portion of it that will be located within the Bob White Farm site. Multifamily garden-type apartments are located adjacent to the high-intensity commercial area, which is appropriate, because garden apartments have the highest use intensity of all residential uses in the Bob White Farm community. Thus, the concept of diminishing density from the perimeter of the site toward the quiet center, and the golf course, is maintained.

Two other commercial sites are proposed at the intersections of major roads; these sites provide for less intense commercial uses such as convenience neighborhood shopping and office centers.

Residential uses throughout the site include townhouse, single-family condominium, and single-family detached dwellings, with the less intense uses proposed along the golf course fairways.

The specific acreages allotted for the preceding land uses within the Bob White Farm development are listed on Exhibit H.

This report and preliminary land use proposals have been prepared within the provisions of the comprehensive plan for DeSoto County. In addition, the planning process has included contact and consultation with the DeSoto County Planning Commission and the representatives of the Whitehaven Country Club.

# APPENDIX

The implementation of the preliminary site plan with respect to zoning is to be accomplished under the provisions of the planned unit development district as outlined in article V, paragraph 12, of the zoning regulations for DeSoto County, Mississippi. This approach has been taken in view of the size of the development and the preference of the DeSoto County Planning Commission.

The title sheet (Exhibit A, Figure 1–2), the preliminary site plan (Figure 1–10), the phasing plan (Figure 1–11), and the text of this Appendix provide the basics for review and approval of the petition for PUD.

As provided under the DeSoto County zoning regulations, certain requirements are spelled out in paragraph 12 of the planned unit development district that are to be included in any petition for rezoning to the PUD district. The purpose of these requirements is to provide the planning commission adequate information and materials on which to base evaluation and approval of planned unit developments. As they pertain to the three documents included in this Appendix, the information requested in these guidelines is discussed next.

### 1. Proposed Land Uses and Population Densities

The preliminary site plan submitted with the rezoning application specifies the proposed land use and density to be permitted within each portion of the Bob White Farm. The land uses proposed are based on previous studies outlined in detail within this report, which substantiate their arrangements and relationships to each other. By the plan, permitted development densities are established for the entire Bob White Farm and for individual use areas in terms of maximum numbers of dwelling units permitted. Proposed densities for all types of uses proposed under the preliminary site plan are generally typical of accepted standards for development of the respective uses and reflect the application of sound planning principles and considerations of development practices and practicalities. On an overall basis the proposed gross residential density of the development would be approximately 3.3 dwelling units per acre, representing 2,502 dwelling units within the 756-acre Bob White Farm community.

In regard to density it is significant that the proposed plan of development provides for the permanent reservation of some 162 acres or 21 percent of the total site for central open space (golf course) use. In addition the plan commits 26 acres to school and park use, 18 acres for church sites, and 6 acres for greenway vistas, which are to provide views of the golf course for through traffic and for neighborhoods in which they are placed. Substantial as it is, this acreage to be devoted to open and semi-open space types of uses will be complemented by open space to be provided within individual use areas of development—open space and recreation areas associated with individual townhouse, single-family condominium, and apartment developments.

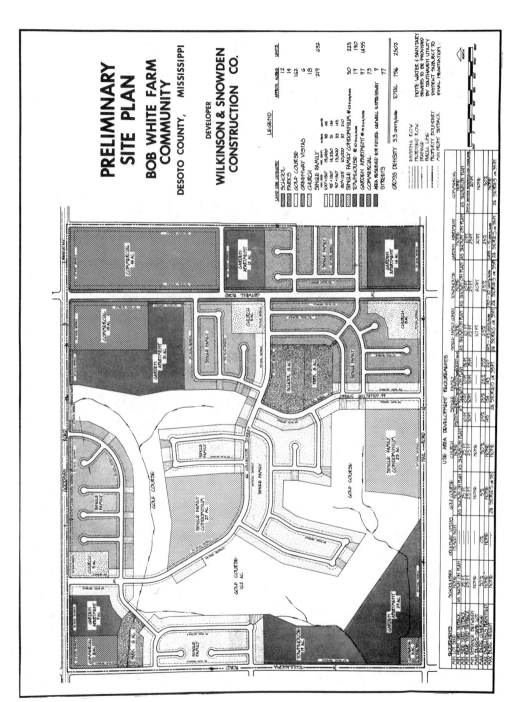

FIGURE 1–10. This preliminary site plan was prepared for a required exhibit to the local authorities.

29

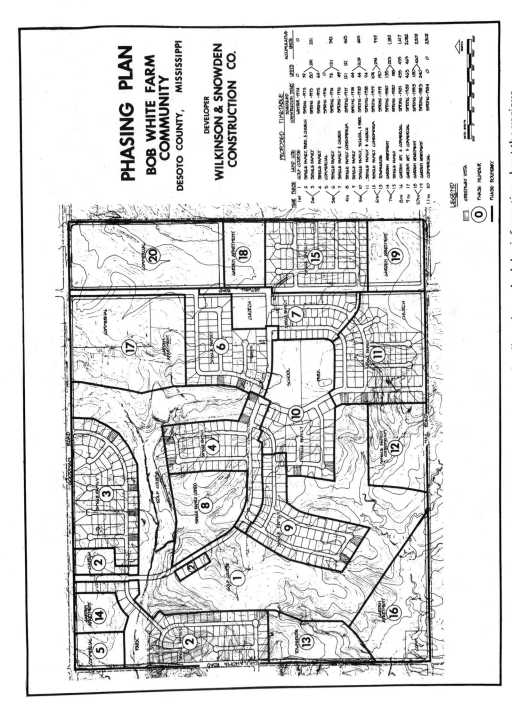

FIGURE 1–11. The phasing plan, as the name implies, gives schedular information about the various components of the site.

A quantative analysis of land use acreages and number of dwelling units proposed for each use is shown in Table 1–2.

## 2. Proposed Primary Circulation Pattern

The primary circulation pattern has been basically established under the Memphis Urban Area Transportation Study (MUATS) for the particular area of north DeSoto County where Bob White Farm is located.

Major roads designated for this area basically follow a grid pattern, spaced 1 mile apart. The location and right-of-way widths of four major roads that influenced the preliminary site plan for Bob White Farm are a part of the MUATS plan and the grid pattern established for this area of north DeSoto County.

Table 1–2. Quantative Analysis of Land Uses for Bob White Farm Community

| LAND USE | | | ACRES | UNITS |
|---|---|---|---|---|
| School | | | 12 | |
| Parks | | | 14 | |
| Golf course | | | 162 | |
| Greenway vistas | | | 6 | |
| Church | | | 18 | |
| Single-family | | | 219 | 632 |

| MINIMUM LOT SIZE | MINIMUM SQ. FT. | ACRES | UNITS | |
|---|---|---|---|---|
| 100′ × 150′ | 15,000 | 58 | 148 | |
| 95′ × 150′ | 14,250 | 51 | 134 | |
| 90′ × 150′ | 13,500 | 53 | 143 | |
| 80′ × 125′ | 10,000 | 57 | 210 | |

| | | ACRES | UNITS |
|---|---|---|---|
| (See Fig 1–12) | | | |
| Single-family condominium 4.5 D.U./AC | | 50 | 225 |
| Townhouse 10 D.U./AC | | 19 | 190 |
| Garden apartment 15 D.U./AC | | 97 | 1,455 |
| Commercial | | 73 | |
| Area reserved for future Getwell expressway | | 9 | |
| Streets | | 77 | |
| Total | | 756 | 2,502 |
| Gross density 3.3 D.U./AC | | | |

The major east-west thoroughfare that will provide the initial primary means of access into Bob White Farm is Goodman Road, which is proposed for a 120-foot right-of-way. Other major roads provided as required by MUATS are Tchulahoma Road, an 80-foot right-of-way that forms the south boundary of the community, and Getwell Road, which will traverse in a north-south direction the eastern third of Bob White Farm. Getwell Road is to be a limited-access facility, ultimately containing 160 feet of right-of-way.

To provide interior circulation within the Bob White Farm community, a collector street system has been established. The collector street system, containing a right-of-way width of 66 feet, is generally spaced at half mile intervals and is basically designed to provide neighborhood access to the major streets.

The minor street system is designed to give satisfactory access for emergency vehicles but to discourage through traffic. This is accomplished by utilizing cul-de-sacs and loop streets. The minor street pattern is planned to minimize walking distance to the school, encouraging school children to use the minor streets in lieu of crossing yards. All of the minor streets will be 50 feet in width.

The location and width of all proposed public streets within Bob White Farm are generally fixed by locations shown on the preliminary site plan.

### 3. Proposed Parks and Playgrounds

The preliminary site plan specifies locations for proposed parks and playgrounds. A 12-acre school and 8-acre park site are provided at the intersection of the two collector streets within Bob White Farm. The 8-acre park will provide for active recreation including facilities for field sports. A 6-acre park is provided in the preliminary site plan at the northwest corner of Bob White Farm adjacent to Tchulahoma Road; this park will provide for more passive recreation such as picnicking and nature trails. The park is in harmony with the general plan for the area, that is, keeping the major drainageways within open space, the drainageways providing a greenbelt system for the area. This 6-acre park would tie into the greenbelt park proposed across the street to the west.

The 162 acres allotted for the golf course will provide, in addition to golfing, opportunities for other forms of active recreation such as swimming and tennis, adding to the overall environment of quality of the development, thereby benefiting all residents.

Six acres of greenway vistas—parcels of land left free of structures—between the golf course fairway and the street allow maximum visibility of the golf course to vehicular and pedestrian traffic. Three church sites within the Bob White Farm community provide additional open space. The proposed plan of development provides for 212 acres or 28 percent of the total site for central open space (golf course, greenway vistas, schools, parks, and churches).

**4. Delineation of the Units or Phases to Be Constructed together with a Proposed Timetable**

It is anticipated that development of 2,502 units proposed in the preliminary site plan will take place over a period of 11 years. The phasing plan delineates the units and phases to be constructed along with a proposed timetable. The development approach to be followed anticipates the initial and immediate installation of the golf course with a collector street to serve it, including sewage, water, and electrical service.

The first eight phases are to be provided sewer service through the north trunk line sewer, which will follow the major drainage way along the north end of Bob White Farm. A separate trunk line sewer will serve the south half of the proposed development with those phases scheduled to be constructed later. The phases have been planned in a sequential order to tie them together, thus allowing good traffic circulation within the community during construction.

The single-family segment of the preliminary site plan is to be the primary initial construction, with the apartment, townhouse, and commercial development phases being the last phases to be constructed in Bob White Farm.

**5. Proposed Means of Dedication of Common Open Space Areas and Preservation of Common Open Space**

The primary open space area under the preliminary site plan is, of course, the 162-acre area designated for golf course, recreation, and open space use. As indicated by the plan this area extends throughout the entire Bob White Farm development and provides a strong element linking all parts of the community together.

It is the developer's intent to build the golf course and then to establish permanent operation and maintenance of the golf course with the Whitehaven Country Club. This approach is intended to assure a quality golf course facility, which is believed the key to success of the overall development. The 6 acres to be devoted for greenway vistas into the golf course are to be left free of structures

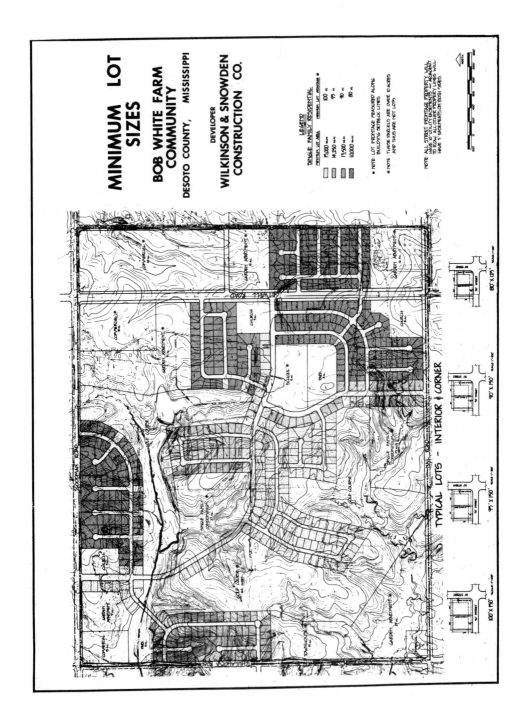

FIGURE 1-12. This drawing shows how the lot sizes are grouped on the project.

34

and are to be owned and maintained by the Wilkinson and Snowden Construction Company. The two park sites are to be made available to the DeSoto County Park Commission.

The 12-acre school site is to be purchased by either a public agency or by private enterprise.

Open space within residential developments will be maintained by their respective owners.

**6. Relation to Land Uses in the Surrounding Area and to the General Plan of the PUD**

The relationship of the Bob White Farm to land uses in the surrounding area is best illustrated in Exhibit E, contained in this report, and on the vicinity map of the title sheet included in the Appendix. The land surrounding the Bob White Farm is primarily used for agricultural purposes and is zoned agricultural district. There is one exception to this, however: an adjacent property zoned R-2, single-family residential district; at this site an extensive residential development is proposed. An existing grocery store is located at the northwest corner of Tchulahoma and Goodman Roads; however, this land is zoned agricultural district.

The general plan of the PUD illustrated on the preliminary site plan follows sound planning principles locating high-intensity use areas adjacent to major thoroughfares around the perimeter of the development, with the intensity of land use decreasing moving away from the perimeter toward the center of the development, that being the golf course.

The preliminary site plan land use proposals have been prepared within the provisions of the comprehensive plan for DeSoto County. In addition the planning process has included contact and consultation with the DeSoto County Planning Commission. Figure 1–12 shows the various lot sizes and indicates how they are grouped on the site.

# TOPOGRAPHIC MAPS

# 2

The shape of the site is called its *topography.* To represent the site graphically, contour lines are used. A contour line is an imaginary line that connects all the points of the same elevation over the site. Thus, contour lines show the different heights and shapes that make up the site: the hills, valleys, flats, etc. Contour lines are typically spaced at uniform elevation intervals, often 1, 2, 5, or 10 feet; this spacing is called *contour interval.*

Typically, every fifth or tenth contour line is heavy and is labeled with its elevation on the uphill side of the line or in an interruption within the contour line. As for the contour numbers, if the sea-level elevation is known at some point on the site, then contours may be noted relative to that point. It is not usually necessary, however, to know the sea-level elevation. Usually an arbitrary elevation at some convenient point on site is taken, and all other contours are then related to that elevation. The completed map is called a *topographic map,* a contour map, or sometimes just a topo. With experience you can glance over the topography map and visualize the shape of the site.

The following basic shapes and their topographic depiction will serve as a beginning vocabulary in studying topographic maps; section views are shown as an aid in relating the topographic views to the various typical shapes found on an actual site (Figure 2–1, A–G).

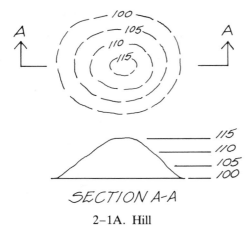

SECTION A-A

2–1A. Hill

FIGURE 2–1. At first topographic maps may appear very complicated. However, with practice the three dimensional shapes of maps may be quickly visualized. Some of the most basic shapes with which to become familiar include hills, depressions, uniform slopes, concave and convex shapes, ridges and valleys.

(Continued)

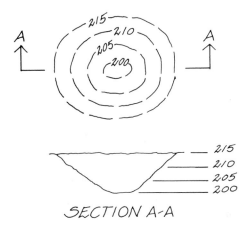

SECTION A-A

2–1B. Depression

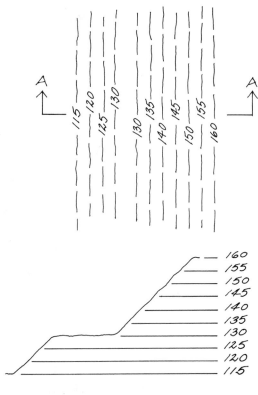

2–1C. Uniform Slope

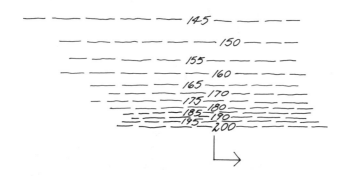

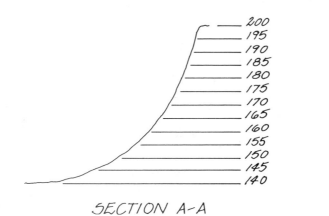

SECTION A-A

2–1D. Concave Slope

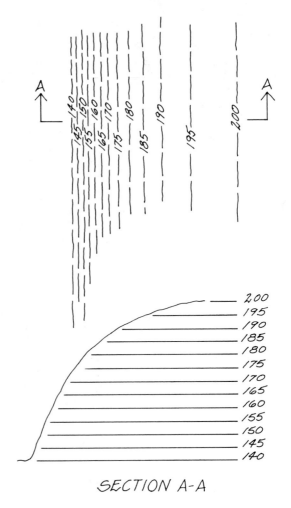

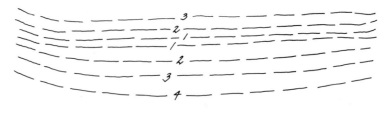

SECTION A-A

2–1E. Convex Slope

2–1F. Valley

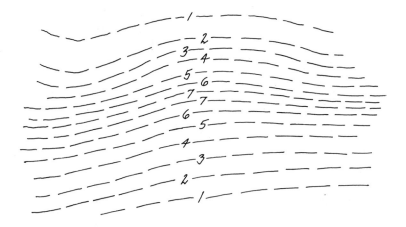

2–1G. Ridge

## Rules

There is no set of rules that, when memorized, will bring proficiency in reading topographic maps. Experience is the best teacher. A study of the foregoing land shapes and familiarization with their topographic representation are a good start. However, a few rules make interpretation of topographical maps a bit more certain.

1. As a rule, contour lines never cross. An overhanging cliff or similar land formation is an exception to the rule.
2. Contour lines never split.
3. Contour lines are closed "loops." Contour lines describe hills and depressions on the site, for example, but the loops may enclose such large areas of land that they close outside the boundary of the site, as in the case of the long ridges or valleys.
4. Rising land is indicated where the contour numbers get larger toward the center of the enclosed land, a hill, for example.
5. Falling land is indicated where the contour numbers get smaller toward the center of enclosed land, a depression, for example.
6. Steepness is usually indicated where parallel contour lines get close together.
7. A concave slope is indicated when the horizontal spacing between parallel contour lines are closest together where the contour numbers are the largest and wider apart where the contour numbers are the smallest.

8. A convex slope is indicated when the horizontal spacing between parallel contour lines are closest together where the contoured numbers are the smallest and wider apart where the contour numbers are the largest.

9. A uniform slope is indicated where parallel contour lines are equally spaced, a levee, for example.

# TOPOGRAPHIC MAPPING

The topographical map is essential to site design. Topographical maps show the site planner surface as it exists. Making the map is a specialized phase of site analysis and it is growing more specialized. Thus, the site planner typically employs specialists to develop the map. However, a basic knowledge of how the maps are made is valuable to the site planner both in interpreting topographical maps and in knowing which specialists are most appropriate for particular sites.

## The Topographic Survey

The purpose of a topographic map is to provide the site planner with a description of the site surface and features that is accurate enough for design purposes. Topographic surveys are necessary to gain the information with which to develop the topographic map. Regardless of the methods used, or the degree of detail used to describe the land surface, the topographical survey may be accomplished by extending a level line from some known point of elevation over the entire site and then recording various elevation points relative to that level line. The known point of elevation may be sea-level, if it is known, or it may be an arbitrarily assigned number.

A detailed study of surveying is not possible here. The reader is instead referred to standard surveying texts. However, the following discussion of the most common equipment and methods used for topographic surveys is essential knowledge for all site planners.

## Surveying Equipment

The transit is the classic surveying tool. In addition to providing a level line, the transit can be used to measure angles and distances; it rotates a full 360 degrees. A target rod is used with the transit; the rod is typically graded in tenths of a foot, inches, or metric measurements.

Given enough time, an almost perfectly accurate description of any land surface could be accomplished by using the transit and rod and recording closely spaced elevation points all over the site, relative to some known elevation point. This practice is not followed because too much detail is a similar handicap to not enough detail. Instead, a grid system is used, with typical spacings of 5 to 25 feet. Thus, the general shape of the land surface can be described within the grid and, where more specific detail is needed for some particular area, it can be gained.

The grid system is usually set in one corner of the property, with the intersection of the $X$ and $Y$ axes over the corner. The $X$ and $Y$ axes are then divided into the chosen intervals. The length of the intervals and the resulting size of the grid squares are determined by the need for detail, as is the number of sitings taken. If, for example, the site changes often and there are a number of features such as creeks, rock formations, and existing structures, a 10-foot grid might be selected and a considerable number of sitings would be necessary to describe the features. Should the land be gently rolling with few features of interest, a 25-foot grid and few sitings would be necessary to describe the land surface adequately. Whatever the grid spacing, the perpendicular lines of the grid are noted where they touch the $X$ and $Y$ axes; one axis is usually noted with numbers and the other with letters (Figure 2–2).

A bench mark is selected after the grid system is set up. A bench mark is a surveyor's mark, a permanent elevation point set on concrete or some other stable surface. All the elevation points that are selected to describe the property relate to this bench mark.

For small, relatively level sites with few dramatic features or site obstruction, it is possible to record all the necessary elevation points from some convenient, single location. More often terrain obstructions such as hills, valleys, rock outcroppings, etc., make it necessary to move the transit and rod around the site to gain the elevation points necessary to describe adequately the site surface and features that impact design.

It is typical to assign the bench mark the value 100, if the sea-level elevation is not known. All elevations will be greater than or less than 100 (except in coincidences where other elevations happen to be exactly 100).

Thus, the transit and rod are the surveyor's basic tools and with them large and complex sites may be accurately described.

For smaller, less complex sites, and for construction work, the builder's level may be used. The builder's level is similar in use and appearance to the transit, but it cannot perform as many functions. Builder's levels are simple to use and are convenient for small lot surveys, foundation stake out, ditch leveling, and similar tasks.

Where local information is needed, a simple survey can be accomplished using a carpenter's square, line level, string, plumb bob, and stakes. At some starting point a stake is driven. A line is stretched from the stake to a distant point, and another stake driven. Using the carpenter's square and the line level to keep the line level, the vertical distance is measured

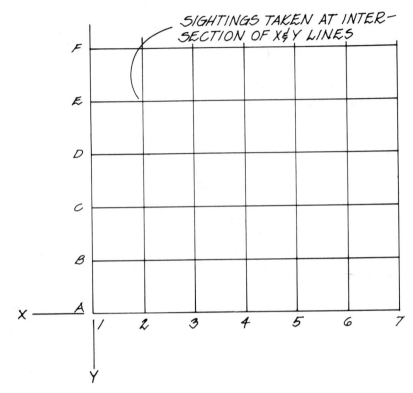

FIGURE 2–2. The grid system usually is set in one corner of the property, with the intersection of the *X* and *Y* axes over the corner. Grid sizes vary according to need for detail: 5, 10, and 25 feet grid squares are common. Elevations at grid intersections are noted and additional elevations can be added as needed.

with a plumb bob and string to the stake. Obviously this method is not highly accurate, but it can be used to gather rough design information such as existing slope grades, possible lot sizes, and so forth. For such purposes it is adequate and cheaper than more sophisticated methods (Figure 2–3).

## Contours

The topographic survey is a systematic gathering of elevation points. By "connecting the dots" or elevation points of the topographic survey, we form contour lines. Contour lines are imaginary lines of equal elevation. With the contour lines in place the symbolic but graphic representation of the site that we call the *topographic map* is created. Using the topographic map, or contour map, the site planner is able to visualize the site in three dimensions (Figure 2–4).

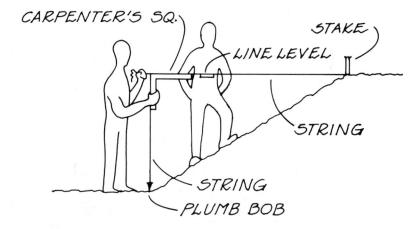

CARPENTER'S SQ.

STAKE

LINE LEVEL

STRING

STRING

PLUMB BOB

FIGURE 2–3. Slopes, location of site features, and other preliminary design information can be gathered quickly with simple equipment.

If all the elevations taken by the surveyor at each grid intersection were whole numbers, the plotting of contours would be much simpler and faster. This, of course, is not the case; rather the reverse is the case, where whole numbered elevations occur at the grid elevations only by coincidence. Thus, the whole-numbered contour lines must be determined by interpolation.

Interpolation of contours is a means of finding even-numbered contours between the grid elevations measured by the surveyor. The most essential contour lines are often drawn in by the surveyor. Even so, the site planner must interpolate contours for particular areas of interest. It is essential, then, that the site planner be familiar with the process of interpolation. Consider the following example of interpolation. Let us say that the four elevation points making up a 50-foot grid square are 103.2 at the top left corner, 104.2 at the top right corner, 103.8 at the bottom right corner, and 103.2 at the bottom left corner.

We want the location of the even-numbered contours, 104.0. We know that contour 104.0 will fall somewhere along the grid line at the top between elevations 103.2 and 104.2 and along the grid line at the right side, between elevations 104.2 and 103.8.

To find where contour 104.0 falls along the top grid line, proceed as follows:

1. Find the total difference in elevation between 103.2 and 104.2 (104.2 − 103.2 = 1).

2. The total horizontal distance between the points was given as 50 feet.

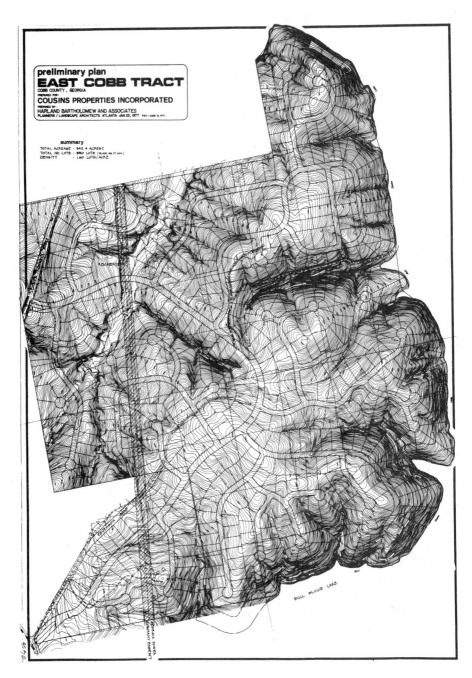

FIGURE 2–4. With experience, the topographic maps provide an accurate three-dimensional view of the land surface and features.

3. Then, the horizontal distance from elevation point 103.2 to 104.0 (the desired even-numbered contour) is

$$\frac{104.0 - 103.2}{104.2 - 103.2} \times 50 = 40 \text{ feet}$$

Thus, contour 104.0 is 40 feet from elevation 103.2 along the top grid line; scale contour 104.0 on the top grid line.

4. Now locate contour 104.0 between elevation points 104.2 and 103.8 similarly:

$$\frac{104.0 - 103.8}{104.2 - 103.8} \times 50 = 25 \text{ feet}$$

Thus, contour 104.0 is 25 feet down from elevation point 104.2, along the grid line at the right; scale contour 104.0 on the grid line at the right.

Now show contour line 104.0 with a dashed line (Figure 2–5).

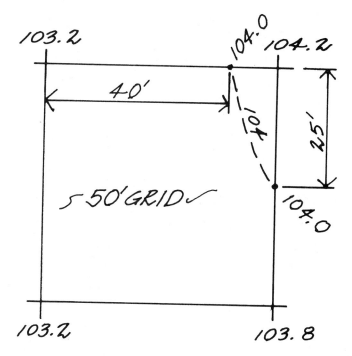

FIGURE 2–5. Interpolation is a means of finding contour lines between points of known elevation.

## AERIAL SURVEYS AND TOPOGRAPHIC MAPS

In a relatively short time the aerial topographic map has become standard with many site planners and other professionals. Aerial topos can be produced quickly, giving the site planner more time for design; the highly graphic quality of photos over conventional drafting techniques is a plus.

To make the maps, a preliminary field survey is first made by conventional methods to identify essential control points. Then an aerial survey is flown. Next, using sophisticated equipment, the aerial surveyor assembles a highly accurate picture of the desired site. The contours may then be drafted by hand but the tendency is toward computerized plotting, which further speeds the process (Figures 2–6 and 2–7).

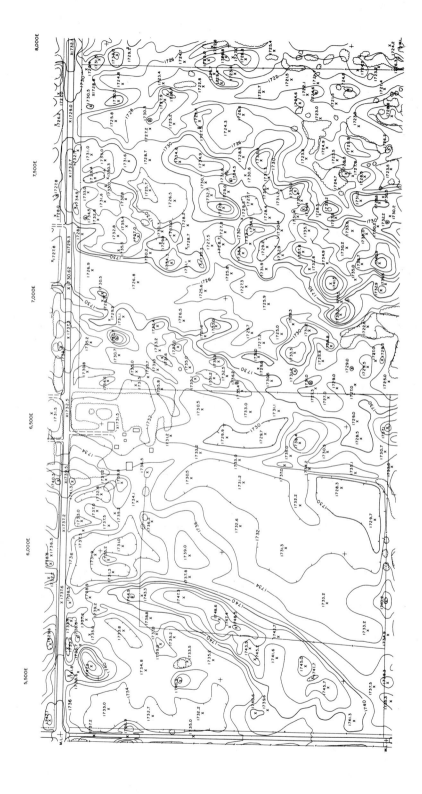

FIGURE 2–6. This topo, made from an aerial survey, was used as part of a comprehensive drainage study for pollution control. Note that particular attention was given spot elevations on tops and in depressions. The contours are at 2 foot intervals.

51

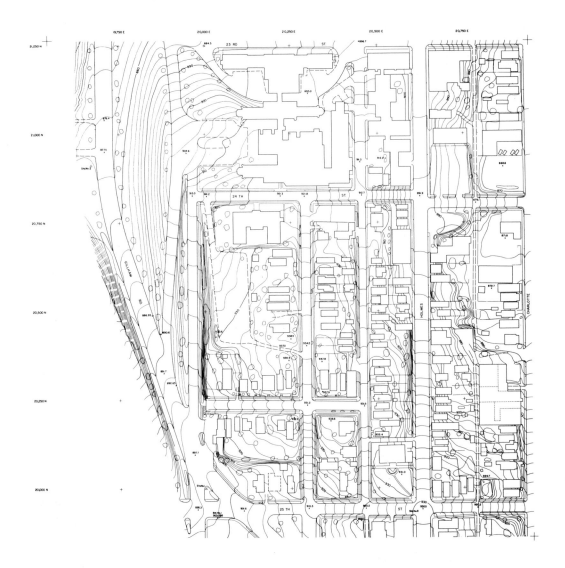

FIGURE 2–7. This topographic map was made for a comprehensive land plan study related to a redevelopment project under the Urban Renewal Program. The scale is 1 inch = 50 feet and the contour interval is 2 feet.

# STREETS AND PARKING

**3**

The obvious function of streets is to provide a means for orderly and safe vehicular travel, safe for motorists and pedestrians alike. One need not drive or walk far from home to notice that even these basic goals are not always met.

Besides the transportation function, streets influence the human activities that take place along them: residing, shopping, selling, sightseeing, eating, working, and so forth. The placement and design of streets either help or hinder any or all these human activities. Streets also are the location of basic services: electric, gas and water lines; storm sewers; sanitary sewers; and telephone lines. There may be bicycle lanes along streets and, in some towns and cities, horse trails. All streets have unique qualities that help define the character of the surrounding area. Conversely the design and placement of new streets can create and predetermine character. Thus, placement and design of streets are worthy of careful study by site planners.

Streets are typically divided into three classes: arterials, collectors, and locals. All three vary in design due mostly to two main design controls: (1) the limitations of rights-of-way due to the type and extent of urban development and (2) zoning or regulatory restrictions. The chief purpose of streets in residential areas is to contribute to a pleasant environment as well as provide safe access. Thus, the technical roadability of residential streets may defer somewhat to gain interest, a beautiful view, and so forth. On larger, more traffic-oriented streets the opposite is the case: Roadability for the motorist is the primary design consideration. The modern expressway is perhaps the most obvious example of a traffic-oriented way, as opposed to the curvilinear, hilly system of some suburbs, where traffic expediency is not the chief concern.

Traffic volume must be considered in street design. Quiet residential streets have a low volume that varies little and thus design is little affected by volume. For heavily trafficked streets that serve industrial and commercial areas, traffic volumes are a major consideration. The design hourly volume (DHV) is figured for some future year when the development of the area surrounding the street is projected to be complete; planning for the future is essential because it is difficult, expensive, and sometimes impossible to modify streets once the surrounding area is built up. Typically DHV is based on estimates 10 to 20 years from the date of construction completion.

Speed is not a major factor for local streets. Speed does become important in the design of collector streets, however. Typically it is desirable to design local streets for 30 mph and collector streets for 40 mph. It is not uncommon to design residential streets in a manner to discourage speed, rather than accommodate it. The importance of higher speeds can be seen in traffic-oriented streets by their gentler curves, less steep hills, and longer sight stopping distances.

It is usually best for residential streets to follow existing terrain as closely as possible. This minimizes the amount of cut and fill, and, where the terrain is rather dramatic, winding, hilly roads are interesting to residents and discourage through traffic, which seeks flatter, straighter, faster streets. Local street gradients should be kept below 12 percent, where possible, and it is preferable that they be below 8 percent. Collector street gradients should be less than 10 percent and preferably less than 7 percent. Any grade over 4 percent tends to make drainage critical, and slopes must be dealt with carefully to avoid erosion. For streets in commercial and industrial areas the flatter and straighter the street, the better; grades should be less than 8 percent and preferably less than 5 percent.

The best intersections meet at a 90-degree angle. Angles less than 60 degrees are undesirable; closely spaced, offset intersections are confusing and undesirable. In residential areas the radius to the outside edge of the payment (at the curb, if there is a curb) should be at least 15 feet, preferably 30 feet. Commercial and industrial radii should be at least 30 feet, preferably more, how much depending on the type vehicles that use the streets. For collector streets the corner sight distance should be at least 300 feet, preferably 400 feet or even more. Local streets need at least 200 feet in corner sight distance, and 300 feet or more is preferable. To achieve adequate corner sight distance, restrictions are often necessary: restrictions on building location and height, fence location and height, and landscaping or other structures that interfere with motorist vision to the corner. The intersection itself in the area where motorists wait to enter the intersection, or turn, should be flat; the approach grade to the intersection should not exceed 5 percent.

## CIRCULATION PATTERNS

Typical circulation patterns for vehicular traffic include the grid, linear, radial, and curvilinear systems. Combinations of these systems also are frequently used.

The names of these systems are indicative of their layout. The grid system may be comprised of equally spaced streets running perpendicular to each other, each grid forming a square block, or the grid may be varied to form different size rectangles to gain some traffic or building layout objective. The street sizes also may be varied to accommodate different volumes and types of traffic, and the grid may be warped to fit topography (Figure 3–1A).

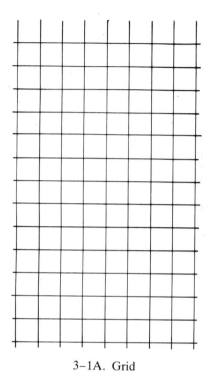

3–1A. Grid

FIGURE 3–1. The grid, linear, radial, and curvilinear vehicular traffic circulation patterns are frequently used in most American cities.

The linear system may be a single, long street or parallel series of streets. All activities—houses, other buildings, etc.—are grouped along one or both sides of the street or road. The linear system is typically used where sight topography or other existing physical constraints make the linear system the most practical approach, along a railroad line or canal, for example, between two sharply rising slopes of land where roads are not feasible, or in agricultural settings, where the highway becomes the logical line along which to develop. The linear system is sometimes modified by the use of loops, cul-de-sacs, and grids or partial grids (Figure 3–1B).

In the radial system, streets spread out from some center. The center is typically some common destination, such as an employment center. The radial system provides the shortest line of traffic to that center. There are modifications to the radial system, such as the addition of rings or branches. The radial system, because it is used to facilitate traffic to and from the center, typically fades into some other pattern at its outer reaches (Figure 3–1C).

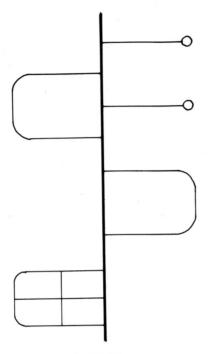

3–1B. Linear

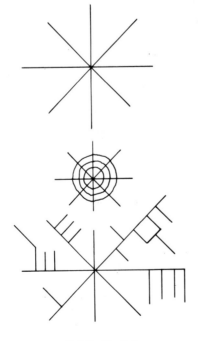

3–1C. Radial

The curvilinear system is not as definitive in form as the other systems discussed. Rather the curvilinear system uses curvilinear streets to discourage through traffic, to create a sense of neighborhood intimacy, or to adjust to difficult sight topography. Thus, the curvilinear system is used more as a supplement or problem solver to one of the other systems rather than a system of traffic movement itself. Used over large areas, the curvilinear system becomes confusing and frustrating to users (Figure 3–1D).

These systems are defined only to aid in gaining a sense of form in road and street layout. In practice the forms are not always geometrically pure and there may be many combinations of the forms. The best solution for a particular development is the system or combination of systems that works harmoniously within the development and relative to the established and ongoing patterns of the surrounding regions.

## COMPONENTS OF ROADS AND STREETS

A typical subdivision street is made up of five components: pavement, gutter, curb, planting strip, and sidewalk (Figure 3–2). But these components vary considerably in form and usage for particular sites and for

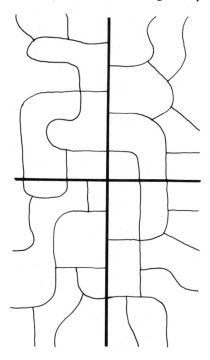

3–1D. Curvilinear

local regulations. Opposite curbs are usually the same elevation (unless there is a median), and the street slopes from the center, or "crown," toward the curb and gutters. Variations in street shape include valley slopes, where the street slopes down toward the center, and slopes to one side (medians increase the possibility of this design).

A 6-inch vertical curb and gutter are often used, although 4-inch roll curbs may still be seen. In low-density residential areas curbs and gutters have sometimes been omitted in favor of shallow, grasslined ditches. When ditches are used, culverts must be employed under every driveway and at intersections; this method is seen less and less, perhaps because curbs make for easier street cleaning and better sanitary conditions and offer better protection to the street edge from crumbling.

## Pavement

Streets and roads are typically asphaltic concrete or concrete. In rural and residential areas, where usage is light and regulations permit, gravel or stabilized soil may be used; stabilized soil is made by mixing portland cement into the soil to a specified depth. Road and street materials preparation, transportation, installation scheduling (especially concerning weather conditions), and installation methods are largely engineering concerns. But the site planner should be familiar enough with the uses and specifications of the various local materials and their installation (including sub-base preparation requirements) to make decisions including material selection and aesthetic appearance and to make sub-base cut-and-fill and cost calculations.

## Dimensions of Roads and Streets

The face-of-curb to face-of-curb dimensions of roads and streets vary somewhat locally. Typically a secondary residential street might be 40 feet;

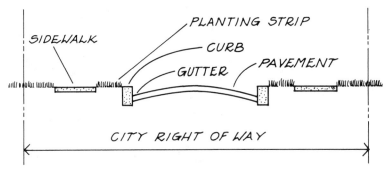

FIGURE 3–2. The typical subdivision street is made up of five components: pavement, gutter, curb, planting strip, and sidewalk.

a minor street, 34 feet; a major street, 64 feet; and a cul-de-sac, 28 feet. Curbside parking, where it is provided, should be a minimum of 8 feet wide, in addition to the traffic lane width required. Planting strip widths vary, depending on usage; *planting* in many cities is synonymous with grass. A 4-foot planting strip where only grass will be used is typical. In addition to appearance, the planting strip sometimes provides an easement for utilities (both above and below grade); separates the sidewalk from the street for ease of walking and safety from traffic; provides a place to pile snow; and provides a temporary staging area for street and utility workmen. If trees are to be installed on the planting strip, it must be widened to accommodate the needs of the particular trees—at least 7 feet wide. When used only as a utility easement, the planting strip is sometimes reduced below the typical 4-foot width, especially in commercial areas.

Public residential sidewalks are typically 4 or 5 feet wide. Private walks to home entries are usually 4 feet wide or less. In areas of dense pedestrian usage, walks must be sized for traffic flow just as streets and roads. Walks are either crowned, like streets, or sloped crossways to drain, typically at one-fourth inch per foot. Walks are typically made of concrete and sometimes of asphaltic concrete and are usually bland and monotonous. However, at little or no extra cost, the appearance of walks may be made more interesting with the use of color mixes and patterns (both by scoring the surface and by the use of varying sized and colored aggregate visible in the material surface). Brick, stone, and other suitable materials may be used for walks, and sometimes a combination of materials is pleasing.

The total public right of way is a summing up of the widths of the street pavement, curb and gutters, planting strip, sidewalks, and sometimes an additional space beyond the sidewalk edge toward the private lots (Figure 3–2).

## Bicycles

Unfortunately provisions for bicyclists are rarely considered. Bicycles are excellent sport and recreation vehicles and offer a serious method of travel for many. Cycleways are typically 12 feet wide and require only light pavement. Gentle curves in grades are preferred. Providing cycleways in cities where they were not initially planned is difficult but not impossible, as some cities have demonstrated. But new developments, especially the larger ones, offer the best opportunity.

## Horizontal Alignment

The center line of roads is measured in 100-foot intervals called *stations*. Intersections, the beginning and ends of curves, and similar significant points along the center line are referenced to this station numbering system. The center line itself is made up of straight lines, called *tangents*, and of segments of circular curves. Site planners sketch the center lines of roads (on tracing paper laid over the contour map or directly on a copy of the contour map if it is not overly detailed), keeping the contours and applicable road design criteria in mind. Once a design concept is arrived at, from the sketches, the site planner may figure the location of roads more accurately (if more accuracy is in fact needed) by understanding the functions of curves.

In Figure 3–3 the elements are as follows:

$PC$ = Point of curvature (beginning of the curve).

$PT$ = Point of tangency (end of curve).

$PI$ = Point of intersection of the two tangents.

$\Delta$ = Deflection angle, as shown. It is equal to the central angle.

$T$ = Distance from $PI$ to $PC$; or $PI$ to $PT$.

$R$ = Radius.

$D$ = Number of degrees turned at the center per 100 foot of curve length.

$L$ = Curve length.

$M$ = Distance from center of curve to center of long cord.

Now, proceed from the sketches to more accurate descriptions of the curves by first measuring the deflection angle, $\Delta$. Then measure $T$. The following formulas may be used for a fairly accurate definition of curve data:

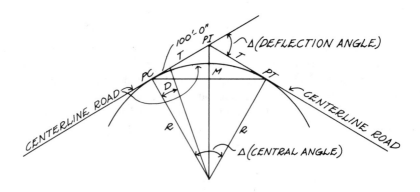

FIGURE 3–3. To accurately compute road and street curves, it is necessary to understand some of the functions of curves.

$$R = \frac{T}{\tan \frac{1}{2} \Delta}$$

$$D = 5{,}730/R$$

$$L = \frac{100 \, \Delta}{D}$$

For example, if $\Delta$ equals 60 degrees and $T$ equals 315 feet, then

$$R = \frac{315}{0.577} = 545.93 \text{ feet}$$

$$D = \frac{5730}{R} = \frac{5730}{545.93} = 10 \text{ degrees} - 30 \text{ minutes}$$

$$L = \frac{100 \times 60.0}{10.5} = 571.43 \text{ feet}$$

Continuing the example, let us say that the *PC* is at station 20 + 00; the *PT* would then be at station 25 + 71.43 (Figure 3–4).

## Vertical Alignment

The center line of a road weaves not only horizontally but also vertically. The up-and-down movement is made up of tangents and curves, similar to horizontal movement. But vertical curves, unlike horizontal curves, are not circular—they are instead parabolic curves. Parabolic curves provide more regular, smooth curves between different grades, which makes

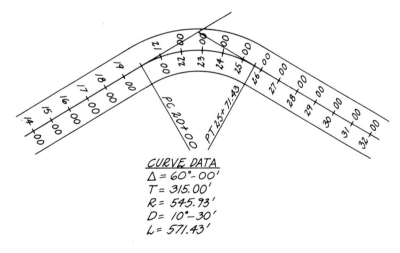

CURVE DATA
$\Delta = 60° - 00'$
$T = 315.00'$
$R = 545.93'$
$D = 10° - 30'$
$L = 571.43'$

FIGURE 3–4. After the curve data is obtained, an accurate drawing can be done.

the road more drivable. Tangent grades may be expressed as percentages, or rise or fall in feet per 100 feet of horizontal distance (run). Typically, uphill grades are called *positive* and downhill grades are called *negative*. Uphill curves may also be called *vertical crests* and downhill curves, *vertical sags*. In drawings, the vertical alignment of a road center line is described by *profiles*, which are sections taken along the length of the road at the center line (Figure 3–5). Cross sections are vertical sections taken perpendicular to the road center lines; cross sections describe cross slopes, shoulders, ditches, etc.

Aligning a road vertically typically involves determining a safe, easily drivable curve between two known, fixed elevations, or one or both the grades may be fixed for driving comfort and safety, drainage, or similar purposes. Vertical curves are parabolic and they may be plotted mathematically by determining a series of points that describe the curve departure from the entering grade tangent and the leaving grade tangent of the curve.

Figure 3–6 shows some essential elements of vertical curves; the elements noted are:

PVC: The beginning of the vertical curve.

PVI: The intersection of grade tangents.

Chord: A line drawn between the PVC and the PVT.

Stations: Reference points along the road center line (see top of drawing).

Elevations: See left side of drawing.

Algebraic difference between the entering and leaving grades: The entering grade minus the leaving grade. For example, the entering grade shown on the drawing is + 4.90 percent and the leaving grade is − 1.00 percent. The algebraic difference then is + 4.90 − ( − 1.00) = 5.90.

Offsets: Distances between the tangent line and the vertical curve at selected intervals. The middle offset is the offset from the PVI to the curve; the end offset is the last offset.

L: The horizontal distance between PVC and PVT.

d: Some segment of L.

PVII: The intersection of the extended tangent with the end offset.

As stated, the vertical curve may be located mathematically. For example, given the information on the drawing:

$$PVC = Station\ 3\ +\ 90,\ Elevation\ 326.36$$

$$PVT = Station\ 6\ +\ 10,\ Elevation\ 330.65$$

$$Entering\ tangent\ grade = 4.90\ percent$$

$$Leaving\ tangent\ grade = 1.00\ percent$$

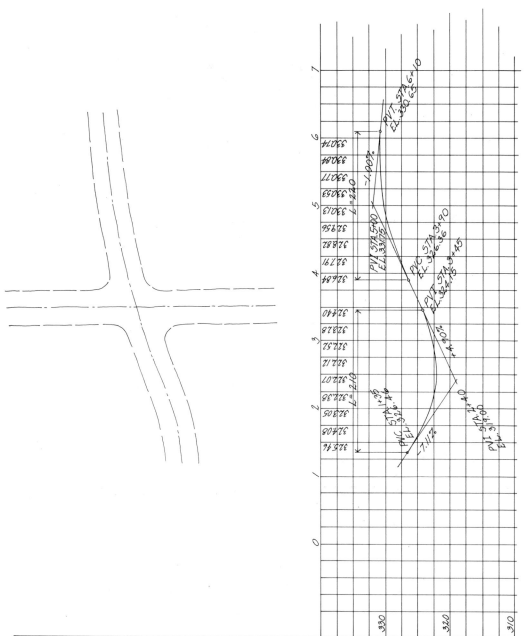

FIGURE 3–5. Profiles are vertical sections taken along the road center line.

65

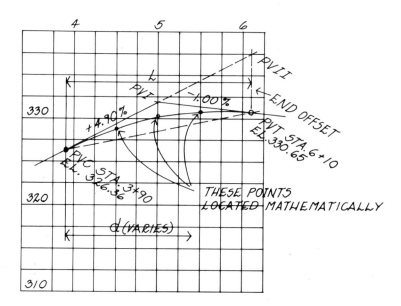

FIGURE 3–6. Vertical curves may be arrived at mathematically or they may be found graphically. For preliminary design purposes, the graphic method often is used. Note the essential elements of the curve.

Find

$$L,$$

PVI station and elevation, and

Elevation of curve at stations 4 + 50, 5 + 00, and 5 + 50.

First, $L$ = station 6 + 10 minus station 3 + 90 = 610 feet minus 390 feet = 220 feet. Next find the elevation of the PVI. Multiplying 4.90 percent (the entering grade tangent) times 220 feet ($L$), we get 10.78. Adding 10.78 to the PVC elevation gives us 337.14, the elevation of the PVI.

Subtracting the PVT elevation from the PVI elevation, we get 6.49, which is the end offset. Now calculate the horizontal distance $d$ from the PVC to the PVI, using the formula

$$d = \frac{\text{end offset} \times 100}{\text{algebraic difference}};$$

the end offset is 6.49 and the algebraic difference is 5.90. Thus,

$$d = \frac{6.49 \times 100}{5.90} = 110 \text{ feet}$$

The station at the PVI is equal to PVC station 3 + 90 plus the distance $d$, which is 110 feet; thus, the PVI station is 5 + 00. The entering grade tangent is 4.90 percent. Multiplying 0.490 × 110 feet, we get 5.39 feet; adding 5.39 to 326.36, we get 331.75, the elevation at the PVI. The middle

$$\text{offset} = \frac{d^2 \times \text{end offset}}{L^2} = \frac{110^2 \times 6.49}{220^2} = 1.62;$$ subtracting the middle

offset distance from the PVI elevation 331.75 gives us 330.13, the elevation of the curve at station 5 + 00; this point may now be plotted.

The elevation of the curve at stations 4 + 50 and 5 + 50 are found similarly. For station 4 + 50 find the offset by the formula

$$\frac{d^2 \times \text{end offset}}{L^2} = \frac{(450 - 390)^2 \times 6.49}{220^2} = 0.48$$

The elevation at the tangent is found by multiplying the entering grade, 4.90 percent, times the distance $d$ of 60, then adding the product to the PVC elevation; thus, the elevation at the tangent at station 4 + 50 is 326.36 + 2.94 = elevation 329.30. Subtracting the offset, 0.48, from the tangent elevation, we get 328.82, the elevation of the curve at station 4 + 50. This point may now be plotted.

For station 5 + 50 find the offset by the formula

$$\frac{d^2 \times \text{end offset}}{L^2} = \frac{(550 - 390) \times 6.49}{220^2} = 3.43$$

The elevation at the tangent is found by multiplying the entering grade, 4.90 percent, times the distance $d$ of 160, then adding the product to the PVC elevation; thus, the elevation at the tangent at station 5 + 50 is 326.36 + 7.84 = elevation 334.20. Subtracting the offset, 3.43, from the tangent elevation 334.20, we get 330.77, the elevation of the curve at station 5 + 50. This point may now be plotted.

Any number of points along the curve may be plotted in this manner. For the example curve discussed here, the several points plotted are enough to draw the curve in with a French curve with reasonable accuracy.

Vertical curves also may be located graphically. In Figure 3–6 we were given

$$\text{PVC} = \text{station } 3 + 90, \text{ elevation } 326.36$$
$$\text{PVT} = \text{station } 6 + 10, \text{ elevation } 330.65$$
$$\text{Entering grade tangent} = +4.90 \text{ percent}$$
$$\text{Leaving grade tangent} = -1.00 \text{ percent}$$

To draw the curve, first draft in the entering and leaving grades at 4.90 feet/100 feet and 1.00 feet/100 feet, respectively; this gives you the PVI.

Now draft the chord from the PVC to the PVT. From the PVT, drop a line vertically to the chord. This line will be bisected by the vertical curve, which therefore gives us a point on the vertical curve. Using a French curve, draft a parabolic curve that passes through the PVC, the center point discussed, and the PVT.

Because profiles are plotted to scale, any point along the curve may be determined relative to other points—including stations and elevations—simply by scaling.

## Superelevation

Superelevation is the practice of banking roads to compensate for centrifugal force as autos drive around curves. The amount of superelevation selected depends on factors such as desired speed and radius of curve (the shorter the radius, the sharper the curve and the greater need for superelevation to maintain regular speed).

The degree of superelevation is the same between the *PC* and the *PT*, but there is a transition length before the *PC* and after the *PT*. The transition length before the *PC* is the same length as the transition length after the *PT*. Transitions simply ease the driver smoothly into and out of the section of fully superelevated curve (Figure 3–7).

There is a formula for superelevation:

$$\frac{e + f = 0.067V^2}{R} = \frac{V^2}{15R}$$

where *e* equals superelevation in foot per foot of road width; *V* equals vehicle speed in miles per hour; *R* equals radius of curve in feet; and *f*

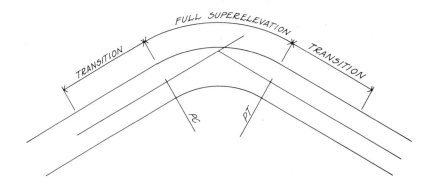

FIGURE 3–7. The degree of superelevation or ''bank'' is the same between the PC and the PT. The transition lengths before the PC and after the PT are the same: the transitions serve to ease the motorist into the fully superelevated portion of the curve.

equals side friction factor (0.16 for 30 miles per hour or less, 0.15 for 40 miles per hour where the superelevation is not over 0.08 foot per foot).

There are other factors besides the one in the preceding formula to consider, however, such as weather, traffic density and type, location.

Generally superelevation is restricted to use on rural highways where it is desirable to maintain uniform, relatively high speeds. Superelevated roads are seldom designed for city areas because they encourage higher than desirable speeds for the intended use of the road (through expressways and four lanes are obvious exceptions).

The site planner must be aware of when superelevation is called for and when it is not. Table 3–1 shows typical design factors for superelevations where the rate of superelevation does not exceed 0.08 foot per foot. Actual design in calculations for superelevated roads usually calls for specialists in road design.

## HORIZONTAL AND VERTICAL ALIGNMENT AND SUPERELEVATION AS A WHOLE

For purposes of study and calculations, horizontal and vertical curves and the technique of superelevation are considered separately. But the streets and highways that we drive, if they are successful in providing us with a safe and pleasant travelway, do not show these elements of design separately. Rather, being on the well-designed street and highway is like being on a giant concrete or asphalt ribbon, smooth and melded into and made one with the landscape. A sense of the whole of street and road design is essential to the site planner. To gain this sense, it is worthwhile to build string models (representing the street center line) or, better, to build models of clay, styrofoam, or similar materials.

### Sight Distance

Minimum forward stopping distance must be maintained for both horizontal and vertical curves; these requirements sometimes make for longer curves than would be necessary for roadability. At night, headlight beam lengths become a factor in sag curves to be sure that they are equal to the minimum sight distance. Allowing for passing sight distance is seldom required for city streets; however, Figure 3–8 shows a method for determining both stopping sight distances and passing sight distances for both horizontal and vertical curves.

Table 3–2 gives minimum stopping sight distances for speeds ranging from 30 to 65 miles per hour; Table 3–3 gives minimum passing sight distances for the same speed range.

## Table 3-1. Values for Design Elements Related to Design Speed and Horizontal Curvature

| D | R | V=30 MPH e | V=30 2-LANE | V=30 4-LANE | V=40 e | V=40 2-LANE | V=40 4-LANE | V=50 e | V=50 2-LANE | V=50 4-LANE | V=60 e | V=60 2-LANE | V=60 4-LANE | V=65 e | V=65 2-LANE | V=65 4-LANE | V=70 e | V=70 2-LANE | V=70 4-LANE | V=75 e | V=75 2-LANE | V=75 4-LANE | V=80 e | V=80 2-LANE | V=80 4-LANE |
|---|---|---|---|---|---|---|---|---|---|---|---|---|---|---|---|---|---|---|---|---|---|---|---|---|---|
| 0°15' | 22918' | NC | 0 | 0 | NC | 0 | 0 | NC | 0 | 0 | NC | 0 | 0 | NC | 0 | 0 | NC | 0 | 0 | NC | 0 | 0 | RC | 240 | 240 |
| 0°30' | 11459' | NC | 0 | 0 | NC | 0 | 0 | NC | 0 | 0 | RC | 175 | 175 | RC | 190 | 190 | RC | 200 | 200 | RC | 220 | 220 | .024 | 240 | 240 |
| 0°45' | 7639' | NC | 0 | 0 | NC | 0 | 0 | RC | 150 | 150 | .022 | 175 | 175 | .025 | 190 | 190 | .029 | 200 | 200 | .032 | 220 | 220 | .036 | 240 | 240 |
| 1°00' | 5730' | NC | 0 | 0 | RC | 0 | 125 | .021 | 150 | 150 | .029 | 175 | 175 | .033 | 190 | 200 | .038 | 200 | 200 | .043 | 220 | 220 | .047 | 240 | 240 |
| 1°30' | 3820' | RC | 100 | 100 | .021 | 125 | 125 | .030 | 150 | 150 | .040 | 175 | 175 | .046 | 190 | 250 | .053 | 200 | 240 | .060 | 220 | 290 | .065 | 240 | 240 |
| 2°00' | 2865' | RC | 100 | 100 | .027 | 125 | 125 | .038 | 150 | 150 | .051 | 175 | 210 | .057 | 190 | 290 | .065 | 200 | 290 | .072 | 220 | 340 | .076 | 240 | 320 |
| 2°30' | 2292' | .021 | 100 | 100 | .033 | 125 | 125 | .046 | 150 | 170 | .060 | 175 | 240 | .066 | 190 | 320 | .073 | 220 | 330 | .078 | 230 | 370 | .080 | 250 | 380 |
| 3°00' | 1910' | .025 | 100 | 100 | .038 | 125 | 125 | .053 | 150 | 190 | .067 | 180 | 270 | .073 | 210 | 330 | .078 | 230 | 350 | .080 | 250 | 380 | D max=2.5° | | |
| 3°30' | 1637' | .028 | 100 | 100 | .043 | 125 | 140 | .058 | 150 | 210 | .073 | 200 | 300 | .077 | 220 | 340 | .080 | 240 | 360 | D max=3.0° | | | | | |
| 4°00' | 1432' | .032 | 100 | 100 | .047 | 125 | 150 | .063 | 150 | 230 | .077 | 210 | 310 | .079 | 230 | 350 | D max=3.5° | | | | | | | | |
| 5°00' | 1146' | .038 | 100 | 100 | .055 | 125 | 170 | .071 | 170 | 260 | .080 | 220 | 320 | D max=4.5° | | | | | | | | | | | |
| 6°00' | 955' | .043 | 100 | 120 | .061 | 130 | 190 | .077 | 180 | 280 | D max=5.0° | | | | | | | | | | | | | | |
| 7°00' | 819' | .048 | 100 | 130 | .067 | 140 | 210 | .079 | 190 | 280 | | | | | | | | | | | | | | | |
| 8°00' | 716' | .052 | 100 | 140 | .071 | 150 | 220 | D max=7.5° | | | | | | | | | | | | | | | | | |
| 9°00' | 637' | .056 | 100 | 150 | .075 | 160 | 240 | | | | | | | | | | | | | | | | | | |
| 10°00' | 573' | .059 | 110 | 160 | .077 | 160 | 240 | | | | | | | | | | | | | | | | | | |
| 11°00' | 521' | .063 | 110 | 170 | .079 | 170 | 250 | | | | | | | | | | | | | | | | | | |
| 12°00' | 477' | .066 | 120 | 180 | .080 | 170 | 250 | | | | | | | | | | | | | | | | | | |
| 13°00' | 441' | .068 | 120 | 180 | D max=12.5° | | | | | | | | | | | | | | | | | | | | |
| 14°00' | 409' | .070 | 130 | 190 | | | | | | | | | | | | | | | | | | | | | |
| 16°00' | 358' | .074 | 130 | 200 | | | | | | | | | | | | | | | | | | | | | |
| 18°00' | 318' | .077 | 140 | 210 | | | | | | | | | | | | | | | | | | | | | |
| 20°00' | 286' | .079 | 140 | 210 | | | | | | | | | | | | | | | | | | | | | |
| 22°00' | 260' | .080 | 140 | 220 | | | | | | | | | | | | | | | | | | | | | |
| D max=23.0° | | | | | | | | | | | | | | | | | | | | | | | | | |

$$e\,max=0.08$$

D—Degree of curve
R—Radius of curve
V—Assumed design speed
e—Rate of superelevation
L—Minimum length of runoff of spiral curve
NC—Normal crown section
RC—Remove adverse crown, superelevate at normal crown slope
Spirals desirable but not as essential above heavy line.
Lengths rounded in multiples of 25 or 50 feet permit simpler calculations.

Design Values for Superelevations Where the Rate of Superelevation Does Not Exceed 0.08 Ft.
Source: AASHO Geometric Highway Design.

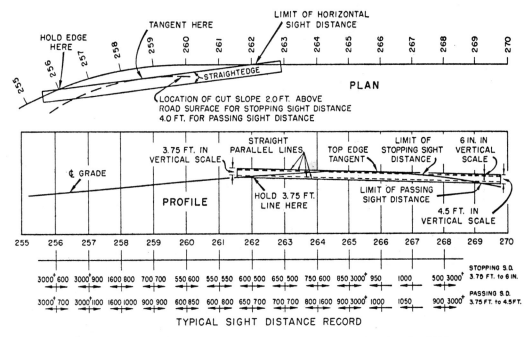

SCALING AND RECORDING SIGHT DISTANCES ON PLANS

FIGURE 3–8. Methods of figuring stopping sight distances and passing sight distances.
*Source:* AASHO Geometric Highway Design

Vertical curves, for a satisfactory aesthetic appearance, roadability, and the minimum stopping sight distance, must not be shorter than $L = KA$, where $L$ is the length of the vertical curve in feet, $A$ is the algebraic difference of grades, and the $K$ values are given in Table 3–4.

## Parking

Parking must be studied as a design element both in itself and as it relates to residential and commercial buildings, pedestrian circulation routes

Table 3–2. Stopping Sight Distances

|  | DESIGN SPEED IN MPH | | | | |
|---|---|---|---|---|---|
|  | 30 | 40 | 50 | 60 | 65 |
| Minimum Stopping Sight Distance in Feet | 200 | 275 | 350 | 475 | 550 |

Source: AASHO Geometric Highway Design

Table 3–3. Passing Sight Distances

| | DESIGN SPEED IN MPH | | | | |
| --- | --- | --- | --- | --- | --- |
| | 30 | 40 | 50 | 60 | 65 |
| Minimum Passing Sight Distance in Feet: 2-lane Highways | 1,100 | 1,500 | 1,800 | 2,100 | 2,300 |

Source: AASHO Geometric Highway Design

and the site as a whole. Typically there is resident, visitor, and service parking to consider. Site terrain and other physical factors often limit parking location and design alternatives. When choices are available, users should not have to approach buildings through a parking lot. Provision should be made for dropping passengers off (such as covered entries at building fronts, etc.). Walking distance from parking to destination should be minimized. Service areas should be separated from parking to reduce accidents, inconveniences, and safety hazards. Efforts should be made to soften the appearance of parking lots with planting when possible.

In locating and designing for parking, the following are typical questions the site planner must investigate.

1. Where is it physically possible to locate parking and how much area is available?
2. What are the different types of parking (such as visitor, resident, and service), how do they relate to each other, and what are the size and circulation requirements of each?
3. What is the walking distance from the various parking areas to the buildings and other destinations?
4. Who will do the actual parking (parking attendants, shoppers, residents, the physically handicapped, the elderly, etc.) and what are their particular characteristics that will affect parking design, location, and stall sizes?

Table 3–4. K Values for Vertical Curves

| | DESIGN SPEED IN MPH | | | | |
| --- | --- | --- | --- | --- | --- |
| | 30 | 40 | 50 | 60 | 65 |
| Minimum K Value for | | | | | |
| Crest vertical curves | 28 | 55 | 85 | 160 | 215 |
| Sag vertical curves | 35 | 55 | 75 | 105 | 130 |

Well-designed vertical curves must not be shorter than $L = KA$, with L the length of the curve in feet, A the algebraic difference of grades, for the K values given in the table.
Source: AASHO Geometric Highway Design

5. What limits, if any, does the budget impose on parking design (large, ground-level parking lots are cheapest; ramp parking structures and parking garages are usually most expensive)?

6. What are the minimum parking square footages for the various site elements (shopping centers, parks, apartments, etc.)?

7. Within the separate parking areas, which stall layout works best in terms of total number of stalls needed, circulation requirements, convenience, and cost (perpendicular; 30-, 45-, and 60-degree parking, etc.)?

8. How will the parking areas be drained? Parking areas usually need at least a 1 percent slope and should not be sloped more than 5 percent.

9. What types of streets and drives must be related to the site and to site parking?

Parking is an important aesthetic and functional consideration in site planning, worthy of considerable design time. It is not possible to establish a set of parking patterns that will work for all sites; even the stall sizes vary considerably. For a more definitive treatment of parking, the reader should consult texts or reference works on the subject. Figure 3–9, A–I illustrates some of the most common parking situations.

## Street Contours

Level streets do not drain well; thus, street profiles always slope somewhat to assure drainage. In cross section, streets are typically crowned in the center, directing runoff to both sides. Less typically street cross sections may slope to a valley at the center or they may be sloped to one side or the other. In urban areas the street is a catchment area (low point), and runoff is directed to curb inlets and hence to the underground storm drainage system. In rural areas just the opposite is the case; streets are high points and runoff is directed over the landscape, because there is no underground drainage system (Figure 3–10).

Street grades, represented graphically by their profile, vary significantly according to locality: A steep grade, acceptable in the Southern California climate, may not be acceptable for Wisconsin winters. Acceptable grades are usually spelled out by the localities, and the site planner works out the best-designed street possible within the fixed parameters. When the profile (grade) is established, streets may be shown on a contour map.

First, note the location of each contour where it crosses the center line of the street. The cross section will be known: crowned street (typical), valley street, or a street sloped to one side. Thus, the site planner knows

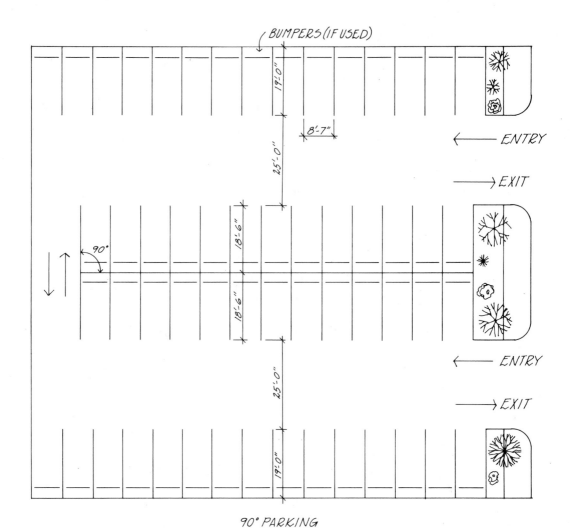

BUMPERS (IF USED)

19'-0"

8'-7"

25'-0"

←——— ENTRY

———→ EXIT

90°

18'-6"

18'-6"

25'-0"

←——— ENTRY

———→ EXIT

19'-0"

90° PARKING

FIGURE 3–9. The exact parking layout used depends on many factors including the number of cars to be parked, the shape and square footage of available parking land, the type development, and the desired circulation patterns. The parking stalls are either perpendicular or angular: typical angles used for parking stalls are 30, 45, 55, and 60 degrees. The examples illustrate only a few of the most common parking layouts possible.

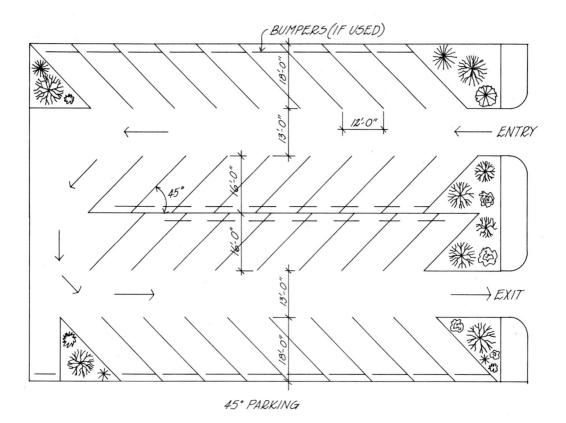

BUMPERS (IF USED)

18'-0"

12'-0"

13'-0"

45°

6'-0"

6'-0"

13'-0"

18'-0"

← ENTRY

→ EXIT

45° PARKING

3–9B.

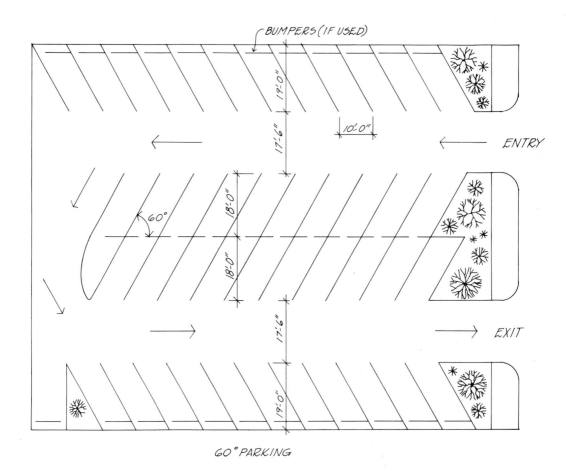

BUMPERS (IF USED)

19'-0"

17'-6"

10'-0"

ENTRY

18'-0"

60°

18'-0"

17'-6"

EXIT

19'-0"

60° PARKING

3–9C.

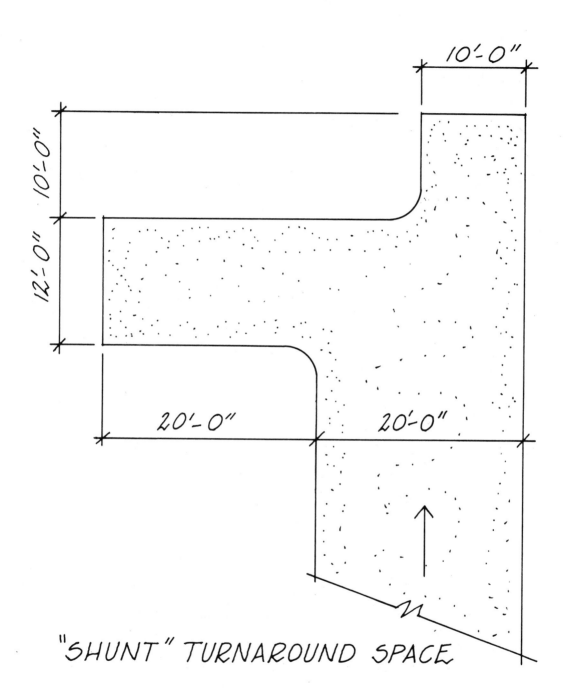

10'-0"

10'-0"

12'-0"

20'-0"

20'-0"

"SHUNT" TURNAROUND SPACE

3–9D.

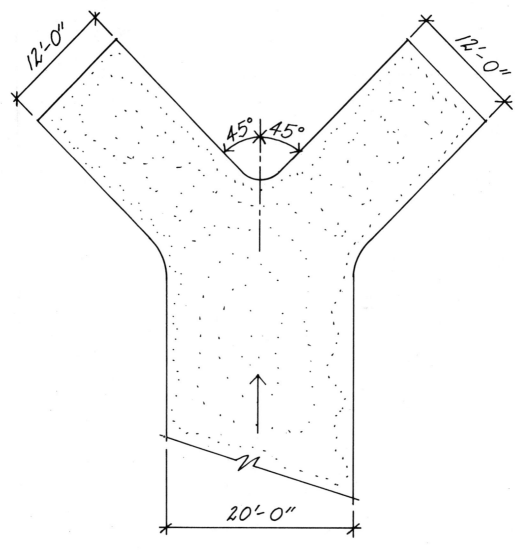

12'-0"

12'-0"

45° 45°

20'-0"

"Y-TURN" TURNAROUND SPACE

3–9E.

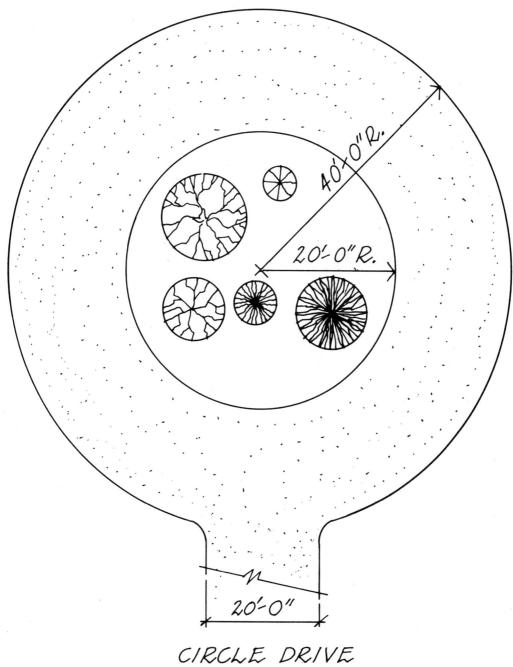

40'-0" R.

20'-0" R.

20'-0"

CIRCLE DRIVE

3–9F.

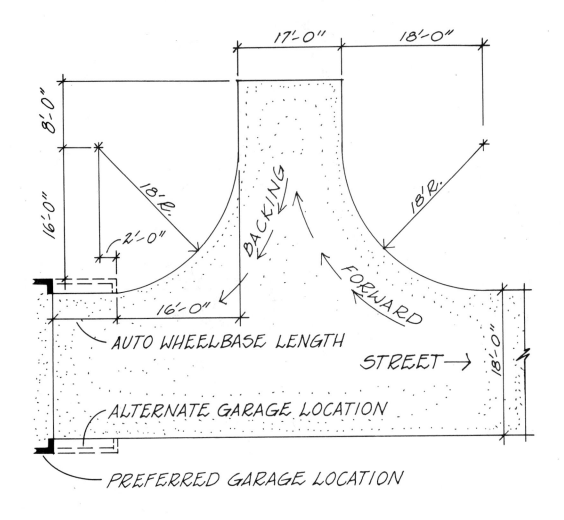

17'-0"   18'-0"

8'-0"

18' R.

BACKING

2'-0"

16'-0"

18' R.

FORWARD

16'-0"

AUTO WHEELBASE LENGTH

STREET →

18'-0"

ALTERNATE GARAGE LOCATION

PREFERRED GARAGE LOCATION

3–9G.

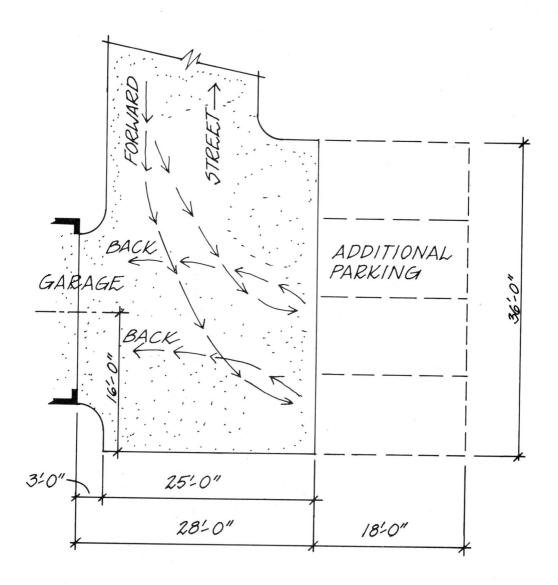

FORWARD

STREET

BACK

GARAGE

BACK

ADDITIONAL PARKING

36'-0"

16'-0"

3'-0"

25'-0"

28'-0"

18'-0"

3–9H.

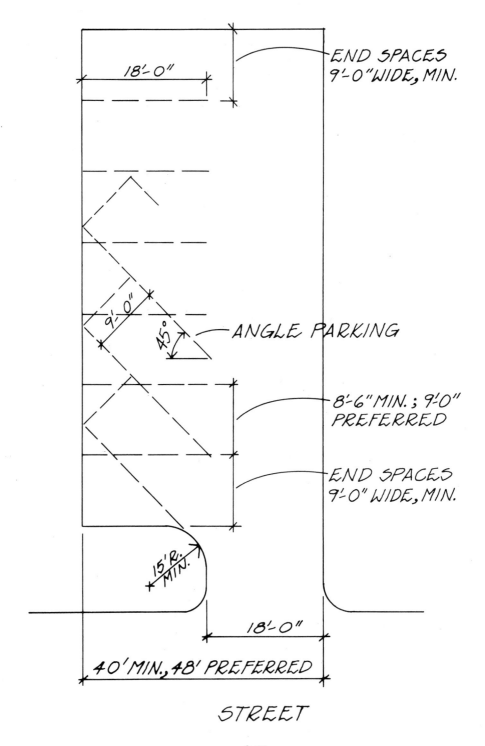

END SPACES
9'-0" WIDE, MIN.

18'-0"

9'-0"

45°

ANGLE PARKING

8'-6" MIN.; 9'-0"
PREFERRED

END SPACES
9'-0" WIDE, MIN.

15' R.
MIN.

18'-0"

40' MIN., 48' PREFERRED

STREET

3–9I.

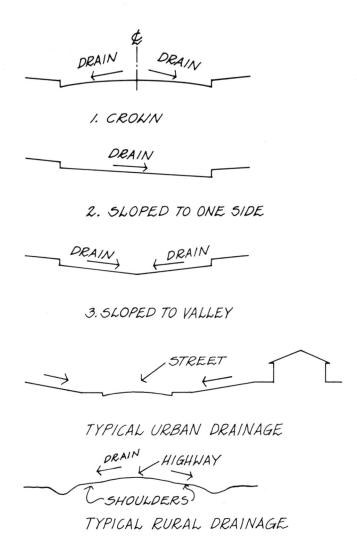

DRAIN | DRAIN

*1. CROWN*

DRAIN

*2. SLOPED TO ONE SIDE*

DRAIN | DRAIN

*3. SLOPED TO VALLEY*

STREET

*TYPICAL URBAN DRAINAGE*

DRAIN | HIGHWAY
SHOULDERS

*TYPICAL RURAL DRAINAGE*

FIGURE 3–10. Streets typically are sloped to drain by crowning the center; sloping to one side or the other; or sloping to a valley in the center.

the relation of curbtop elevations to center line elevations and so forth. To draw the street contours, the planner notes with tick marks where the land contours cross the center line, top of curb, and gutter. The street contour line may then be drawn freehand.

This general technique may be used to relate land contours to any fixed surface such as game courts, parking lots, terraces and patios, driveways, ditches, and similar surfaces. The technique involves locating the points where the land contours cross the fixed elevation points (fixed due to drainage or usage) and then adjusting the land contours accordingly.

# GRADING, EARTHWORK, AND CONSTRUCTION LAYOUT

# 4

Site program objectives almost always make some grading necessary. Surface water must be directed away from buildings and activity areas. Concentrated runoff from building roofs, parking areas, streets, walks, and other built elements must not be allowed to cause problems to surrounding properties. Erosion must be prevented. To accomplish these and other site goals, the land must be reshaped from its natural state. A good grading plan must consider many factors and solve many problems. Whenever possible, positive drainage should be provided for.

The existing natural drainage patterns must be thoroughly understood so that these natural patterns may continue to be used as much as possible, thus reducing costs and preserving the natural appearance of the site, when desirable. Existing vegetation must be considered. Grade changes near trees and plants are often harmful and may kill them. The grading plan should attempt to utilize the natural grades near trees and plants. Where this is not feasible, tree wells, retaining walls, or other devices that maintain the original grade near the trees and plants should be used.

Deep cuts and fills to accommodate structures are expensive. Therefore, the finished elevations of building first floors, streets, walks, and so forth should be carefully considered. Grading should be designed to minimize the use of retaining wells, terraces, banks, and similar structures; these structures are aids to drainage and site usage, not substitutes for good grade planning. Long flights of steps are difficult for the elderly and sometimes dangerous; they should be avoided.

Finally, grade design is an aesthetic endeavor: an effort to harmonize the reshaped land, the existing land, and the built site elements. These goals are not meant to be conclusive but rather are presented to give an idea of the many considerations that go into the making of a grade plan.

# DEFINITIONS

The following definitions are basic to an understanding of grading and earthwork.

*Cut.* A cut, as the term implies, is the removal of soil. On the contour map, a cut is the soil that is removed between an existing contour line (dashed) and a proposed contour line (solid). A cut is a measurable quantity; its length, height, and width can be measured and its volume determined.

*Fill.* A fill is the addition of soil. On the contour map a fill is the soil that is added in the space between an existing contour line and a proposed contour line. A fill, like the cut, has a prescribed length, width, and height, and its volume can be determined (Figure 4–1).

*Gradient.* Sometimes called simply *grade*, gradient is the amount of rise or fall in the land over some horizontal distance. If, for example, the land rises 5 feet over a horizontal distance of 100 feet, then the gradient is 5 feet:100 feet = 1:20 slope; the gradient can also be expressed as a percentage. Using the preceding figures, the vertical

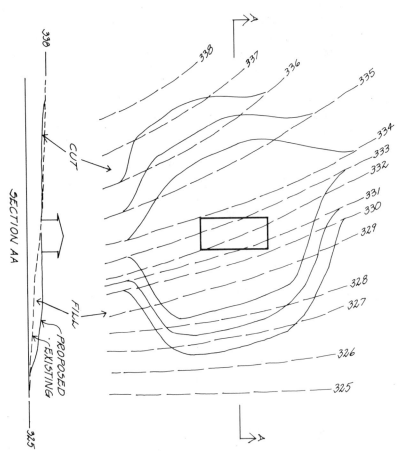

FIGURE 4–1. To quickly recognize cut and fill areas on a grading plan, remember: proposed contour lines made by moving away from existing contours toward higher numbers are cuts. Proposed contour lines made by moving away from existing contours toward smaller numbers are fills.

distance 5 feet, divided by the horizontal distance 100 feet, gives a 5 percent slope. All this can be expressed in simple formulas: where the vertical distance $= V$, the horizontal distance $= H$, and $G$ is the gradient, the formula becomes $V{:}H = G$. To express the slope as a percentage, the formula becomes $\dfrac{V}{H} = \%$ slope.

Percentages are usually used to express minimal slopes. Steep slopes, greater than 1:1, are usually expressed as gradients. The important thing is that the site planner be able to determine the existing site grades, determine what grades are necessary for the desired site activities, and evolve the simplest, cheapest, most aesthetically pleasing set of grading solutions and drainage aids to accommodate these activities. The following example is a simple but typical grading problem.

Let us say that a span of land is 100 feet in length and its high elevation is at contour 105. The site planner has determined that the desired usage for the area requires a 3 percent slope to drain properly. Manipulating the formula $\dfrac{V}{H} = \%$ slope, to $V = \%$ slope $H$, we have $V = 100$ feet times 3 percent; thus, we know that the lowest contour must be 3 feet less than the highest contour to drain properly. Therefore, the low contour is 105 $- 3 = 102$. Of course, this simple formula can be manipulated further, to yield $H = \dfrac{V}{\%}$ slope.

In this example the span of land was 100 feet. This was for convenience in illustrating use of the formula to solve a problem. But what happens if a 3 percent grade or less were necessary for the activity, you could get only a 3-foot vertical drop over the span of land, and the span of land were 150 feet, instead of 100 feet? Using the formula $\dfrac{V}{H} = \%$ slope and substituting 3 feet for $V$ and 150 feet for $H$, we see that the slope would only be 2 percent instead of the necessary 3 percent. Because the critical need for the activity is a 3 percent grade, the designer must hold the grade at 3 percent and determine what drainage aid (such as an area drain or catch basin) to use; otherwise the surface cannot be manipulated to drain adequately.

The grading plan is evolved with drainage, activity requirements, cost, and aesthetics simultaneously in mind.

*Grading.* Grading is cutting into an area of existing grade or filling over it. It is possible to accomplish site grading by cutting the entire site or by filling the entire site. The advantage of cutting the entire site is that the soil uncovered is well compacted and stable, thus reducing erosion and settling. The disadvantages are that the topsoil must be stored and then replaced for areas where vegetation is desired, because the topsoil supports the growth of vegetation; erosion is a problem when soil is redistributed over the site in large quantities; and it is costly to dispose of large quantities of unused soil.

Grading entirely by fill is usually done only when there is no other way to provide for drainage or site usage. This method is typically used for relatively small areas because the associated costs are high and because of other difficulties. Compacted fill under buildings, for example, is always avoided and when it cannot be avoided, the fill must be installed with strict engineering methods.

Thus, the most economical method of grading (short of no grading at all, which would perhaps be ideal) typically involves both cutting and filling. Using a combination of cuts and fills minimizes the problems associated with grading entirely by cut or entirely by fill.

*Rough Grading and the Subgrade.* The contractor must grade deeply enough to allow for the placement of streets, walks, sod, and other finish surface materials. The depth to which this rough grading goes is called the *subgrade.* The closer the subgrades are to parallel with the finished surface materials, the better.

Rough grading also typically includes cutting trees below ground (trees that cannot be saved); making any cuts and fills needed; compacting appropriately any fill needed; scarifying and otherwise preparing existing slopes to accept fill so that it does not slip; and removing debris, organic matter, or other unwanted materials that might hinder site development.

*Finish Grading and the Finish Grade.* The grading plan prepared by the site planner shows finished grades. Finished grading involves smoothing the subgrade parallel to the finished grade in anticipation of the finished materials.

Finish grading typically includes scarifying the subgrade where it is necessary to ensure a bond between the subsoil and the finish soil; providing finish soil proper and workable for the planned vegetation; and providing proper soil compaction to accommodate usage but minimize settlement.

## Spot Elevations

Spot elevations are supplementary elevation points. They are used to note exact location of elevation variations in items of interest between contour lines—existing small ponds, low points, rises, trees, wells, rock outcroppings, and similar items. Preliminary spot elevations are set by the site planner as an aid in developing the grading plan.

Finished spot elevations are noted at critical points to guide the contractor in implementing the grading plan. Typical finished elevation locations are top and bottom of curves, gutters, and walls; location of trees and natural elements to be saved; finished first-floor elevations of buildings; corners of buildings; door stoops; top and bottom of sloping walks; top and bottom of ramps; and rim and invert elevations of catch basins, manholes, and other storm and sanitary structures.

Spot elevations are usually noted to the hundredth decimal point: 100.25, 100.53, and so forth.

## Profiles

A profile is the line formed by the intersection of a vertical plane at some point along the ground. Profiles are a method of studying and describing specific areas; roads, for example, are studied and described by a series of profiles.

## The Grading Plan

The grading plan is a graphic representation of what the site planner thinks the new site should look like and be, having studied the existing site in depth; it is the key drawing on which the contractor will depend to build the new site.

It is not unusual for site planners to work out several conceptual grading plans before the final grading plan is evolved. The plan is typically begun by setting a number of preliminary spot elevations, then studying how they relate to each other; then contour lines are drawn. For conceptual drawings such as these, it is a waste of time to show every contour line. Rather, for 1-foot contour intervals, it is typical to show every fifth line. By showing every fifth line, the site planner can determine fairly quickly whether the plan is feasible without wasting time on unnecessary detail. When the conceptual plan is acceptable, the remaining lines are drawn in.

Some of the spot elevations are givens. Existing buildings, for example, with their drainage requirements, are often starting points in a grading concept. To such given elevations and grading beginning points, the site planner may add another list of proposed elevations that represent site goals: special views to be created or maintained; special trees and natural features to be preserved; and other site givens, with their corresponding elevations, that appear to be critical to the overall success of the new site.

All such preliminary spot elevations are shown on a conceptual grading plan that at the beginning may be no more than a freehand sketch;

there is no point in wasting time "hard lining" a conceptual drawing at the early stages. This beginning drawing is studied to determine concept feasibility.

Almost any grading plan can be made to work. But a good grading plan is aesthetically pleasing, functions well, and can be built within the budget. There are early indicators of an infeasible concept. For example, a grading plan that depends on a large number of retaining walls to drain properly probably needs further study; retaining walls are expensive and rarely need to be used in wholesale fashion in order for the site to drain properly. Excessive use of steps is another tip-off that further study should be done. Grading plans that rely on steep slopes are undesirable. A grading plan that results in an extreme unbalance of cut or fill—all cut or all fill, for example—often needs further study. Slopes that drain toward buildings are suspect. Any plan that requires removal of large amounts of vegetation is likely to be defectively planned; vegetation is initially expensive and is expensive to plant and often does not fare as well as the vegetation that was in place at first. These examples, of course, are merely indicators that more planning may be necessary; they are not rules. Sites are much too varied to have their planning reduced to a set of rules.

It was mentioned that an extreme unbalance of cut or fill is suspect, and that further planning may be necessary when this condition is discovered. It is simply good conventional grading practice, on typical sites, to avoid hauling large volumes of soil to or away from the site. Thus, it is necessary to calculate the amount of cut or fill with some frequency as site grading planning proceeds. If an unfavorable balance is calculated for some area of the site, that area must be restudied to assure that the imbalance is necessary to achieve a good overall plan. It is appropriate at this time, then, to consider the methods used to calculate cut and fill.

## Calculating Cut and Fill

There are several methods of calculating cut and fill, including the contour-area method, the end-area method, and the borrow-pit method.

The first method—contour-area—is good for large areas, has the advantage of being graphic, and proceeds directly from the conceptual grading plan. The end-area method is especially useful for linear earth work calculations such as roads. The last method—borrow-pit—is good for building or similar excavations; it is the least graphic of these methods of calculating cut and fill.

*Contour-Area Method.* To determine the amount of cut and fill by the contour-area method, first shade all the areas of cut and fill. Shade cut in one color and fill in another. Do this on tracing paper laid over the grading plan or directly on a copy of the grading plan. Number each area between contours—typically C–1, C–2, C–3, etc., for cuts and F–1, F–2, F–3, etc., for fills (Figure 4–2). Next determine the corresponding surface area for each of the numbered areas between contours. You can determine area by using a fine graph paper or by using a planimeter; if graph paper is used, simply count the squares.

Both the graph area and the planimeter give the area in square inches. Therefore, you must convert the square inch areas to square feet. To get square feet from your square-inch calculations, simply multiply the square-inch planimeter or graph paper reading by the plan scale squared. For example, if you have a graph paper or planimeter reading of 2.25 square inches, and the drawing scale is 1 inch equal to 20 feet, the square-foot reading for the area is $20 \times 20 \times 2.25 = 900$ square feet.

When you multiply the surface area by the contour interval, you get volume in cubic feet. Because earth work is usually computed in cubic yards, you must then divide by 27. For example, using the given numbers,

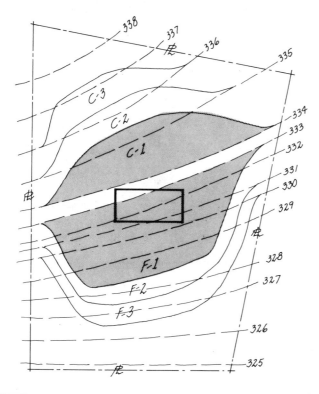

FIGURE 4–2. To determine the amount of cut and fill by the contour-area method, first shade all the areas of cut and fill. For simplicity, only one area of cut and one area of fill have been shaded in this illustration.

say that you have computed an area of cut to be 900 square feet. The contour interval on your conceptual grading plan is 5 feet. The volume of cut would then be 5 times $\frac{900}{27}$, or 167 cubic yards.

As a procedure it is probably safest first to write all the graph or planimeter area readings in square inches—one column for cuts and one column for fills. Then compute the cut-and-fill volumes. Finally determine whether your plan requires that earth be hauled away or brought to the site by simply subtracting the smaller from the larger volumes.

*End-Area Method.* The end-area method of computing cut and fill utilizes the formula

$$V = A_1 + \frac{A_2}{2} \times L$$

where $V$ is volume, $A_1$ and $A_2$ are vertical cross sections, and $L$ is the length of cut or fill considered (Figure 4–3). In highway work the distance

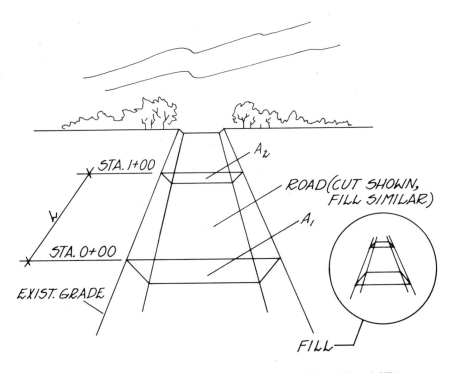

FIGURE 4–3. To find the cut volume between STA. 0 00 and STA. 1 00, use the following formula:

$$\text{volume} + \frac{A_1 + A_2}{2} \times L.$$

*L* between the two cross sections is usually one station or 100 feet. The formula, however, may be used to compute any similar longitudinal cuts and fills.

*Borrow-Pit Method.* The borrow-pit method is often used to compute the amount of cut or fill under buildings or similar excavations. Using this method, first overlay the area to be computed with a convenient grid (Figure 4–4).

Where a grid corner occurs at only one square, letter it *a*; letter grid corners that are common to two squares *b*; letter grid corners that are common to three squares *c*; and grid corners that are common to four squares *d*. Next compute the existing elevations of all grid corners. From each grid corner, subtract the bottom of excavation; the bottom of excavation is the elevation where the building will rest. This difference gives you the height of all the *a*'s, *b*'s, *c*'s, and *d*'s. Compute the sum of all the *a*'s, *b*'s, *c*'s, and *d*'s, keeping them separate.

Volume equals the area of 1 square over 27 times the sum of *a*'s plus 2 sum *b*'s plus 3 sum *c*'s plus 4 sum *d*'s all over 4. A numerical example follows.

Given a grid of 20 feet and a bottom of excavation of 105.0, first compute the elevations of all the grid corners (Figure 4–4). Next compute the heights of the grid corners by subtracting the bottom of excavation (105.0) from the grid corner elevations.

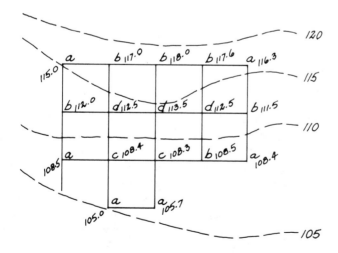

FIGURE 4–4. Choose a grid of any convenient size. Compute the elevations at the grid corners. Compute volume of earthwork as described in text.

| | | | | | |
|---|---|---|---|---|---|
| *a*'s: | 115.0 | 116.3 | 108.4 | 105.0 | 105.7 |
| | − 105.0 | − 105.0 | − 105.0 | − 105.0 | − 105.0 |
| | 10.0 | 11.3 | 3.4 | 0.0 | 0.7 |

| | | | | | | |
|---|---|---|---|---|---|---|
| *b*'s: | 117.5 | 118.0 | 117.6 | 112.0 | 111.5 | 108.5 |
| | − 105.0 | − 105.0 | − 105.0 | − 105.0 | − 105.0 | − 105.0 |
| | 12.5 | 13.0 | 12.6 | 7.0 | 6.5 | 3.5 |

| | | |
|---|---|---|
| *c*'s: | 108.4 | 108.3 |
| | − 105.0 | − 105.0 |
| | 3.4 | 3.3 |

| | | | |
|---|---|---|---|
| *d*'s: | 112.6 | 113.5 | 112.5 |
| | − 105.0 | − 105.0 | − 105.0 |
| | 7.6 | 8.5 | 7.5 |

Sum of *a*'s = 25.40 feet

Sum of *b*'s = 55.12 feet

Sum of *c*'s = 6.70 feet

Sum of *d*'s = 23.60 feet

Using the formula

$$\text{Volume} = \frac{\text{area of 1 square}}{27} \times \frac{\text{sum } a\text{'s} + 2 \text{ sum } b\text{'s} + 3 \text{ sum } c\text{'s} + 4 \text{ sum } d\text{'s}}{4},$$

we get

$$V = \frac{400}{27} \times \frac{25.4 + 2\,(55.12) + 3(6.7) + 4\,(23.6)}{4} = 250.14 \text{ cubic yards}$$

These three methods of computing cut and fill are simple, if tedious, and will suffice for much of the rough earth work calculations that the site planner makes in the design stage of the grading plan. Small, regular areas of cut or fill may be computed by simply comparing them to some geometric shape and applying the appropriate formula for finding volume.

The excavation of a rectangular building or similar excavation may be computed similarly to the grid method discussed, but substituting the building corners for the grid. The formula is $V = $ average height $\times L \times W$, where $L$ is the length of the building, $W$ the width, and average height is the average height of excavation.

For example, let us say that you wish to compute the volume of cut for a 40 by 80 foot building. Assume a bottom of excavation of 102.5. The building is located on the contours shown on Figure 4–5.

First compute the building corner elevations; they are 122.5, 113.3, 107.5, and 113.3, as shown in the drawing. Now find the average height

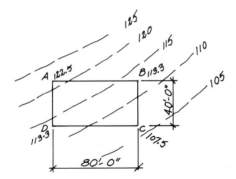

FIGURE 4–5. Excavation volumes for rectangular buildings (or similar shapes) may be computed by finding their average height of excavation and then using the formula volume = average height of excavation × length of building × width of building.

of excavation. Do this by subtracting the bottom of excavation figure (102.5) from each of the building corner elevations, then finding their average:

$$
\begin{array}{cccc}
A = 122.5 & B = 113.3 & C = 107.5 & D = 113.3 \\
-102.5 & -102.5 & -102.5 & -102.5 \\
\hline
20.0 & 10.8 & 5.0 & 10.8
\end{array}
$$

$$20.0 + 10.8 + 5.0 + 10.8 \div 4 = \frac{46.6}{4} = 11.7 \text{ feet}$$

Using the formula $V$ = average height × $L$ × $W$, we get $V = 11.7 \times 80 \times 40 = 37{,}440$ cubic feet. Dividing 37,440 by 27, we get a volume of 1,387 cubic yards.

In evolving a grading plan, as in all analytical work of site planning, site planners must manage their design efforts efficiently, because these efforts are expensive and time-consuming. A rough sketch with the cut-and-fill areas shaded in will sometimes—at a glance—be sufficient to eliminate a poor concept before more time is spent on it, when, for example, an existing imbalance of cut or fill, for the project in question, would make its construction outside the proposed budget. But for concepts that appear promising, continuing data are accumulated, and more accurate cut-and-fill volumes are computed.

## Subgrading and Topsoil

Subgrading for walks, roads, buildings, parking lots, game courts, and other structures sometimes adds up to enough volume to affect cost estimates seriously; obviously the larger the project, the more important subgrading calculations become.

To compute the volume of subgrading, outline the area of the subgrade, then compute its area with a planimeter or by using graph paper. Next convert the square-inch figure that you get by multiplying by the plan scale squared; the figure will be square feet of area. Multiply square feet of area by the depth of the soil to be cut or filled; that figure will be volume in cubic feet. Divide by 27 to get cubic yards.

Sometimes it is necessary to remove topsoil (which must be stored somewhere on site). Compute the topsoil volume the way that you compute the subgrade volume: outline; find the area (square inches); convert to square feet, then multiply by depth. Divide the cubic feet figure by 27 to get cubic yards.

## Fill Shrinkage

A cubic yard of cut, hauled to a fill area, will not completely fill a cubic yard void when placed as fill. After weathering for some time it will shrink further. Shrinkage typically ranges from 3 to 5 percent, the exact amount depending largely on the type soil and thus its stability. When calculating shrinkage as it affects the cut-fill balance, 4 percent is typically used.

The data are for typical site and soil conditions. A knowledge of soil types for the particular site is necessary to predict soil shrinkage accurately, especially on large sites where much fill may be needed.

## Fill Compaction

Developers always hope to find stable, naturally compacted soil as the subgrade. Such "good" soil cuts down on expenses. Where the soil is not naturally stable enough to support the desired structures, it is sometimes necessary to remove the unstable soil and replace it with more stable soil, which is typically laid and compacted in shallow layers. The volume of imported fill must be computed, as it is a cost. Hauling the fill and installing are, of course, also costs.

Estimating project costs is conceptually simple but involves a great number of items to be summed up: land clearing, cut and fill amount, compacted fill, finish grading, drainage structures, and so forth. Estimating project costs is a vital function of site planning.

## Layout and Grading of Sports Fields

Sports field layouts vary according to usage; younger players, for example, often need smaller fields than adults. Sex may also influence field layout and dimensions.

The layouts in this section illustrate general form and space requirements for some of the more popular sports (Figure 4–6, A–I). In general the fields are graded very gently (the outfield of a baseball field slopes at 2 percent away from the bases toward the outfield). Both layout and grading requirements should be checked with the appropriate ruling authority as well as the eventual users.

In the design stage the site planner is concerned with selecting the best location on the site for the required sports fields. A baseball field or track and football field, for example, requires a relatively level space. If there are choices of locations, such fields should be located where extremes of cut and fill can be avoided—you would not want to slice into a hillside or fill a large depression to install a baseball or football field, if there were other more level choices of land that fit with the desired overall circulation pattern of the site.

After the general location for the sports fields are determined, the site planner may adjust the grades surrounding the sports field so that overall drainage is accomplished while maintaining the particular requirements of the sports field.

## CONSTRUCTION LAYOUT

### The Surveyor

Specialization is important in construction. Building tasks overlap enough to make the job flow, but the variuos skills are distinct. The contractor who grades the site, for example, is interested in foundation work to the extent necessary to dig the proper subgrades. But the grading contractor is not concerned with, say, the techniques used to erect the buildings.

"The surveyor" may be one person or several persons and may be a full-time surveyor or only perform surveying as part of general job responsibilities, as in the case of the civil engineer. Reference points for design and construction, however, fall in the province of surveying. All the built elements of the site—grades, terraces, retaining walls, lakes, buildings, streets, parking lots, and so forth—are located on the plans relative to distances from known objects. These objects may be existing, such as building corners, or public bench marks, or they may be created by the surveyor in the form of new bench marks, stakes, etc.

The surveyor establishes initial reference points that site planners, architects, engineers, and others use to design the project. As the project plans progress, the surveyor is called on to establish additional reference points for design or construction use. All the reference points used must be appropriate for the particular skill or trade that needs them.

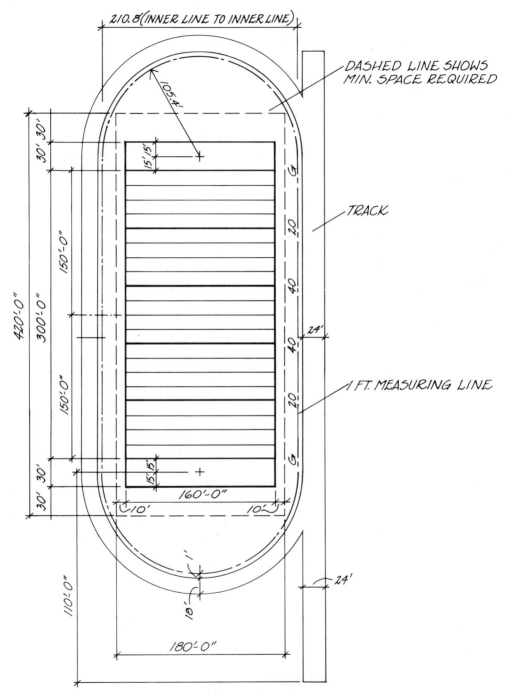

FIGURE 4–6A. Football field/440 yard track.
Note: The sports layouts shown should be used only for preliminary design work. Before final layouts are done, check the current and approved dimensions of the governing athletic organizations and/or other authorities in charge of standards.

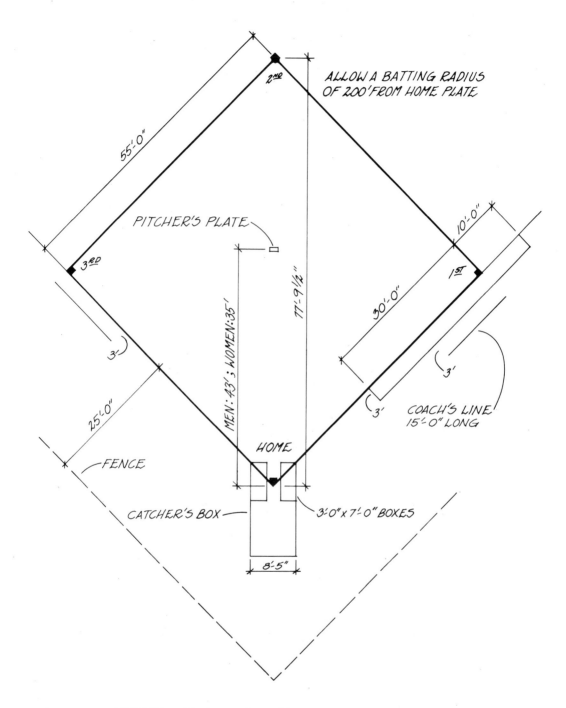

FIGURE 4–6B. Regulation softball field. A field for young people may be built similarly but using 45 foot base lines instead of the 55 foot shown and by reducing the distance to the pitcher's plate to 35 feet.

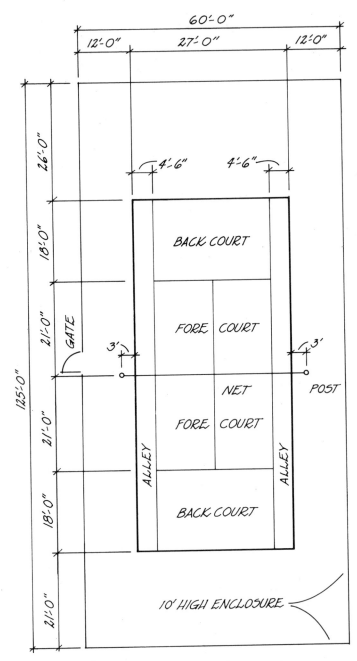

TYPICAL TOURNAMENT TENNIS COURT

FIGURE 4–6C. The sizes of tennis courts vary somewhat depending on factors including usage and materials. Check local requirements for the most desirable orientation of the court. It usually is best to arrange multiple courts side-by-side, rather than end-to-end.

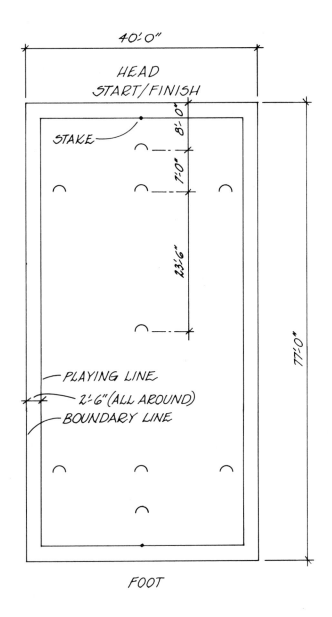

FIGURE 4–6D. Lawn croquet court.

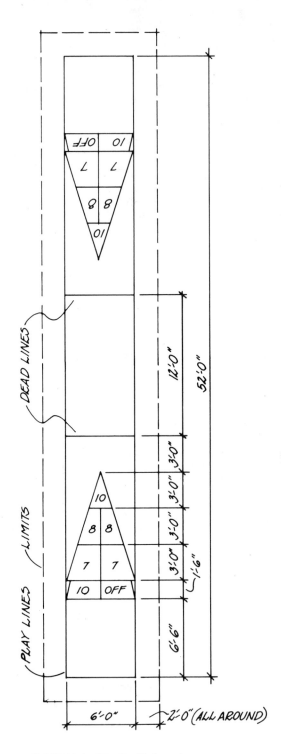

FIGURE 4–6E. Shuffleboard court.

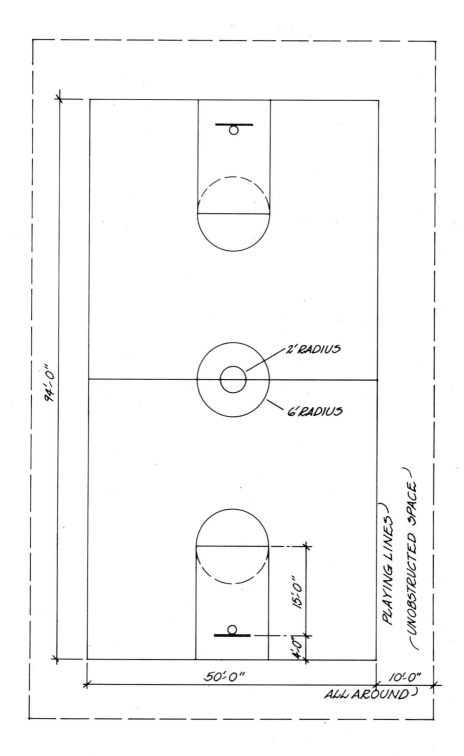

FIGURE 4–6F. Collegiate basketball court.

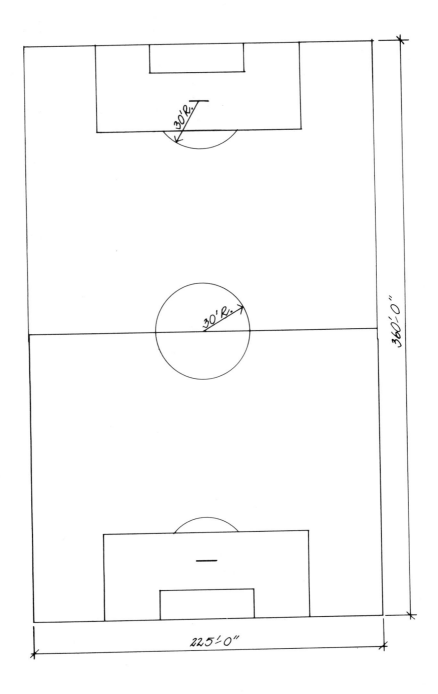

FIGURE 4–6G. Soccer field.

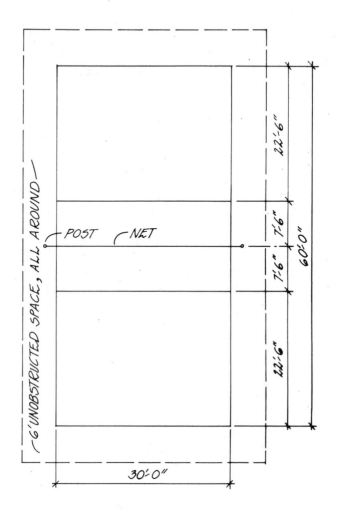

FIGURE 4–6H. Volleyball court.

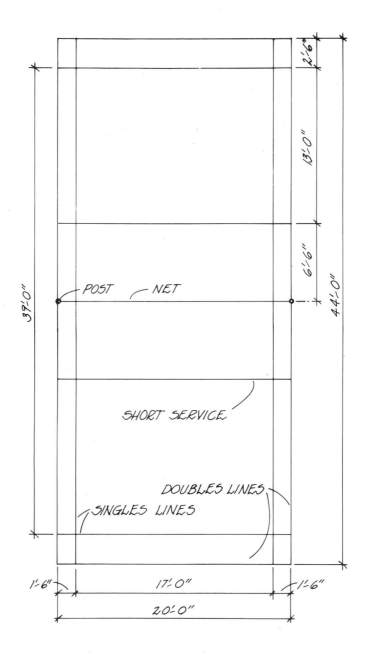

FIGURE 4–6I. Badminton court.

Most construction work involves alteration of the earth surface. Site planners strive to keep a reasonable balance between cut and fill. The surveyor provides the initial elevations from which the topographic map or contour map is made and from which the site planner derives the preliminary site plan.

## Stakes

Once the plan is finalized, stakes must be located in the field to guide the various contractors in their work.

*General.* Stakes are necessary to guide the various contractors in building the site per the plans and specifications. Sometimes the stakes are graphic in their use, almost like drawings on the site surface (as in the case of street and ditch centerline stakes), and other times they are more symbolic than graphic (as in the case of grid stakes and reference stakes). When and where stakes are needed, how many are needed, and how they are installed are decisions best left to surveyors and engineers. Staking takes time and costs money in itself; if it is not done carefully and correctly, very costly errors can be made by equipment operators.

The following, though not conclusive, gives an idea of how stakes are used for construction layout on typical sites.

*Grid Stakes.* The form, features, objects on, and other identifying characteristics of a site may be located with grid stakes. The stakes are arranged in squares over the site; typical spacings range from 5 to 100 feet. The grid arrangement may vary over a given site, where more information is needed in particular areas than over the site as a whole.

*Location Stakes.* As the name implies, these stakes locate objects on the site. The objects may be man-made, such as buildings and parking lots. Or they may be natural objects, such as ponds, lakes, and rock outcroppings. Other uses include lot corner stakes and stakes for building setback lines. Location stakes locate both existing features and proposed features of sites.

*Bench-mark Stakes.* Bench marks are fixed reference points. For contour maps and other preliminary design work, the initial bench mark may be a tree trunk, a building corner, or some similar permanent or semipermanent point of elevation. On small jobs and jobs where the site is fairly level and all elevations may be viewed by placing the leveling instrument at some known high point, it may not be necessary to move the instrument further.

But most jobs, especially large ones, need additional bench marks as work progresses. Roadwork and streets, for example, typically involve many checks for level and inherently demand movement of the instrument in both the layout and construction phases. These additional "working" bench marks are often stakes placed where they can be easily viewed from each new position of the instrument.

*Reference Stakes.* Where stakes are likely to be destroyed or where they must be removed to facilitate construction, reference stakes may be used to reset the original stakes. For example, where excavation within the building corner stakes is necessary, the corner stakes may be reset by the use of reference stakes placed relative to each corner of the building.

*Ditch Stakes.* Ditches for storm sewers, sanitary sewers, and other gravity systems require accurate digging. There are several ways of staking and digging ditches. One way is to plot the profile of the land above where the pipe will be laid with stakes. From some starting point, elevations are taken along the ditch profile; the station system is used, beginning with station $0+0$ and continuing the length of the ditch. Intermediate elevations are taken as required, depending on the building conditions. A stake every 25 feet is common, more often if necessary.

The stakes may be laid out directly above the pipe centerline or to either side of the ditch or to some convenient offset line from the ditch. The amount of cut at any station may be determined by subtracting the bottom elevation from the surface elevation.

*Grading Stakes.* The amount of cut and fill desired for different areas is figured and marked on the stakes. Strips of cloth tied to the fill stakes save the operator from having to climb down from the machine to check whether the stake is cut or fill.

*Street Stakes.* The first stakes employed for streets are typically those along the centerline and along the outer limits of the street. The centerline stakes note cut and fill. The outer stakes show the outer limits that must be cleared for the street.

As the work proceeds and the subgrade is approached, centerline stakes are replaced and shoulders (if any) and gutters are staked. Bluetops are used for finish grades; bluetops are stakes driven so that their tops are at the desired grade, typically the subgrade. They are colored blue for better operator visibility.

## Batter Boards

Batter boards are a convenient field reference system. Set back from the actual work area, the boards may be marked or notched where the alignment strings are; the strings may then be removed and replaced, should the work make it necessary. When footings are dug, for example, and heavy machinery is present, the strings may be removed. Using the marks or notches on the batter boards, the strings may be replaced to help locate construction points such as the foundation wall face and height of floor slabs—any horizontal or vertical points (Figure 4–7).

While the boards are being erected, they may be checked for square by measuring the diagonals from their corners. If the diagonals are equal, the corners are square, that is, the corners are 90 degrees (Figure 4–8).

To aid in erecting the boards, some builders use a 3-4-5 right triangle. The triangle may be built on the job using 1 by 4's or similar stock. The triangle may be any convenient multiple of 3-4-5: 3 feet by 4 feet by 5 feet, 6 feet by 8 feet by 10 feet, etc. (Figure 4–9).

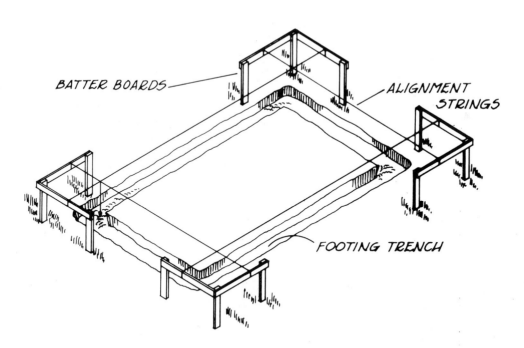

BATTER BOARDS

ALIGNMENT STRINGS

FOOTING TRENCH

FIGURE 4–7. Batter boards and alignment strings are a convenient method of keeping footing trenches level and square. The boards should be located far enough from the trenches to be out of the way of workers and equipment.

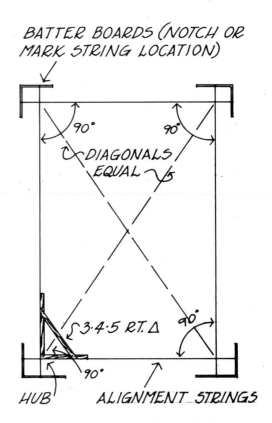

BATTER BOARDS (NOTCH OR MARK STRING LOCATION)

90°   90°

DIAGONALS EQUAL

3·4·5 R.T. Δ   90°

HUB   90°   ALIGNMENT STRINGS

FIGURE 4–8. Individual corners may be checked for squareness by measuring along the legs of the 3–4–5 right triangle: then check to see that the hypotenuse is the correct length. Measuring major diagonals is another check; if they are equal, the corners are square.

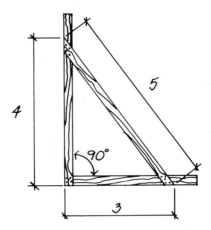

5

4

90°

3

FIGURE 4–9. A 3–4–5 right triangle, made of 1 × 4's or similar members, is a simple way to assure square corners for trench work, footings, foundation walls, and similar tasks.

# DRAINAGE 5

## Storm Drains

A storm drainage system is designed to collect, direct, and dispose of runoff. Runoff occurs both during and shortly after rains. The storm drainage system makes use of natural site drainage—as much as is practical—and is composed of a number of manmade components both above and below ground.

Aboveground drainage is usually cheaper because of the cost associated with underground pipe and its installation. Thus, the site planner tries to manipulate the ground surface to drain away from the buildings and other areas where water is undesirable and to direct the water to acceptable disposal points.

Belowground drainage systems are used where surface drainage alone cannot collect, direct, and dispose of runoff satisfactorily. For sites large enough to justify the services of a site planner, drainage is typically accomplished with a combination of above- and belowground drainage components. The site planner tries to minimize the use of underground components, contributing to economy, without eliminating significant development objectives and aesthetic appeal.

To help visualize the storm drainage system, study a local development with which you are familiar. Study the site during a rain, beginning your observations with the buildings, houses, and similar structures. Watch how the rainwater drains from the buildings and houses. Rain moves down roof slopes to gutters, then to downspouts. The downspouts may empty onto the ground or they may go underground to a drain pipe; they may do both.

Grassy areas, walks, parking lots, and similar areas are sloped to direct runoff to final disposal points, perhaps being first collected in swales, ditches, or catch basins. Try to trace all the rainwater patterns to their final disposal points.

Some drainage is not visible, such as the rainwater that moves through the soil, the rainwater that evaporates, and the rainwater that is used in the transpiration process. But most of the runoff is directed over and under the site surface to final disposal points and you can observe this, although it may take several trips. Final disposal points may be underground drain lines at the street, open ditches or canals, streams and lakes, or other site runoff exits.

It is important to realize that final disposal points are final only relative to the particular site. On many sites the site planner will be called on to design, it will be necessary only to design the best way to tie the site storm drainage system into the public storm drain lines; little analysis beyond a particular site and its immediate neighbors is required in such cases. But on large-scale developments, or on an areawide plan, where considerable storm water is directed to streams and other disposal points—which may alter natural levels and water speeds with harmful effects—considerable analysis and study are required to determine the effects of the particular site storm drainage plan on the larger environment.

In analyzing the storm drainage system of your study site, first consider how rainwater affects the site components: the buildings, parking areas, activity areas, open spaces, all designed and natural site components. Study the routes and materials that the site planner designed to direct the rainwater to final disposal points. Analyze the use of swales, ditches, catch basins, and other drainage aids. Then, after you understand the storm drainage system of the site, take a trip to the local planning department and observe how the particular site relates to the drainage of the surrounding areas.

Designing a storm drainage system for a particular site is a process of choosing among many relatively simple but important water-routing methods and materials. Your choices impact the site development program, have cost consequences to your client, and have environmental consequences to the public.

## STORM DRAINAGE COMPONENTS

### Building Drains

Gutters and downspouts are the typical method of draining rainwater off houses in all areas of the country. Similarly, commercial, industrial, institutional, and other structures collect rainwater at the roof and direct it to interior and exterior downspouts. Downspouts for houses, buildings, and other structures often empty rainwater out at the ground, where it is collected and directed away from the building and ultimately directed to final disposal points. Or the downspouts may go underground to drain pipes or there can be some combination where part of the rainwater from the roof empties onto the ground and part of it goes to underground drain lines. The design of a roof drainage system is determined by factors such as building size (which may be a single house or may be an industrial building or buildings occupying many acres of land and significantly influencing drainage), roof design, site activities around the building, and weather.

# Slopes

Manipulating surface slopes is a primary method of achieving good storm drainage. Positive drainage, drainage design that directs rainwater away from structures in activity areas, is best. Positive drainage is often a requirement of local and federal regulating authorities, and these authorities publish recommended slope gradients for particular usages. The site planner must become familiar with applicable requirements.

The following slope gradients are often desirable, but local conditions may vary:

1. Grassy areas sloping away from houses or buildings: Maximum 21 percent. Minimum 5 percent.
2. Building entry stoops: Maximum 2 percent. Minimum 1 percent.
3. Main entry walks to buildings: Maximum 4 percent. Minimum 1 percent.
4. Swales: Maximum 10 percent. Minimum 2 percent.
5. Secondary or collector walks: Maximum 8 percent. Minimum 1 percent.
6. Mowed grassy slopes: Maximum 3:1 slope.
7. Unmowed grassy slopes: Maximum 2:1 slope.
8. Patios and sitting areas: Maximum 2 percent. Minimum 1 percent.
9. Service areas: Maximum 5 percent. Minimum 0.5 percent.
10. On-site parking: Maximum 5 percent. Minimum 0.5 percent.
11. Ramps: Maximum 10 percent. Minimum 1 percent.
12. Grass-covered recreational areas: Maximum 3 percent. Minimum 2 percent.
13. Streets: Maximum 8 percent. Minimum 0.5 percent.

These gradients are not definitive but are presented to give an idea of how structures and site surfaces relate to each other in terms of storm drainage.

# Swales

Drainage swales are used to collect and direct runoff. Generally speaking, drainage swales are wide, rather shallow, with rounded bottoms. They may, however, have flat or V-shaped bottoms and can slope steeply, depending on drainage needs. The steeper the swales, and the more water they carry, the more attention is required to surfacing. Gentle swales for residential use may be surfaced with grass or other ground covers. Steeper swales may need rocks, concrete, or similar surfaces. If the swale is used to disperse water over the ground, it should be kept wide and should slope gently. Narrow, steep swales are used to direct water to catchment areas. For all uses, swales typically begin wide and shallow at the top, for highest elevation, and become somewhat deeper, wider, and slope down more toward the bottom where the greatest runoff collects—this prevents ponding.

## Catch Basins and Area Drains

Both catch basins and area drains are used to transfer water directed to them to underground drain lines. They are typically located at the lowest point in catchment areas. From above, catch basins and area drains look about the same. Both of them are fitted with some kind of grate to keep out debris and avoid clogging. But area drains are built similarly to household sinks; the water goes through the grate directly into the drain line. Catch basins on the other hand have rather deep, box-shaped pits under the grates. This pit catches leaves, sediment, debris, and so forth and is used where periodic clean-out is necessary.

## Dry Wells

A dry well is a pit or "well" filled with coarse gravel or masonry rubble that allows water to run down through it quickly, thus avoiding ponding. The diameter and depth of the dry well depend on the amount of water that it will have to absorb, the type of soil, and the location of the water table. The bottom of the dry well must be above the water table at its seasonal height. Dry wells should be kept as far as possible from buildings and other structures that would be harmed by the water concentrated in and around dry wells.

## Trench Drains

Trench drains are typically flat-bottomed, uniformly sloping, linear drains. They are usually a drainage supplement or a link between larger drainage components. For example, trench drains may be used periodically across long links of sloping sidewalks to carry runoff to underground drain lines. Or they may be used across the top or bottom (or both) of flights of steps or similarly at the top and bottom of ramps. They may also be used at the intersection of two oppositely sloped drainage areas, such as where a steep driveway meets the street. Trench drains may empty into underground drain lines or they may empty onto the landscape; they usually are equipped with metal or concrete grates and they sometimes employ clean-out pits at the juncture of the underground drain, if they are so connected.

## Culverts

Culverts are pipes used to carry runoff under structures such as roads, driveways, and walkways. Culverts are usually made of metal or concrete. The diameter varies with the amount of water to be carried; typical sizes begin at about 1 foot and range up to several feet.

## Underground Drain Pipes

Underground drain pipes transport water received from collection points such as area drains and catch basins. The pipes vary greatly in size, from several inches to several feet, depending on usage; for example, a 6-inch-diameter underground pipe that receives water from a residential area drain may transport water to a storm drain pipe of several feet in diameter at the street. The pipe is made of several materials, including concrete, clay, and plastic.

## Terraces

Terracing is a method of slowing the flow of surface water on slopes. In some cases terraces can be made by grading the earth to form the terraces and using a ground cover such as grass on the surface. For steep slopes it may be necessary to use retaining walls to hold the terraces in place; retaining walls are expensive and usually avoided if other solutions are possible.

## Baffles

Baffles, like terraces, are devices to slow the flow of surface water over slopes or areas subject to erosion. They are built of any material appropriate to the function required and to the landscape design; cross ties, stone, and masonry rubble are typical baffle materials. The baffles are installed in a manner to slow and divert surface water as it moves down slopes. Baffles are usually used on less dramatic slopes than are terraces and are simpler and less expensive to build.

## Curbs and Gutters

Curbs and gutters are used to direct street runoff to catch basins or other runoff collection points. The streets themselves may be drained by several methods or combinations of methods. Perhaps the most common method is to build a "crown," that is, a higher surface in the center of the street, thus directing the water to each side of the street, where it is further directed by curbs and gutters. Another method of draining streets is to build the street flat and slope it along the length; the water is eventually picked up and redirected by some other drainage device. Some streets are flat and slope to one side or the other, where curbs and gutters carry surface runoff to catch basins or other collection points. Although curbs and gutters in streets are a familiar scene all over America, the localities may vary considerably in their design; local authorities usually publish their requirements, which are available to anyone concerned with street and road design.

## Manholes

A manhole is a structure built into a storm drain or sewer line to provide access for cleaning and maintenance. Manholes are often precast concrete components, but they may be made of brick, concrete block, poured concrete, metal, or other suitable materials. The covers are usually 24 inches or larger in diameter. The bottoms are usually solid but may be perforated or made of gravel, if percolation is desired.

## Detention Ponds

Detention ponds are man-made or natural depressions designed to store storm runoff and then slowly release it over time after the rain subsides. The purpose of detention ponds is to make individual developments more responsible for their own drainage, thus reducing the size and expense of the overall public storm drainage system and lowering the risk of downstream flooding.

Detention ponds can be designed to be aesthetically pleasing, treated, in effect, as small, on-site lakes. With large commercial and industrial buildings, detention ponds or holding basins may be incorporated on flat roofs. Underground storage tanks are possible where the roof design is not conducive to water storage. In any case detention ponds are usually equipped with a slow-release water exit (such as small drain pipes or similar devices), typically at the low point of the pond or basin; a method of overflow must also be provided in the design.

The description applies to temporary detention ponds. Where soil conditions permit, detention ponds may be designed to hold the water until it is disposed of through percolation; even in such permanent water detention situations, an acceptable route must be provided for overflow in stormy conditions.

# Drain Fields

Drain fields are subsurface lines to which runoff is directed; perforations in the drain lines allow the water to percolate through the soil. Soil tests must be made to determine whether this method will work. The size of the drain field, size of the drain pipes, and method of installation depends on a number of factors such as area to be drained; ability of the soil to soak up the runoff; local weather and rain conditions; and duration of rainfall.

# DRAINAGE SYSTEMS

We know that a storm drainage system is designed to collect, direct, and dispose of runoff. And we know that there are both above- and belowground methods of controlling runoff. We have noted some of the drainage components and aids to drainage systems. Now let us consider some of the advantages and disadvantages of the drainage systems and the usages of some of the drainage aids and components previously discussed.

## Surface Drainage System

A surface drainage system is formed by manipulating the site's earth surface in such a manner as to collect and direct runoff from paved and unpaved areas to acceptable disposal points. The main advantage to this system is cost: It is cheaper to build a surface drainage system than any other system. The main disadvantage is that erosion may occur if proper methods are not used to protect the surface drainage routes, such as swales and ditches.

Some of the typical devices for protecting the surface over which runoff travels are terraces and baffles, which slow runoff and can direct its flow. Drain fields may be built to absorb runoff, where soil conditions permit. And temporary and permanent detention ponds may be used to help control the velocity of runoff from the site. Ground covers are an aid in erosion control in areas where runoff is not too swift for them. Some forms of paving, such as concrete, or semipaving, such as stone or masonry rubble, slow water and help prevent erosion in steep swales and ditches. Where paved areas direct water onto grassy areas, steps must be taken to prevent erosion of the grassy areas.

## Enclosed Underground Drainage System

The enclosed underground drainage system collects and directs runoff from paved and unpaved areas to underground pipes through which the water moves to disposal points. The main advantage of the enclosed underground drainage system is that surface water is prevented from building up much volume or velocity before it is brought to underground pipes. Thus erosion is prevented. There are several disadvantages to this system. The cost is usually higher than surface drainage systems. And although surface runoff volume and velocity are decreased, the volume is concentrated in the underground pipes and the velocity is considerable there; thus, there is potential for erosion at the points where the pipes empty. Another disadvantage is sediment, which builds up in the pipes from unfiltered site runoff. This sediment is a maintenance problem on-site and must be removed from runoff before the runoff enters the underground municipal storm drain.

## Enclosed Underground Drainage System with Detention Pond

The addition of a detention pond slows the velocity of runoff to off-site disposal points, eliminating erosion concerns, as well as removing sediment before it reaches the municipal system. This system has the advantage of little site erosion, typical of enclosed systems. Cost and potential maintenance remain the main disadvantages.

## Combination Drainage System

The combination system uses an underground system for runoff from paved areas and a surface system for unpaved areas. Thus, the total volume of runoff is shared by the two systems. Because of the reduced volume and velocity in the enclosed system, part or perhaps all of the enclosed runoff may be directed to the surface drainage routes. If velocity remains a problem where the water leaves the site and if there is considerable sedimentation, it may be necessary to incorporate a detention pond in the design.

Combination systems relieve erosion concerns where paved areas meet grassy areas, but the soil where the enclosed pipes empty onto the surface areas may have to be stabilized. And as in all systems with underground pipes there are maintenance requirements and potential maintenance problems. Cost is also a disadvantage of this system. But the combination system probably offers the most environmentally sound and aesthetically pleasing system of the storm drainage choices available.

It is impossible—and undesirable—to reduce grading and drainage plans to a set of rules and formulas. However, several typical plans are often used. These plans are shown in Figure 5–1, A–D.

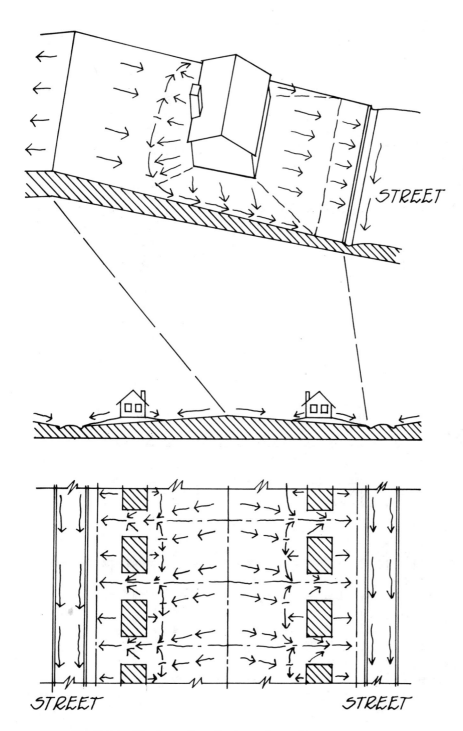

FIGURE 5–1A. Block grading. Drainage from ridge along rear lot lines to street.

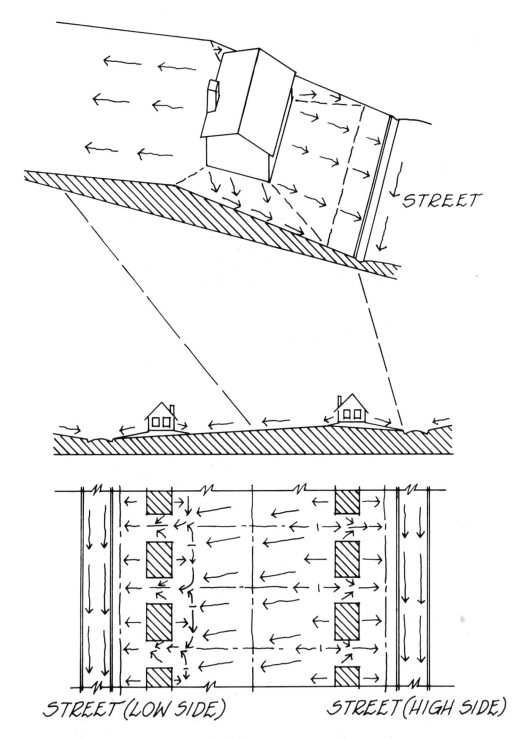

STREET

STREET (LOW SIDE)          STREET (HIGH SIDE)

FIGURE 5–1B. Drainage across a gentle cross slope.

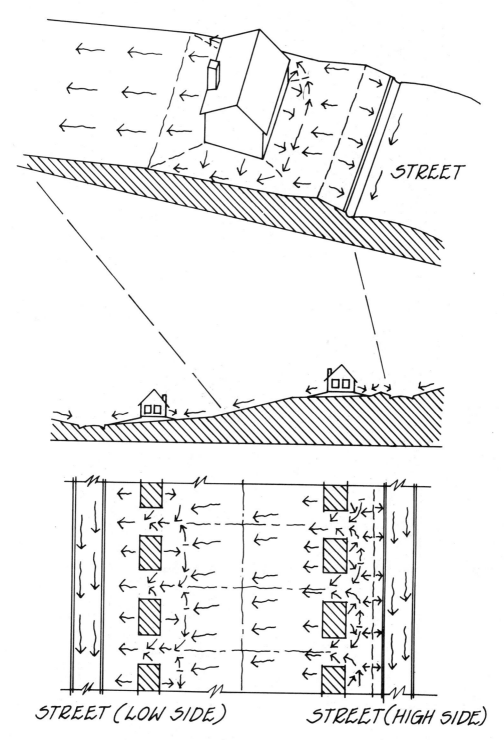

STREET

STREET (LOW SIDE)          STREET (HIGH SIDE)

FIGURE 5–1C. Drainage across a steep cross slope.

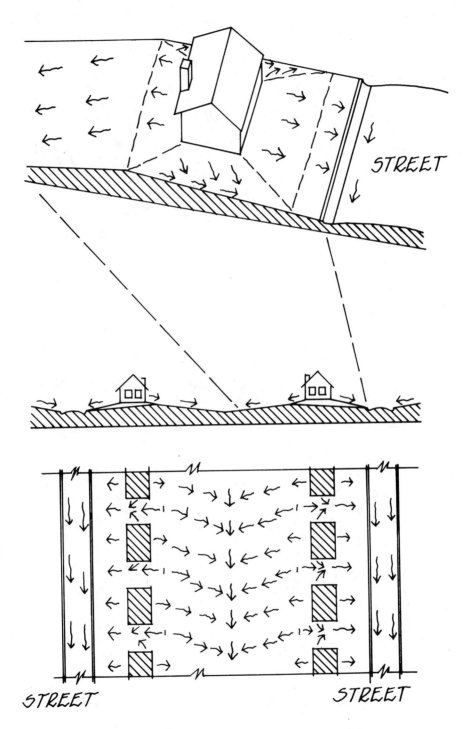

FIGURE 5–1D. Drainage down valley along rear lot lines.

# SIZING STORM DRAIN PIPES

To size storm drain pipes, we must first know something about rainfall. There are two key factors to be considered in rainfall: amount and intensity. The amount of rainfall is the total rainfall per incident; the intensity is the amount of rainfall for a given unit of time. Both amount of rainfall and intensity vary within a given region and from region to region.

Thus, the site planner must study weather data from the appropriate region to compute storm drain pipe sizes. This is sometimes called *choosing the year of storm*. In a 5-year storm the probability of a given intensity occurs every 5 years; in a 10-year storm, once every ten years; and so forth. Local regulations often specify storm years, which are based on factors such as safety and value: A residential area, for example, might require a 10-year storm design and a shopping center, a 25-year storm design.

When rain reaches the ground, a building roof, or some other designed surface, it becomes runoff. Runoff computations are affected by the amount, intensity, and duration of rainfall—plus the ability of the surface to shed water.

For our purposes, one formula, the Manning chart, and rainfall storm data suffice to compute storm drain pipe sizes. The formula is $Q = CIA$, where $Q$ is the storm water runoff of a given area, in cubic feet per second; $C$ is the coefficient of runoff; $I$ is intensity; and $A$ is area in acres. The Manning chart is shown in Figure 5–2. Figure 5–3 gives a listing of runoff coefficients. Figure 5–4 shows rainfall data.

## Example

Given: A 2-acre asphalt parking lot to be drained by one subsurface pipe that slopes 0.2 percent to the main storm drain at the street. The property is located in Miami. Find the pipe size for a 10-year storm.

In the formula $Q = CIA$, the runoff coefficient for asphalt, $C$, is 0.95; $I$, intensity, is found from the rainfall 10-year storm map to be 3.25. Thus, $Q = 0.95 \times 3.25 \times 2 = 6.18$ cubic feet per second. Consulting the Manning chart, we see that 6.18 cubic feet per second flow through a pipe of slope 0.2 percent requires a 20-inch pipe.

Any pipe size to drain a given area can be computed in this manner. Simply determine the area of the catchment area in acres or portions of an acre; determine the appropriate runoff coefficient; determine the intensity, based on weather experience for the area and based on the appropriate degree of safety against flooding for the particular property; then

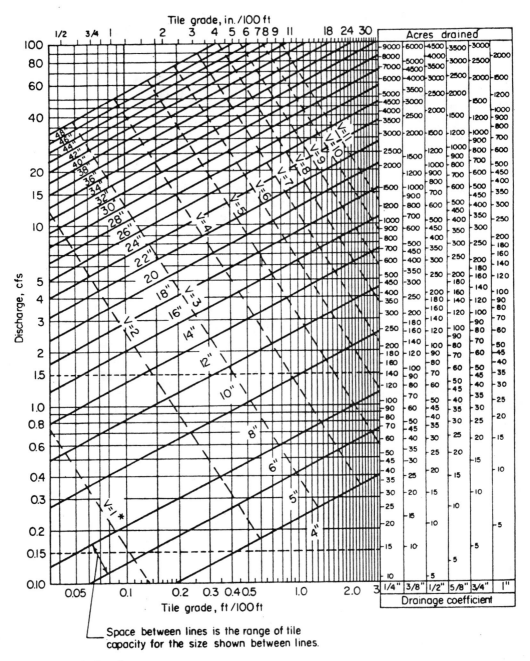

Space between lines is the range of tile capacity for the size shown between lines.

*V = velocity, fps

FIGURE 5–2. Drain-tile design chart. For more information, see *The Flow of Water in Drain Tile,* by D. L. Yarnell, U.S. Dept. Agr. Bull. 854, 1920.

Developed Areas

| Type of drainage area | Runoff coefficient, C |
|---|---|
| Lawns: | |
| Sandy soil, flat, 2% | 0.05–0.10 |
| Sandy soil, average, 2–7% | 0.10–0.15 |
| Sandy soil, steep, 7% | 0.15–0.20 |
| Heavy soil, flat, 2% | 0.13–0.17 |
| Heavy soil, average 2–7% | 0.18–0.22 |
| Heavy soil, steep, 7% | 0.25–0.35 |
| Business: | |
| Downtown areas | 0.70–0.95 |
| Neighborhood areas | 0.50–0.70 |
| Residential: | |
| Single-family areas | 0.30–0.50 |
| Multiunits, detached | 0.40–0.60 |
| Multiunits, attached | 0.60–0.75 |
| Suburban | 0.25–0.40 |
| Apartment-dwelling areas | 0.50–0.70 |

| Type of drainage area | Runoff coefficient, C |
|---|---|
| Industrial: | |
| Light areas | 0.50–0.80 |
| Heavy areas | 0.60–0.90 |
| Parks, cemeteries | 0.10–0.25 |
| Playgrounds | 0.20–0.35 |
| Railroad-yard areas | 0.20–0.40 |
| Unimproved areas | 0.10–0.30 |
| Streets: | |
| Asphalt | 0.70–0.95 |
| Concrete | 0.80–0.95 |
| Brick | 0.70–0.85 |
| Drives and walks | 0.75–0.85 |
| Roofs | 0.75–0.95 |

FIGURE 5–3. Runoff coefficients, C, for formula $Q = CIA$.
*Source:* The American Society of Civil Engineers

## Rural Areas

| Topography and vegetation | Open sandy loam | Clay and silt loam | Tight clay |
|---|---|---|---|
| **Woodland** | | | |
| Flat (0–5% slope) | 0.10 | 0.30 | 0.40 |
| Rolling (5–10% slope) | 0.25 | 0.35 | 0.50 |
| Hilly (10–30% slope) | 0.30 | 0.50 | 0.60 |
| **Pasture** | | | |
| Flat | 0.10 | 0.30 | 0.40 |
| Rolling | 0.16 | 0.36 | 0.55 |
| Hilly | 0.22 | 0.42 | 0.60 |
| **Cultivated** | | | |
| Flat | 0.30 | 0.50 | 0.60 |
| Rolling | 0.40 | 0.60 | 0.70 |
| Hilly | 0.52 | 0.72 | 0.82 |

plug the factors into the formula $Q = CIA$ and apply the resultant cubic foot per second figure to the Manning chart to get the pipe size.

It should be noted that this method for sizing storm drainage pipes is not meant to be definitive. It is rather a quick method by which a site planner may determine preliminary pipe sizes in order to estimate cost, velocities within the pipes, and similar factors that can influence the design of the final site plan. Final calculations for the storm drainage plan and other utilities are usually done by engineers specializing in these systems.

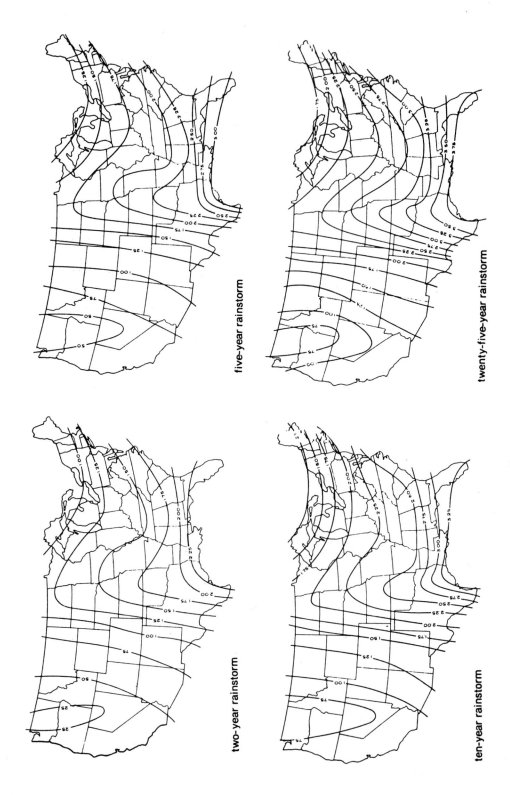

five-year rainstorm

twenty-five-year rainstorm

two-year rainstorm

ten-year rainstorm

FIGURE 5–4. Rainfall intensity-frequency map. These maps are available from the USDA, The National Oceanic and Atmospheric Administration, and in publications of the U.S. Weather Bureau.

# LANDSCAPING
# AIDS FOR GRADE
# CHANGES

**6**

Builders and developers hope to achieve good drainage and acceptable lot grades by grading alone, manipulating the surface of the lots. They want to shape the lots by grading alone because this is the cheapest solution and thus helps increase profits and allows more flexibility in establishing sales and rental prices.

When acceptable grades cannot be achieved by grading alone, when grading results in slopes that are too steep for desired homeowner activities, or when the slopes are too steep to walk safely or create drainage and erosion problems, grading must be supplemented. The supplements typically are terraces, steps, ramps, retaining walls, and baffles.

## TERRACES

Terraces are typically a series of level or nearly level grades within a steeper overall slope. Terraces are, in effect and appearance, giant "steps"; the treads of these steps may be several yards from one elevation to the next, or dozens of yards, or even more, depending on lot size (Figure 6–1).

The "risers" of these steps are actually minor slopes, formed most cheaply by grading. When walking up or down a terraced slope, some provision must be made to negotiate the elevation changes at the minor slopes, or risers, to continue the step comparison; the provisions are usually steps, stepped ramps, or both. In cases where the differences between the terrace elevations are too great to allow a graded slope, retaining walls must be used.

The terraces themselves may be surfaced with a variety of materials, depending on usage. In general the cheapest solution is grass or some other

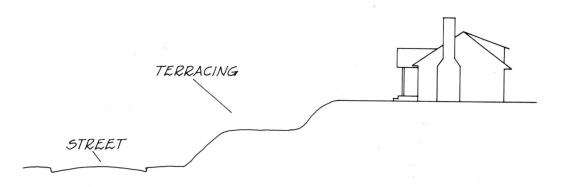

FIGURE 6–1. Terraces may be used like giant steps to soften a steeper overall slope.

hardy ground cover, if no specific activity is to be planned for. Otherwise each activity has its own best set of materials.

The following slopes are typical in many areas of the United States for the respective uses. These relationships are not exhaustive and may vary somewhat locally, but they should give the reader a feel for when terracing may be necessary and what the range of slopes are for some typical activities (Figure 6–2).

- Mowed grassy slopes: Maximum 3:1 slope.
- Unmowed grassy slopes: Maximum 2:1 slope.
- Patios and sitting areas: Maximum 2 percent. Minimum 1 percent.
- Rear and "casual" walks: Maximum 8 percent. Minimum 1 percent.
- Main entry walk: Maximum 4 percent. Minimum 1 percent.
- Parking areas: Maximum 5 percent. Minimum 0.5 percent.
- Ramps: Maximum 10 percent. Minimum 1 percent.
- Grassy recreational areas: Maximum 3 percent. Minimum 2 percent.

## STEPS AND RAMPS

Steps and ramps function to allow passage of people and equipment between grades of different elevations in safety and comfort. That statement may seem heavy for a building component as apparently simple to locate and construct as a set of steps or a ramp. They are simple to build, but careful attention must be paid to their design. Consider the following set of basic guidelines for designing steps.

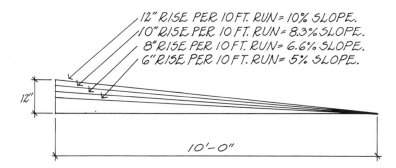

FIGURE 6–2. For comfortable transition of grades, either stairs, ramps, or combinations of stairs and ramps must be used. A walk with a slope of 5% or more is considered a ramp. If the grade is more than 8.3%, a ramp should be combined with steps for comfortable walking.

1. Typical tread and riser relationships are as follows: 7-inch riser, 11-inch tread; 6½-inch riser, 13-inch tread; 6-inch riser, 15-inch tread; 5½-inch riser, 16-inch tread; 5-inch riser, 17-inch tread; 4½-inch riser, 18-inch tread; 4-inch riser, 19-inch tread. Avoid risers less than 4 inches or more than 7 inches; avoid treads less than 11 inches deep. Where possible to achieve, a good outdoor tread and riser relationship is a 6-inch riser with a 15-inch tread.

2. Keep the tread and riser relationship the same throughout the flight (a flight is two or more steps).

3. Do not taper treads and risers. For example, a 6-inch riser should be 6 inches for the width of the steps; a 15-inch tread should be 15 inches for the width of the steps.

4. Pitch outdoor treads to drain, approximately ⅛ inch per foot.

5. Steps should be the same width as the walks that they join.

6. For safety, where possible, steps that join walks or drives at right angles should be set back at least 2 feet from the walk or drive.

7. Landings between flights of steps should be the same width as the steps.

8. Where a series of step flights are connected by walks or ramps, the lengths of the walks or ramps between the flights of steps should be kept the same, if possible.

9. Stair railings are recommended for flights greater than 30 inches.

These guidelines are rudimentary, not conclusive. Figures 6–3 and 6–4, A–F detail some commonly used outdoor stairs.

Ramps perform the same function as steps: transporting people across elevation changes. But ramps are more convenient in areas where wheeled

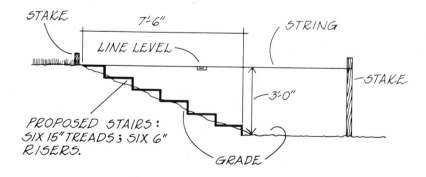

FIGURE 6–3. Outdoor stairs may be planned with simple instruments: wood stakes, a line level, and perhaps a plumb bob for measuring vertical distance.

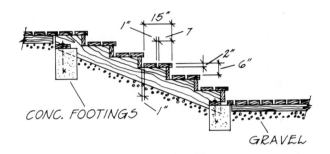

FIGURE 6–4A.  A variety of materials and combinations of materials may be used to build outdoor stairs between grade changes. The stairs may be built into the grade; or, it may be better to span over the ground, depending on the steepness of the grade.

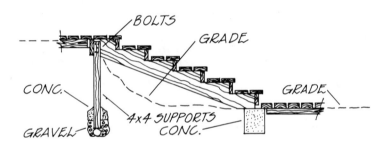

FIGURE 6–4B.

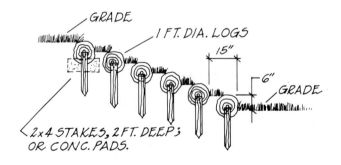

FIGURE 6–4C.

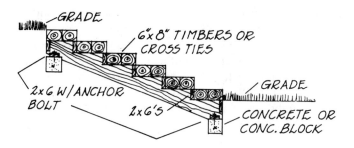

FIGURE 6–4D.

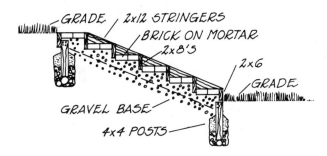

FIGURE 6–4E.

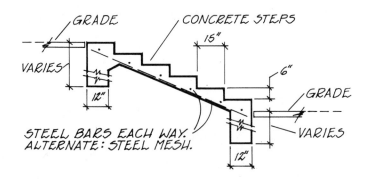

FIGURE 6–4F.

equipment must be transported or where the handicapped and the elderly travel. The topography may also call for a ramp: where the change in elevations to be transcended is too low for steps (where the risers would be less than 4 inches, for example) but where the subject slope is too steep for a normal walk. Generally speaking, walks that slope approximately 5 percent or more are considered ramps.

Stepped ramps are ramps used in series. Stepped ramps may transcend elevation changes with a single riser, several risers, or flights, depending on the slope to be negotiated (Figures 6–5 and 6–6). Obviously, gentle slopes require fewer risers than the steeper slopes.

Topography, weather conditions, type of materials used, and users and usage are typical considerations in determining what ramp slopes are appropriate within the range of physical possibilities. Typical ramp slopes range between 5 and 10 percent slopes: a 6-inch rise in a 10-foot run gives a 5 percent slope; 8 inches, a 6.6 percent slope; 10 inches, an 8.3 percent slope; and 12 inches, a 10 percent slope. A 5 percent ramp of broom-finished concrete might be called for by an unaided user in a wheelchair, while a 10 percent ramp would work for the nonhandicapped.

Ramps and stepped ramps require somewhat more demanding specifications than do walks with steps. The following guidelines are basic, not conclusive.

1. Steps between ramps should be 3 risers high or be 3 flights of 2 risers each. All risers should be the same height; all treads, the same depth.
2. Risers should not exceed 6 inches.
3. Ramps between flights should be the same length.

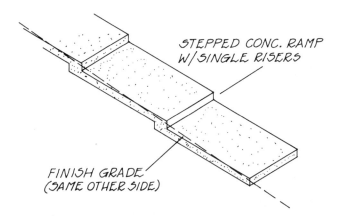

FIGURE 6–5. Stepped concrete ramp with single risers. Hold finish grade to ⅔'s height of risers, as shown.

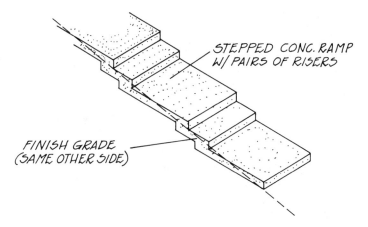

STEPPED CONC. RAMP
W/ PAIRS OF RISERS

FINISH GRADE
(SAME OTHER SIDE)

FIGURE 6–6. Stepped concrete ramp with pairs of risers. Hold the finish grade to the line connecting bottom of upper riser of each pair of risers, as shown.

4. Where ramps are connected by single risers, the ramp length should allow two comfortable foot paces (approximately 6 feet long). Where ramps are connected by flights of 2 risers, allow for 3 comfortable paces (approximately 9 feet long).

5. Ramps and stepped ramps should be the same width as the walks that they join.

6. The approaches to ramps should be clear, level, and approximately 5 feet long to allow for wheelchair and child stroller maneuvers and to provide for general safety.

7. Handrails, when used, should extend 18 inches beyond the top and bottom of the ramp.

8. Ramps should be at least 3 feet wide, wider where there is heavy traffic and where the ramp will be used by service people.

9. Planting should be located so as not to cast shadows on ramps, thus increasing ice buildup in winter.

10. Low curbs at the sides of ramps are desirable where wheeled equipment will travel.

11. Ramps should be well illuminated to ensure night safety; illumination is particularly important at ramp approaches.

## 155    RETAINING WALLS

Retaining walls may be called for when the slope of a lot is too steep to be handled by a series of terraces, at the property line of a steeply sloping lot, or similar situations. In general, retaining walls are avoided if other acceptable solutions are available because retaining walls are expensive to build and must be built with considerable care.

The height of the retaining wall and the angle of the earth on its high side are two critical factors in designing a retaining wall. The higher the wall, the more structural strength must be built into it. The more steeply the earth slopes up from the high side of the wall, the more structural strength is required. Surcharges increase the structural requirements further (surcharges are additional forces that the wall may encounter, such as vehicles, buildings, and driveways located near the wall).

In addition to these factors, other important considerations in building retaining walls include drainage, soil, and weather conditions. A well-designed retaining wall uses the most economical material that is compatible with the overall design of the project in a manner that meets the structural needs.

There are four common types of retaining walls: the gravity retaining wall, the cantilever retaining wall, the counterfort retaining wall, and the buttressed retaining wall.

## Gravity Retaining Walls

Gravity retaining walls utilize their own weight and positioning to achieve stability (Figure 6-7). Typically the fill side of the wall slants down from the top, into the fill. The side opposite the fill is usually vertical (most retaining walls are built with a slight slant toward the fill side, not for structural purposes but to offset the visual impression that the wall is leaning toward the lower side, which happens when the wall is built perfectly vertical). The great width of gravity walls, at the bottom, and their weight (gravity walls are usually masonry or concrete or both) keep them in place against the resistance of the earth.

Gravity walls often require no steel reinforcement but, because of the massive amount of masonry used, can be expensive. Where large amounts of native stone or suitable material are available, gravity walls may be used economically. Gravity walls require less skilled labor than walls requiring steel reinforcement.

## Cantilever Retaining Walls

Cantilever retaining walls are shaped similarly to an inverted T (Figure 6-8). Earth, resting on the footing portion, helps hold the stem of the wall in place. Cantilever retaining walls are often reinforced concrete and may be veneered with other materials, if desired. Because these walls have steel reinforcement, they are much thinner than gravity walls and require less material. They do, however, require professional design; skilled labor is required to construct them.

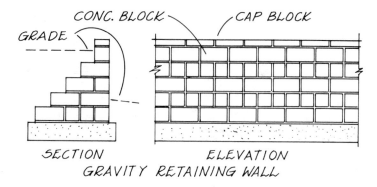

SECTION                ELEVATION

GRAVITY RETAINING WALL

FIGURE 6–7. Gravity retaining walls depend on mass for structural stability: they may be built of masonry, stone, concrete, or any substantial, heavy material.

## Counterfort Retaining Walls

Counterfort retaining walls utilize a series of vertical supports (post or columns) and spanning panels (Figure 6–9A). A typical example of this system would be reinforced concrete posts with concrete panels spanning from post center to post center; steel cables attached to the fill side of the posts would run down, at an angle, to a concrete foundation, where they would be anchored. The steel cables would hold the posts in place, which would hold the panels in place. The panels would have enough structural strength to withstand the earth fill. The cables in this system are in tension.

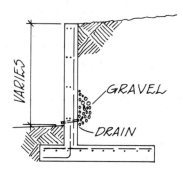

CANTILEVER RETAINING WALL
(STEEL REINFORCED)

FIGURE 6–8. Cantilever retaining walls are shaped similarly to an inverted "T". They usually are reinforced with steel and may be built of masonry or concrete.

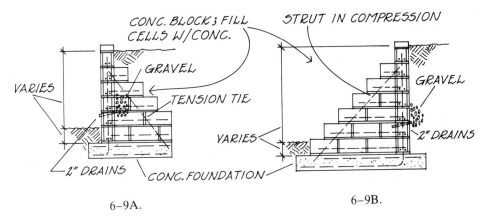

6–9A.          6–9B.

FIGURE 6–9. The retaining wall on the left is a counterfort wall; note the steel tie in tension. The right retaining wall is a buttressed wall; note the strut in compression.

## Buttressed Retaining Walls

Buttressed retaining walls are similar in construction to the counterfort walls (Figure 6–9B). However, the buttressed wall, as the name implies, uses structural buttresses to maintain structural stability. The structural buttresses, located opposite the fill side of the wall at periodic intervals, keep the wall from toppling over; these buttresses are in compression.

Drainage is important to all retaining walls; in areas subject to frost heave, it becomes especially important. The typical method of drainage is to build a series of drainage holes (weep holes) through the wall near the base. These holes prevent the buildup of water on the fill side of the wall. To protect the holes from stoppages, wire or other filters may be used on the weep holes on the fill side; gravel is required around the weep holes to aid drainage and is recommended all along the fill side of the wall.

Where weep holes cannot be used, a drain pipe with periodic entries may be laid at the base of the wall on the fill side. The entries should be protected from stoppages similarly to weep holes. The drain pipe runs to some acceptable disposal point.

In areas subject to frost heave, the soil on the fill side of the wall should be checked. If the soil is largely clay, the wall may have to be lined over its entire fill side surface with gravel or with a sandy soil; clays are particularly susceptible to frost heave and, in extreme cold, can topple the best retaining walls, if precautions are not taken.

Retaining walls often require building permits, especially those over 3 feet tall. Engineering consultation and design usually are necessary to avoid damage to the wall or injury to people. The cost of engineering services is small because builders can easily spend more on guesswork design than they would for economically designed walls that do not waste steel reinforcement or other costly materials.

Retaining walls that are 3 feet high, or less, with a mild slope at the high side, may be built with somewhat less concern for structural strength and may be built with a variety of materials and methods. Figure 6–10, A–D, detail some practical and handsome timber, masonry, and stone retaining walls.

# BAFFLES

Baffles are materials used on slopes to slow and divert the flow of water, preventing erosion. Any material suitable to the use and to overall design may be employed: masonry rubble, stone, broken concrete, cross-ties, etc. Effective baffles with an acceptable appearance also may be built with combinations of the materials.

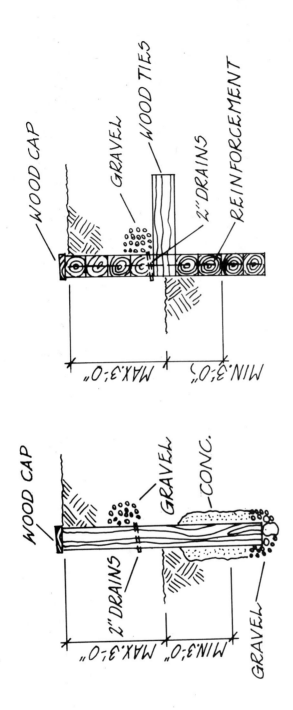

FIGURE 6–10A. Timber retaining walls are simple to build and long-lasting, if the wood is treated properly. The wall on the left uses timber ties at each joint all along the bottom course. Vertical steel reinforcement is used at 3 feet on center, horizontally. The wall on the right is all vertical members, set in concrete.

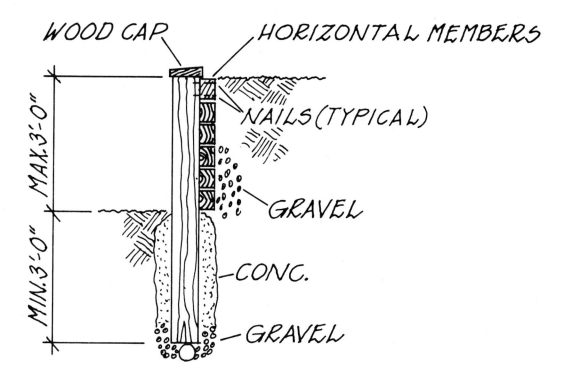

FIGURE 6–10B. This timber retaining wall uses vertical supports at 8 feet on center, set in concrete. The horizontal members are spaced about an inch apart for drainage.

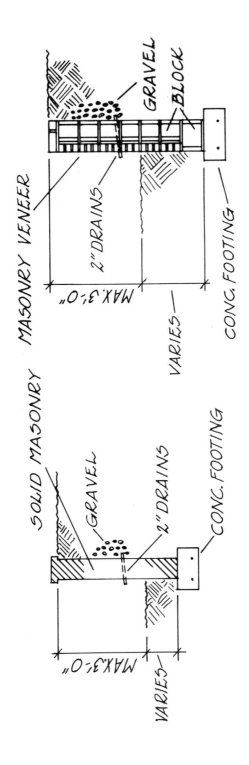

FIGURE 6–10C. Low retaining walls may be built of solid masonry without reinforcement, if the earth at the top is level or nearly level. For a more finished appearance, a masonry veneer may be applied.

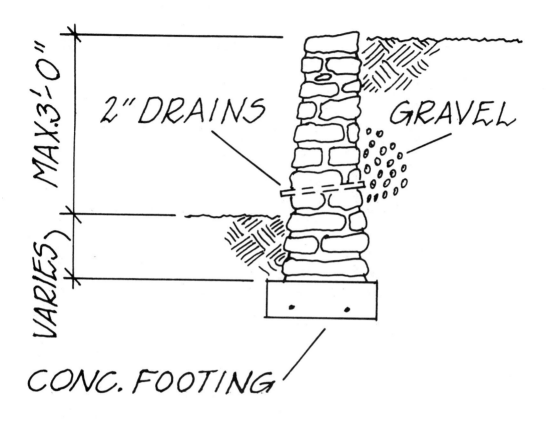

MAX. 3'-0" (VARIES)

2" DRAINS

GRAVEL

CONC. FOOTING

FIGURE 6–10D. Stone retaining wall on reinforced concrete footing.
The drains have gravel on the back side to prevent clogging.

# THE SEWAGE DISPOSAL SYSTEM

# 7

Sanitary sewers, although they are similar in layout and design to storm sewers, are a completely separate system. The purpose of separate sanitary lines is to transport raw sewage—such as that from toilets and sinks—to sewage treatment plants or disposal systems (raw sewage cannot be directed to rivers, streams, and lakes), thus reducing the volume that sewage treatment plants must process and preventing the possible backup of sewage onto developments and the landscape. At the treatment plant or disposal system, raw sewage is converted to an effluent that can then be discharged into the rivers, streams, and lakes.

Sanitary drainage systems are always a closed system. There are no open inlets to the sanitary system. The system is typically continuous, composed of straight or gently curving (horizontally) pipes that ultimately lead to the treatment plant or disposal system. Toilets, sinks, and other connections to the system are equipped with traps that prevent sewer gases and odors from escaping into the houses, buildings, etc. Manholes occur, depending on the engineering situation and local regulations, at changes in slope, changes in direction, and other locations necessary for proper drainage and maintenance of the system. In some localities, simpler, cheaper clean-outs may sometimes be used in place of manholes.

## SELF-CONTAINED SEWAGE DISPOSAL

A self-contained sewage disposal system is composed as follows. A sewer or sewers from the building or house served to a septic tank. A manhole is usually required in the middle of sewer links exceeding 300 feet. Separate building lines to grease traps are needed, where the traps are necessary. From the septic tanks an effluent sewer line proceeds to a distribution box from which the effluent sewage may travel to a subsoil disposal field, to leeching cesspools, or to a sand filter.

Figure 7–1 diagrams these essential components. A discussion of each of the component parts follows.

### Building Sewer

The building sewer carries raw sewage from the building to the septic tank. Cast-iron pipe with lead-filled joints is the best pipe material and is required where potable water supply is nearby or where trees or other growth might work into other type pipes. Other typical sewer pipe materials are glazed clay tile and cement. In any case, cast-iron pipe is used for approximately 5 or 6 feet out from the building foundation. The size of the pipe and the slope at which it is laid vary with the amount of sewage transported and with local weather conditions.

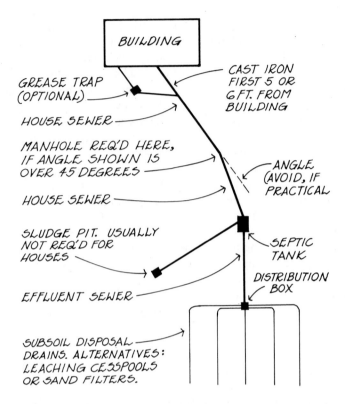

FIGURE 7–1. An individual disposal system, as a minimum, is composed of a septic tank, a distribution box, some type of disposal area, plus all the lines required to tie the system together. Grease traps and sludge pits also may be necessary.

## Grease Traps

Grease traps do what the name implies. They separate grease and oil from the building waste. Grease traps are optional but reduce maintenance. The degreased waste line ties back into the building sewer, which proceeds to the septic tank (Figure 7–2).

## Manholes

Manholes are required to turn the sewer where direction changes exceed 45 degrees. Angles in the line less than 45 degrees may be turned with one-eighth or one-fourth bend. Additional manholes may be required to facilitate drainage (Figure 7–3, A–B).

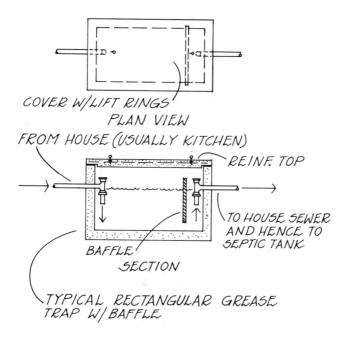

COVER W/LIFT RINGS
PLAN VIEW
FROM HOUSE (USUALLY KITCHEN)

REINF. TOP

TO HOUSE SEWER
AND HENCE TO
SEPTIC TANK

BAFFLE
SECTION

TYPICAL RECTANGULAR GREASE
TRAP W/BAFFLE

FIGURE 7–2.  The grease trap functions to separate grease from other waste and provide a means for periodic cleanout by way of a removable top.

## Septic Tank

Septic tanks are simply built, boxlike structures. They are commonly built of concrete, steel, and other materials and may be either constructed on the job or purchased as manufactured units. In either case care must be taken to match the size of the tanks to site needs (Figure 7–4, A–C).

The septic tank operates as a kind of natural processor. Raw sewage from the building sewer enters the septic tank, where the heaviest matter settles to the bottom. Anaerobic bacterial action takes place, forming three layers of sewage in the tank. The lowest layer, at the bottom, is a sludge; the middle layer is a liquid; and at the top is a layer of scum, which seals off air and aids the bacterial action.

As more raw sewage enters the tank from the building sewer line, the effluent sewage is pushed up and flows over into either a siphon tank or directly into the effluent sewer line, which goes to the disposal system. Siphon tanks are typically used for tanks of 1,000-gallon capacity or more and are always used when the disposal system utilizes sand filters. Siphon

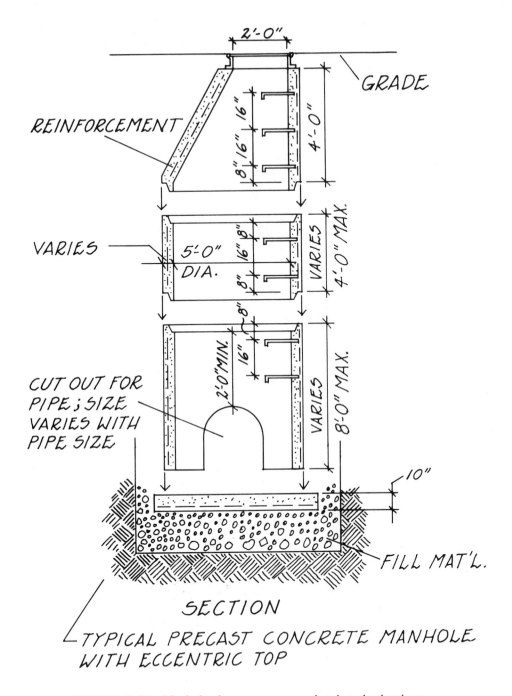

2'-0"

GRADE

REINFORCEMENT

8" / 16" / 16"

4'-0"

VARIES

5'-0"
DIA.

8" / 16" / 8"

VARIES
4'-0" MAX.

CUT OUT FOR
PIPE; SIZE
VARIES WITH
PIPE SIZE

8" / 16"

2'-0" MIN.

VARIES
8'-0" MAX.

10"

FILL MAT'L.

SECTION

TYPICAL PRECAST CONCRETE MANHOLE
WITH ECCENTRIC TOP

FIGURE 7–3A. Manhole shapes vary somewhat but the local authorities usually have standard designs which are available to builders and others. Manholes may be built on the job of masonry, concrete, or other suitable materials. Most builders opt for the simplicity of precast units.

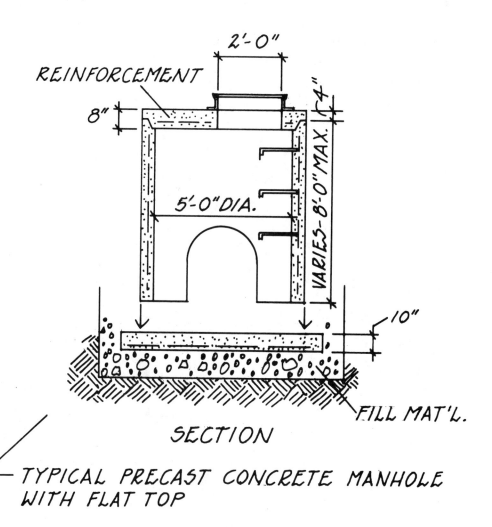

SECTION

TYPICAL PRECAST CONCRETE MANHOLE
WITH FLAT TOP

FIGURE 7–3B.

157

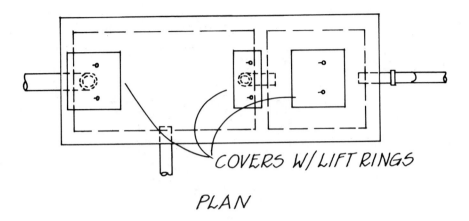

COVERS W/ LIFT RINGS

PLAN

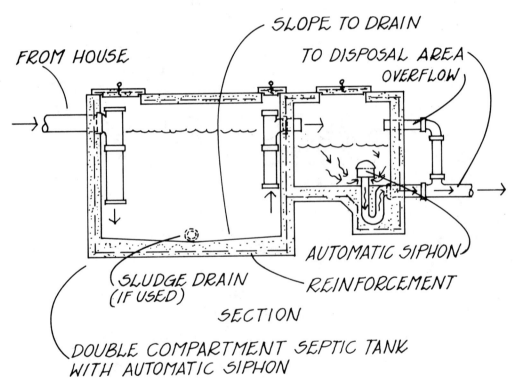

FROM HOUSE

SLOPE TO DRAIN

TO DISPOSAL AREA
OVERFLOW

AUTOMATIC SIPHON

SLUDGE DRAIN
(IF USED)

REINFORCEMENT

SECTION

DOUBLE COMPARTMENT SEPTIC TANK
WITH AUTOMATIC SIPHON

FIGURE 7–4A. The double compartment septic tank with automatic
siphon is a convenient and frequently-used residential septic tank.

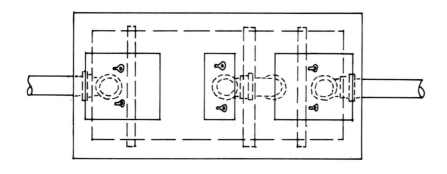

PLAN

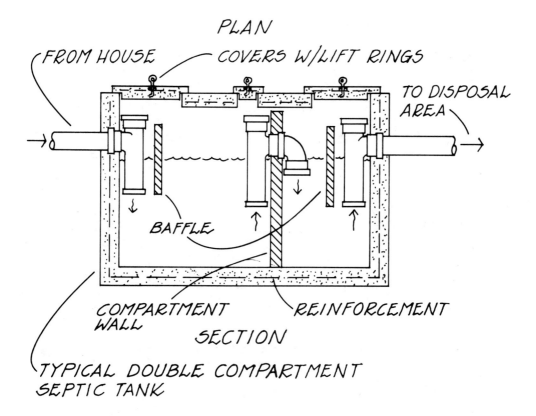

FROM HOUSE

COVERS W/LIFT RINGS

TO DISPOSAL AREA

BAFFLE

COMPARTMENT WALL

REINFORCEMENT

SECTION

TYPICAL DOUBLE COMPARTMENT SEPTIC TANK

FIGURE 7–4B. Shown above is a double compartment septic tank without an automatic siphon.

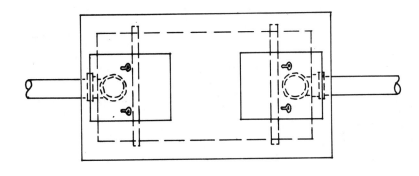

PLAN

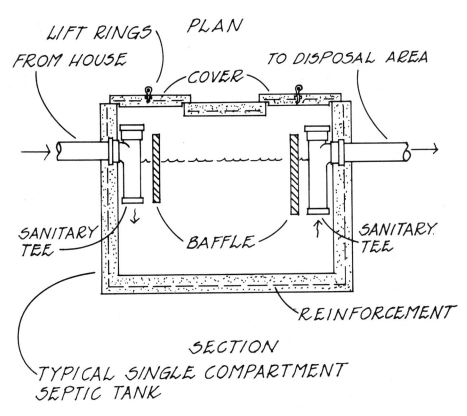

LIFT RINGS

FROM HOUSE

TO DISPOSAL AREA

COVER

SANITARY
TEE

BAFFLE

SANITARY
TEE

REINFORCEMENT

SECTION

TYPICAL SINGLE COMPARTMENT
SEPTIC TANK

FIGURE 7–4C. The single compartment septic tank is the simplest and initially the cheapest of all the septic tanks; there is, however, greater danger of malfunction and attendant expense than with the double compartment designs.

tanks may be required for residences in some localities. In form, siphon tanks are a separate compartment in the septic tank, collecting overflow from the septic tank and discharging it to the effluent sewer line by means of an automatic siphon. The purpose of the siphon tank is to regulate the flow of effluent to the disposal system, preventing overloads, and thus preventing saturation of the system with the accompanying bad smells.

## Sludge Pits

The sludge pit is a boxlike structure, similar in form but smaller than the septic tank. A sludge drain, located at the bottom of the septic tank, runs to the sludge pit, which must be located adequately away from and below any water supply. Sludge may be removed from the sludge pit by way of a cover at the top. The sludge pit is optional. Its purpose is to provide a convenient way of cleaning the tank without having to shut down the system while this cleaning is under way (Figure 7–5).

## The Effluent Sewer

The effluent sewer line is similar to the building sewer line. The effluent sewer line is a closed pipe that transports effluent from the siphon tank or the septic tank to a distribution box, from which the effluent moves to the disposal system.

## Distribution Box

The distribution box, like the sludge pit, is similar in form but smaller than the septic tank. The purpose of the distribution box is to accept effluent from the effluent sewer line and direct it to the various parts of the disposal system. The number of distribution box outlets to the disposal system varies (Figure 7–6).

# THE DISPOSAL SYSTEM

The following is a discussion of three common types of disposal systems: leeching cesspools, subsoil disposal beds, and sand filters. (Figures 7–7, A–B, 7–8, and 7–9).

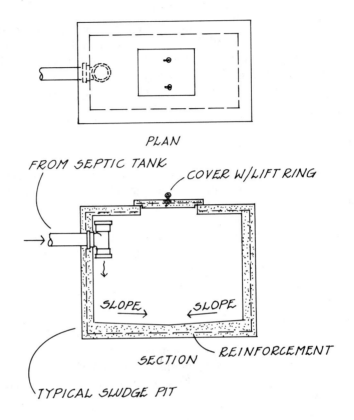

PLAN

FROM SEPTIC TANK

COVER W/LIFT RING

SLOPE

SLOPE

SECTION

REINFORCEMENT

TYPICAL SLUDGE PIT

FIGURE 7–5. Sludge pits are built very similarly to single compartment septic tanks and function to provide less maintenance on the
septic tank (and possible temporary shutdown) by removing sludge
that accumulates on the septic tank bottom.

Leeching cesspools are typically round, underground, masonry structures similar in appearance to a manhole structure. The joints of the structure are laid open and the bottom is an absorptive surface. A 4-inch layer
of graded stone is typically laid all around the cesspool. Effluent from the
distribution box is transported to the cesspools, where it gradually passes
through the masonry joints and through the absorptive bottom into the
surrounding soil.

This system offers several advantages to the site planner: It takes up
less land area than any other system; it can be used on any site slope; the
construction cost is low; and maintenance is seldom needed.

The typical restrictions of leeching cesspools are as follows: Cesspools
require soil with good absorptive qualities and must be located where the
groundwater level is 8 feet or more below grade or 2 feet or more below

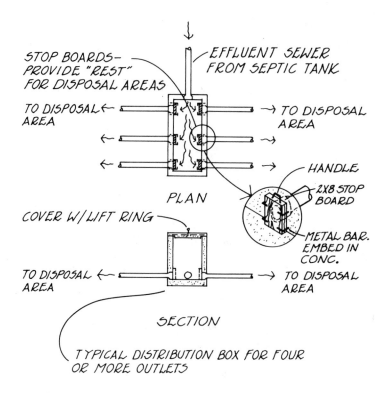

STOP BOARDS—
PROVIDE "REST"
FOR DISPOSAL AREAS

EFFLUENT SEWER
FROM SEPTIC TANK

TO DISPOSAL
AREA

TO DISPOSAL
AREA

HANDLE

2X8 STOP
BOARD

PLAN

COVER W/LIFT RING

METAL BAR.
EMBED IN
CONC.

TO DISPOSAL
AREA

TO DISPOSAL
AREA

SECTION

TYPICAL DISTRIBUTION BOX FOR FOUR
OR MORE OUTLETS

FIGURE 7–6. Distribution boxes do what the name implies: they distribute the effluent material from the septic tank, preventing overload to any particular area of the disposal system.

the bottom of the cesspool. Cesspools must be located well away from potable water supplies and away from buildings.

## Subsoil Disposal Beds

The subsoil disposal bed is a system of open, jointed drain pipe through which effluent sewage passes into the surrounding soil.

Subsoil disposal beds can be used in soils that absorb too slowly to use leeching cesspools. When used in soils that absorb well, only distribution sewage lines need be used. Subsoil disposal beds may be used on level to fairly steep slopes by varying the arrangement of the lines. The disposal beds require little maintenance if the septic tank is kept in good operating order.

If the soil is semi-impervious, collection drains must be used in addition to the distribution lines. Collector drains transport the filtered ef-

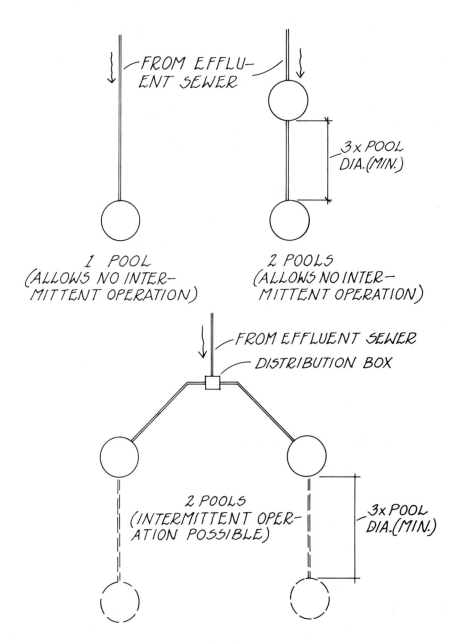

TYPICAL LEACHING CESSPOOL ARRANGEMENTS

FIGURE 7–7A. The number of cesspools used depends on the amount of waste they must process. The arrangement is chosen to provide continual operation of the system while maintenance or cleanout is underway.

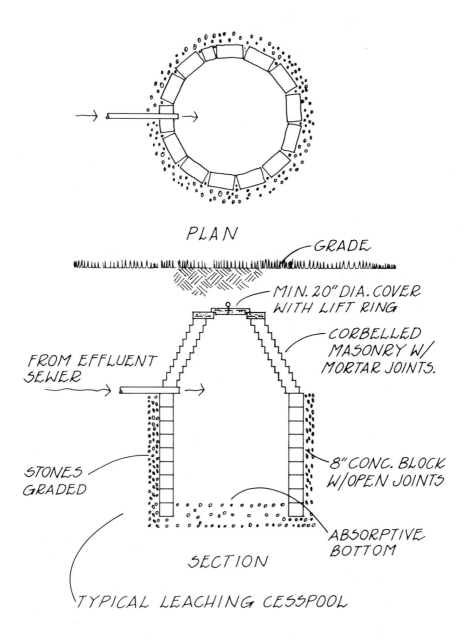

PLAN

SECTION

TYPICAL LEACHING CESSPOOL

FIGURE 7–7B. The leaching cesspool is similar in size and form to a manhole. However, the cesspool is designed to allow the gradual escape of its contents.

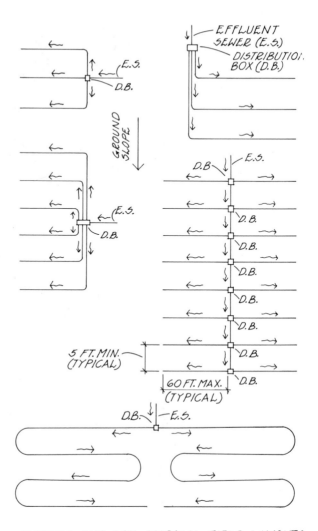

TYPICAL SUB-SOIL DISPOSAL FIELD LAYOUTS

FIGURE 7–8. Sub-soil disposal fields probably are the most frequently-used residential disposal method. There are a variety of layouts, the one chosen depending largely on topography and space available.

fluent sewage to soil that drains better or transports it to some nonpotable water disposal point; this of course is an added expense and takes up more land area. The beds must be located where the groundwater level is more than 2 feet below grade. Subsoil disposal beds cost more to build than leeching cesspools and the land area required is greater than that for leeching cesspools or sand filters.

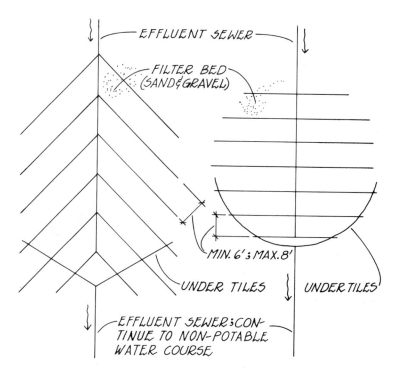

TYPICAL SAND FILTER LAYOUTS

FIGURE 7–9. Sand filters are expensive, relatively difficult to install and are chosen only if there is no other disposal system that will work.

## Sand Filters

The sand filter system is presented last because it is typically used only when the other two systems are not feasible—when soil absorbs too poorly to use leeching cesspools or subsoil disposal beds.

To utilize sand filters, the impervious soil in the whole area that will be the filter must be excavated and then filled with filtering material, typically sand. Both distribution and collection lines are used: the collection lines carrying the filtered effluent to a nonpotable water disposal point, to leeching cesspools, or to subsoil disposal beds in soil with better absorptive qualities. Sand filters are expensive, compared to the other two systems. Sand filters require less area than subsoil disposal beds and more area than leeching cesspools.

# PLANTING PLAN, SURFACE PREPARATION, AND EQUIPMENT

**8**

The planting plan is what many homeowners think of as site planning: arranging trees, shrubs, and grass or some other ground cover on their lawns, after the houses are ready to live in. Site planning is vastly more complicated than any of its single aspects, including the planting plan. But even the planting plan is more complicated and worthy of more thought than most clients realize.

Trees, shrubs, and ground covers are the basic materials worked with on many but not all sites. Many trees, for example, will not flourish or even survive in semiarid regions. To force plants onto environments that are not hospitable to them invites maintenance problems. There is another problem with translocating plants to unlikely locations—a subjective problem. That is, some plants simply do not look right when moved from their typically native locations; to give an extreme example, imagine the streets of New York lined with palm trees. Even if it were possible to maintain the trees, the appearance would be ridiculous. Unfortunately most of the planning decisions are not as clear-cut as deciding not to plant palm trees in New York. The problem just described is when and if to use "exotics." An *exotic* is simply a plant not native to some local site. However, many plants can be introduced to new areas and flourish. Thus, beyond avoiding obvious extremes in planting, the selection of plants involves the subjective judgment of the designer.

In addition to their ability or lack of ability to live and prosper in a given location, and in addition to their subjective qualities in the minds of designers and homeowners, all plants have certain qualities of form and scale: giant oak trees, spindly crepe myrtles, low-lying junipers, bermuda grass, and a myriad of ground covers—all these plants have particular shapes and sizes that must be carefully considered both as to how each of them relates to the site in terms of form and scale and also how they relate to each other. An oak sapling, planted in the patio garden of an apartment or condominium development, will someday be as out-of-place as palm trees in New York. The oak tree, planted in close proximity with trees of lesser scale and trees with conflicting forms (such as a weeping willow), usually does not look right (Figure 8–1, A–D).

This is not to suggest that there are "rules" that must be followed in the selection and arrangement of plants on a given site. Talented designers consistently break conventional planting procedure and come up with fine designs. However, when good designers violate convention, they do so to gain some specific objective in the plan—not just to be different.

Trees, shrubs, and ground covers, then, each have their own quality of form (regularity of form, shagginess, etc.) and scale (size); have certain parameters of soil and environment in which they survive or prosper; and

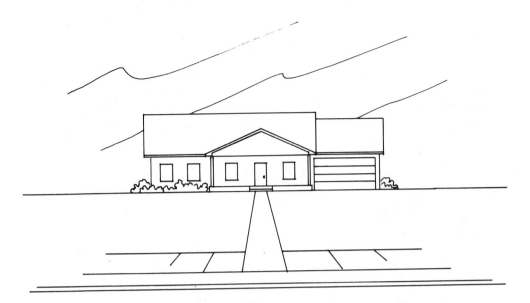

## LANDSCAPE WITHOUT TREES

FIGURE 8–1A. With good planning, the trees selected will prosper, perform their function (such as shading and screening), and will be a pleasing element of the overall house and landscape composition.

## TREES TOO SMALL FOR HOUSE

FIGURE 8–1B.

TREES TOO LARGE FOR HOUSE

FIGURE 8–1C.

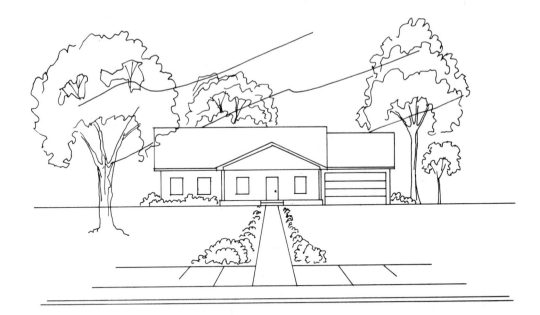

TREES IN GOOD SCALE RELATIVE TO HOUSE

FIGURE 8–1D.

evoke certain subjective qualities in the minds of their viewers, (Figure 8–2).

In addition to these considerations, plants are often used to perform or aid some specific function or functions. Trees, for example, may be chosen primarily because shade is needed or just for their appearance. Grass may be chosen as a ground cover for an area where heavy foot traffic and sports are contemplated; conversely an ivy may be chosen for some expanse of land where there will be little or no foot traffic and where the owner does not wish to spend the maintenance time required of grass. Other ground covers or shrubs may be used for specific functions, such as preventing erosion on steep slopes. Some plants may be chosen for their ability to prosper in poor soil or in extreme light or shade conditions.

Thus, if given proper consideration, the planting plan is arrived at by using design procedures similar to those used to plan the site and buildings. Some designers compare individual landscapes to the house interior: Lawns are similar to house floors; shrubs are compared to furniture and room dividers; trees form the exterior walls or provide major separation of areas. Function can also be included in this comparison: What is the function of the lawn "floor"? Will it receive heavy traffic or rarely be

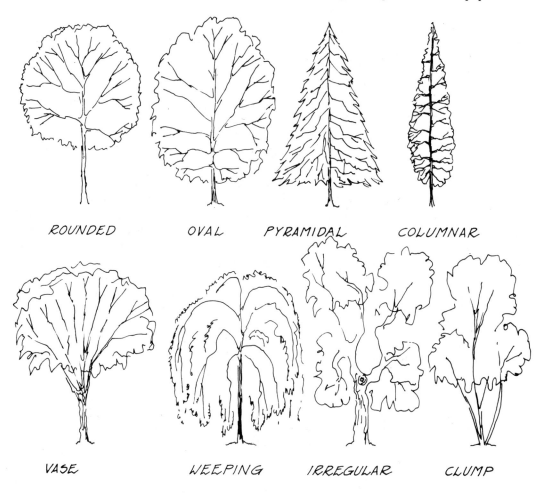

ROUNDED        OVAL       PYRAMIDAL      COLUMNAR

VASE              WEEPING       IRREGULAR       CLUMP

FIGURE 8-2. Tree forms are not entirely consistent. Each species does, however, have a particular "habit of growth" or general form by which they usually may be quickly identified. The forms shown are typical for many frequently-used trees.

walked on? You would not use a fine oriental rug in the kitchen; neither should you "floor" a badminton court with some delicate ground cover. If the occupants will be elderly and will rarely use the lawn except visually, then high-maintenance grass is not appropriate. This comparison can effectively be used for establishing general design parameters and starting points, all the way down to final detail work (the stone borders around flower beds, for example, are roughly similar in appearance and quite similar in function to house baseboard trim).

## OUTDOOR MATERIALS

Trees, shrubs, and ground covers are the typical outdoor materials with which the designer works. The following is a listing, though by no means a complete listing, of some of the much-used materials, with remarks about their usage.

### Trees

The following is a restricted list, restricted to trees that in maturity reach over 40 feet in height; that can withstand temperatures to minus 20 degrees Fahrenheit or less—and thus will grow in the majority of regions of the United States; that are not extremely short-lived, not particularly subject to diseases; and that require only reasonable maintenance. The list is further restricted to those trees that are particularly handsome (a subjective decision) for landscape use. In many cases local trees not found on this list may be preferable to designers and owners. Such lists are often given alphabetically, using the scientific name; however, because this list is for illustrative purposes and in view of the previous discussion emphasizing form and function, the trees are listed in descending order of height, popular name first (Figures 8–3 and 8–4).

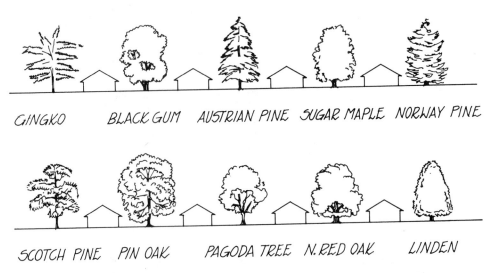

GINGKO      BLACK GUM   AUSTRIAN PINE   SUGAR MAPLE   NORWAY PINE

SCOTCH PINE   PIN OAK    PAGODA TREE   N. RED OAK    LINDEN

FIGURE 8–3. Trees usually are the most visually dominant of the plants used by landscape designers and site planners. The trees shown are quite hardy in many areas of the United States, are not short-lived or particularly subject to diseases, and require only normal maintenance.

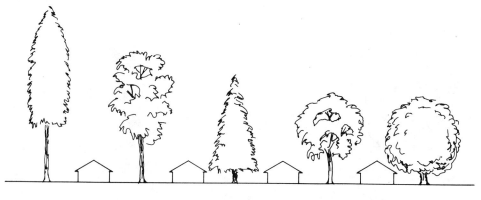

DOUGLAS FIR    TULIP TREE    WHITE FIR    AMERICAN ELM    EUROPEAN BEECH

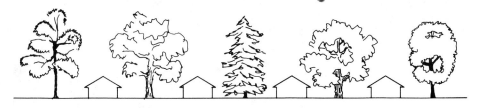

WHITE PINE    SYCAMORE    E. HEMLOCK    WHITE OAK    WHITE ASH

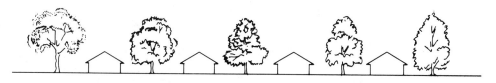

LOCUST    RED MAPLE    N. CATALPA    HORSE CHESTNUT    KATSURA

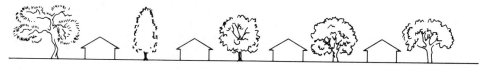

BLACK PINE    E. RED CEDAR    NORWAY MAPLE        CORK TREE

TREE OF HEAVEN

WEEPING WILLOW

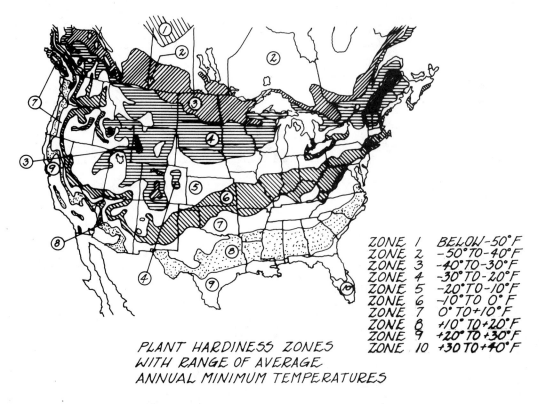

ZONE 1    BELOW -50°F
ZONE 2    -50° TO -40°F
ZONE 3    -40° TO -30°F
ZONE 4    -30° TO -20°F
ZONE 5    -20° TO -10°F
ZONE 6    -10° TO 0°F
ZONE 7    0° TO +10°F
ZONE 8    +10° TO +20°F
ZONE 9    +20° TO +30°F
ZONE 10   +30 TO +40°F

PLANT HARDINESS ZONES
WITH RANGE OF AVERAGE
ANNUAL MINIMUM TEMPERATURES

FIGURE 8–4. Trees and other plants prosper only within certain tolerances of soil, light, water, and temperature conditions. The plant hardiness zones shown are generally accurate, but specific local requirements should be verified.

*Douglas Fir (Pseudotsuga taxifolia).* The tree reaches heights of 200 feet, with a 20-foot spread; it is shaped like an elongated pyramid. The branches are quite short, relative to the height of the tree, and begin about one-third the way up the tree. The branches are dense and have blue-green needles; cones are in clusters. The tree grows rapidly when young, preferably in moist, somewhat acidic, light soil in full sunlight. The mountain variety is hardy to minus 20 degrees Fahrenheit. This tree may live 700 years, or longer, but is subject to wind damage. Tree is evergreen.

*Tulip Tree (Liriodendron tulipifera).* This tree reaches heights of 150 feet, with a 70-foot spread. This tall tree has relatively short branches; first branches are a considerable distance from the ground. The trunk is straight and the branches form an irregular, oblong shape. The leaves are broad and shiny, pale underneath, and somewhat darker on top. The leaves turn yellow in the fall. This tree produces a tuliplike blossom from which it gets its name; the blossom is greenish-yellow with orange markings. The tulip tree is large, lives a long time, and requires rich, moist soil. The tulip tree requires only ordinary maintenance and is quite resistant to disease and insect problems. It is hardy to minus 20 degrees Fahrenheit.

*White Fir (Abies concolor).* The tree reaches heights of 120 feet by 60 feet; it is shaped like an elongated pyramid. Downsloping, dense branches reach all the way to ground. It has blue-green needles. The tree tolerates heat or shade and needs moist soil. It grows between 1 and 2 feet per year. An evergreen, it is hardy to minus 20 degrees Fahrenheit.

*American Elm (Ulmus americana).* This tree is regarded by many, both professional designers and amateurs, as one of the most beautiful trees in the United States. It is vase-shaped up to an umbrella-like top, offers excellent shade, and blends well in both urban and suburban use. Unfortunately this tree is subject to two diseases that may, if the tree is not frequently used, result in extinction. Therefore, it is recommended that this tree be used but in coordination with other trees; if the tree becomes disused, we may lose the species.

*European Beech (Fagus sylvatica).* This tree reaches heights of 100 feet by a 70-foot spread. This is a wide, almost oval tree. Branches go all the way to the ground with dense, small, dark green leaves that turn bronze in the fall. It lives 300 years or more and requires rich, moist, well-drained soil. This species transplants readily but cannot tolerate fill or compaction around roots. It is hardy to minus 20 degrees Fahrenheit.

*White Pine (Pinus strobus).* The tree grows to heights of 100 feet, with a 40-foot spread. This tree grows from a pyramidal shape to an almost cylindrical shape at maturity, then spreads out in old age. It is an evergreen with green needles. Branches are rather widely spaced. The ground underneath the tree will be covered with brown pine needles. The tree will grow in a variety of moist, well-drained soils but it needs sun. Tree is long-lived but subject to white pine blister rust and weevils. This is a popular and durable tree, hardy to minus 35 degrees Fahrenheit.

*Sycamore (Platanus acerifolia).* This sycamore reaches heights of 90 feet, by a 60-foot spread. The sycamore is easily identified: The branches and trunk are white, spotted with patches of light gray; the branches spread out from the trunk and grow quite long; leaves are large. This tree grows rapidly when young. An excellent shade tree and hardy, it prospers in city, country, and seashore environments. It will adjust to a variety of soils but prefers rich, moist soil. The tree is subject to anthracnose and canker. Easy to transplant, it is hardy to minus 15 degrees Fahrenheit.

*Canadian or Eastern Hemlock (Tsuga canadensis).* This hemlock attains heights of 90 feet, with a 30-foot spread. This is an evergreen with an elongated pyramid shape; the branches, however, are not particularly dense and thus there are open spots through the tree. Branches grow all the way to the ground. When pruned, many small branches will grow—it is a good tree for screening. It will grow in shade; it grows from 1 to 2 feet per year. The needles are short and thin, dark green on top and lighter green underneath. This tree does not prosper in urban air. It needs moist, deep soil. Otherwise it is long-lived and hardy to minus 40 degrees Fahrenheit.

*White Oak (Quercus alba).* The oak grows to 80 feet, with a 60-foot spread. It has a rounded shape with wide, spreading branches; the trunk and branch structure is visible through the branches and rather craggy in appearance. This tree needs considerable space to grow. Dark green leaves turn rusty and wine-red in fall. Bark is rough and light gray in color. The tree prefers somewhat dry, sandy, or gravelly soil but grows in other soils; it can be used in coastal areas. Transplanting is difficult if not done when the tree is young. It is hardy to minus 30 degrees Fahrenheit.

*White Ash (Fraxinus americana).* The ash reaches 80 feet, with a 50-foot spread. This tree can tolerate poor soil and polluted city air. Branches angle upward; the overall shape of the tree is almost oval. Branches start rather high off the ground. Large leaves turn purple or yellow in fall. The tree is subject to oyster scale and should be sprayed. It is hardy to minus 35 degrees Fahrenheit.

*Gingko (Gingko biloba).* The gingko grows to 80 feet by a 40-foot spread. Branches create open appearance. This tree cannot be missed in the fall: The leaves, about the size of half-dollars and fan-shaped, turn a brilliant, uniform yellow. This tree is particularly good for city use because it requires little, if any, maintenance, tolerates city air well, and transplants easily. Some say that this is the oldest surviving tree species. It is hardy to minus 25 degrees Fahrenheit.

*Black Gum (Nyssa sylvatica).* The gum reaches heights of 80 feet, with a 40-foot spread. The shape varies: It may be pyramidal or cylindrical; round tops are common. The tree has rather short, craggy horizontal branches; dark bark; and dark green leaves turning brilliant red in fall. Birds are attracted by the fruit. This tree needs wet, rich, acid soil and tolerates coastal areas. It is difficult to transplant unless tree is small. The roots are shallow and thus the tree may be pushed over if in exposed area where winds are a problem. The tree requires little maintenance and is hardy to minus 20 degrees Fahrenheit.

*Austrian Pine (Pinus nigra).* This tree has heights of 80 feet by a 40-foot spread. This evergreen starts out pyramidal in shape and gradually the top flattens. Branches spread horizontally and grow close to ground.

Dark green needles are long and thick. The tree needs full sunshine but tolerates poor soil, acid, and lime soil. It tolerates coastal areas, must be transplanted carefully, and is hardy to minus 30 degrees Fahrenheit.

*Sugar Maple (Acer saccharum).* The maple grows to 75 feet with a 40-foot spread. A beautiful tree, especially in fall, it has an oval top and a thick, wide shape. The trunk is short, with branches fairly close to ground. The large leaves are dark green on top and whitish-green underneath; in fall they turn brilliant shades of red, orange, and yellow. Yellow flowers bloom in spring. This tree transplants easily, even when large, but needs moist, well-drained soil, full sunshine and pure air. It is hardy to minus 30 degrees Fahrenheit.

*Norway Pine (Pinus resinosa).* With a height of 75 feet and 40-foot spread, this pine characteristically is tall, with a straight stem; branches angle downward from the tree and grow close to ground. It has an elongated pyramid shape and is open in appearance. This evergreen requires little maintenance and tolerates poor soil. It grows 1 to 2 feet per year and needs full sunshine. Long-lived, it is hardy to minus 50 degrees Fahrenheit.

*Scotch Pine (Pinus sylvestris).* This pine grows to 75 feet with a 40-foot spread. This evergreen grows from a pyramidal shape to a roundish, bristly shape at maturity. It has rather open, irregular branches, with blue-green needles. Bark is reddish at maturity. The tree prospers in coastal areas, it grows one to two feet per year and is hardy to minus 50 degrees Fahrenheit.

*Pin Oak (Quercus palustris).* The tree grows to 75 feet and a 40-foot spread. Cylindrical with horizontal branches, it has lower branches that droop downward and shed with age. Green leaves turn red in fall. Dense tree, stately in appearance. It prefers moist, nonalkaline soil, transplants well, and is hardy to minus 20 degrees Fahrenheit.

*Pagoda Tree (Sophora japonica).* At a height of 70 feet, with a 50-foot spread, the tree has a roundheaded, graceful, delicate appearance, with bright green leaves, yellowish white flowers in late summer, and yellow pods in winter. It is a decorative but tough tree and tolerates heat, poor soil, and city environment. It transplants easily, lives in dry soil, and is hardy to minus 30 degrees Fahrenheit.

*Northern Red Oak (Quercus borealis).* The oak grows to 70 feet, with a 40-foot spread. Its short trunk spreads into several strong branches forming round-topped, irregular shape. Lowest branches are fairly high off ground. Fine green leaves turn dark red in fall. It tolerates city environments and is hardy to minus 20 degrees Fahrenheit.

*Little Leaf Linden (Tilia cordata).* At a height of 70 feet and spread of 50 feet, the tree is pyramidal but rounded at the top. Branches go all the way to ground and are dense, especially when pruned. The tree has small, bright green leaves; yellow flowers at first of summer attract bees. It should have moist soil. Aphids and leaf-eating insects are problems; spray. An excellent shade tree, it is hardy to minus 30 degrees Fahrenheit.

*Moraine Locust (Gleditsia triacanthos inermis moraine).* The tree reaches 70 feet with a 30-foot spread. Loose branches are roundheaded. The tree has a delicate appearance, with no thorns or pods. Leaves are rather late in coming and shed early in fall. Long-lived, it is a popular city tree because it transplants easily, tolerates poor soil and air, and requires little maintenance. It is hardy to minus 25 degrees Fahrenheit.

*Red or Water Maple (Acer rubrum).* This maple grows to 60 feet, with a 40-foot spread. It has an oval, sometimes round shape. Branches are dense and angle upward. It produces small red flowers in spring. In fall the leaves turn brilliant red, orange, and yellow. The tree grows in sun or shade and tolerates coastal areas. Wet ground is best, but the tree can adapt. It grows rapidly, as much as 2 feet per year, and transplants easily. It is hardy to minus 40 degrees Fahrenheit.

*Northern Catalpa (Catalpa speciosa).* With a height of 60 feet and a spread of 40 feet, it has an irregular, elongated pyramid shape; irregular, horizontal branches are easily seen. The tree has large green leaves, spotted white flowers in summer, long slender pods in winter. It tolerates poor soil and city environments and grows rather slowly—less than 1 foot per year. It tolerates heat and drought and is hardy to minus 20 degrees Fahrenheit.

*Horse Chestnut (Aesculus hippocastanum).* The tree grows 60 feet tall and 30 feet wide. It is pyramidal with a round top. Trunk and branch structure are visible; it is an open tree with large leaves and creamy flowers in spring; nuts shed around tree. It tolerates city environments and coastal areas and transplants easily. It needs sunlight and rich, moist soil and is hardy to minus 35 degrees Fahrenheit.

*Katsura Tree (Cercidiphyllum japonicum).* With a 60-foot height and 30-foot spread, the tree has a loose outline; branches grow close to the ground. The leaves are close to the branches; the tree is reddish in spring, blue-green in summer, and changes to red and yellow in fall. It grows 2 feet or more per year and requires little maintenance. It needs rich, moist soil and plenty of sun and is hardy to minus 25 degrees Fahrenheit.

*Japanese Black Pine (Pinus thunbergi).* The pine grows to 60 feet, with a 30-foot spread. It is an irregular, spreading, dense tree, with craggy trunk and branches. This evergreen transplants easily, tolerates poor soil and coastal areas, and is good for mass planting as screen, area definition, etc. It is hardy to minus 5 degrees Fahrenheit.

*Eastern Red Cedar (Juniperus virginiana).* The cedar grows 60 feet high and 20 feet wide. It has a straight, narrow shape. Small green leaves eventually turn rusty brown. The tree has red bark and produces berries that attract birds. It tolerates coastal areas and almost any soil except swamps. This evergreen grows slowly, sometimes less than 1 foot per year; it can become a tree or can be used as a shrub, depending on type soil, climate, and maintenance (pruning). It is hardy to minus 50 degrees Fahrenheit.

*Norway Maple (Acer platanoides).* At a 50-foot height and 40-foot spread, it has a roundish, regular shape. It produces yellow flowers in spring. It grows 1 to 2 feet per year, transplants easily, and tolerates coastal areas and city environments (can be used at street). A limited number of plants will grow under the tree. It is hardy to minus 40 degrees Fahrenheit.

*Tree of Heaven (Ailanthus altissima).* The tree grows to 50 feet, with a 30-foot spread. Coarse, spreading branches create an open appearance; in winter the structure is stark. There are large, bright green leaves. The tree produces flowers, which become a reddish fruit. It is self-seeding, tolerates almost any soil and city environments, and requires little maintenance. However, it lasts only 25 to 30 years; in open acreage or large lots this would not be too important, because the tree replenishes itself—for single usage, the short life becomes more important. Also, the tree grows rapidly, over 2 feet per year. It is hardy to minus 20 degrees Fahrenheit.

*Amur Cork Tree (Phellodendron amurense).* The tree grows 40 feet high, with a 40-foot spread. The open tree has a low trunk, branches angling upward, and a rounded top. Medium green leaves grow at the ends of branches. Female trees produce black fruit. Sun penetrates the tree (light shade). It transplants easily, tolerates poor soil and city environments, grows over 2 feet per year, and is hardy to minus 35 degrees Fahrenheit.

*Weeping willow (Salix babylonica).* With a 40-foot height and 40-foot spread, the tree has limber branches bending to the ground and a round, umbrella-like shape. A graceful tree, it sways with the slightest breeze and provides light shade. Valued primarily for decorative quality, it is easily toppled in storms due to shallow roots. Roots seek out drain and sewer pipes—and can penetrate open or loose-jointed pipes and clog. Not a rugged tree, it requires considerable maintenance and is subject to disease and insect damage. It grows over 2 feet per year, transplants easily, and requires moist ground. It sheds leaves if ground becomes dry. It is hardy to minus 20 degrees Fahrenheit.

## Shrubbery

In undisturbed areas of land a wide range of plant sizes makes up the visual and spatial quality of the setting. Tall and medium trees make up the higher levels, then smaller trees, then shrubs of varying level, and finally small plants and groundcovers. For illustrative purposes here, shrubs, in size and form, fall between trees and ground covers.

Shrubs should be selected with the same care as trees. The following listing of shrubs certainly is not complete. As with the tree listing, these are popular shrubs that flourish in many regions of the United States. The intent here is not to provide a "recipe" for planting but rather to aid the reader in gaining a feel for plant selection within the planting plan design process.

### Azaleas

There are a variety of azaleas, including Chinese azalea (Rhododendron molle), Japanese azalea (Rhododendron jamponicum), Korean azalea (Rhododendron mucronulatum), and Azalea Pinxter (Rhododendron nudiflorum).

These azaleas are deciduous, bear fragrant blossoms, and need light shade and rich loam soil. Chinese, Japanese, and Pinxter prefer acidic soil. The Korean variety is adaptable—it grows in acid or neutral soil but always rich loam.

Chinese azalea grows 3 to 4 feet high and produces yellow flowers in spring. It is hardy to about minus 5 degrees Fahrenheit.

Japanese azalea grows to about 6 feet high and produces brilliant flowers in red, yellow, or orange colors in spring. It is hardy to about minus 10 degrees Fahrenheit.

Korean azalea grows to about 5 feet high and produces rosy-purple flowers in spring. The leaves turn yellow, bronze, or red in the fall. It is hardy to about minus 20 degrees Fahrenheit.

Pinxter grows to about 5 feet and produces white or pink flowers in spring. It is hardy to about minus 20 degrees Fahrenheit.

### Lilac

There are a variety of lilacs, including Chinese lilac (Syringa × chinensis), Common lilac (Syringa vulgaris), and Persian lilac (Suringa × persica).

These lilacs are graceful, open shrubs. Persian lilac grows to about 6 feet, the others 12 to 15 feet high. They need full sun and average soil. Deciduous shrubs, in the spring they produce clusters of fragrant flowers, typically white, purple, or lavender. They may be trimmed to about 3 feet for hedge use. They also are good for screens or use against fences or columns. Chinese is hardy to minus 10 degrees Fahrenheit; Common to minus 35; and Persian to minus 35.

*Japanese Quince (Chaenomeles speciosa lagenaria).* It grows 6 to 10 feet high. Deciduous, it has abundant red, white, pink, or orange flowers in spring and yellow-green fruit, about 2 inches in diameter. It is a good decorative shrub alone, in groups, or against walls, fences. It needs full sun or light shade. Adaptable to various soils, it is hardy to minus 10 degrees Fahrenheit.

### Rhododendron

There are a variety of rhododendrons. Carolina Rhododendron (Rhododendron carolinianum) and Catawba Rhododendron (Rhododendron catawbiense) are good for general use in many areas of the country. Both of these prosper in light shade but do not like full sun. They produce white, purple, or pink flowers in spring. With lustrous green leaves, it needs acid soil, rich loam, and watering. Carolina grows to 15 feet, Catawba to 8 feet. Carolina is hardy to minus 10 degrees Fahrenheit, Catawba to minus 20.

*Heather (Calluna vulgaris).* This is the popular Scottish heather. It grows to 3 feet high. Branches grow upward; it has silver-gray, pinkish-bronze foliage. Colorful, it needs full sun or light shade. Growing in acid, light sandy soil, this evergreen is hardy to minus 10 degrees Fahrenheit.

*Daphne (Daphne mezereum).* It grows to 3 feet high. Deciduous, it produces fragrant, rosy-pink flowers in winter in the south, spring in the north; red fruit close to branches in fall. It needs full sun and acid soil. It is hardy to minus 10 degrees Fahrenheit.

*Witch-Hazel (Hamamelis virginiana).* It grows to 15 feet high. Deciduous, it produces yellow flowers in fall that tumble over the branches, with a spicy fragrance. It needs full sun or light shade and grows in average soil. It is hardy to minus 20 degrees Fahrenheit.

These shrubs were selected as illustrations of widely available and hardy shrubs that prosper in much of the United States. It also should be noted that flowering times vary; a combination of shrubs may be selected so that there will be green, flowering growth in all four seasons. These shrubs are only a few of dozens of choices.

## Ground Covers

There is no practical reason for attempting a hard-line distinction between shrubs and trees, even if such a distinction were technically possible. Some trees may be pruned to achieve the size and usage of shrubs; conversely some shrubs may be "taught" to function as small trees. Similarly shrubs and ground covers may sometimes overlap in function. Low-lying shrubs may sometimes be used effectively as ground covers, and ground covers may be groomed to function as shrubs. The following listing, though not definitive, should help the reader consider ground covers from a design standpoint.

*Grass*

For many homeowners, and even professional site planners, grass is *the* ground cover. Indeed there perhaps is no other ground cover as versatile and hardy as grass. Whole volumes are available that describe the varieties of grass and installation and maintenance procedures for various uses: individual lots, common areas in large developments, sports and recreational areas, and other large areas where a hardy ground cover is needed. Thus, grass is the most widely used of all the ground covers. And grass often is overused.

*Grass*
*Alternatives*

On large areas where foot traffic is less frequent than for preceding uses, or infrequent, and minimum maintenance is desired, other ground covers may be appropriate. The following listing of ground covers also may be used in transition areas between large high-use grassy areas and areas of lesser foot traffic such as wooded areas or utility areas (parking lots, driveways, etc.).

*Goutweed (Aegopodium podagraria)*. This grows in a dense mat about 6 inches high. It has small, delicate green leaves (also available with mixture of white and blue-green leaves). Leaves shed in winter, return in spring. Carrotlike flowers bloom in early summer. This spreads vigorously and may need periodic thinning, tolerates poor soil and drought and grows in sun or shade (more slowly in shade). It requires mowing only two or three times per year. It is hardy to minus 35 degrees Fahrenheit.

*Bugleweed (Ajuga reptans)*. This grows in a low mat, formed by oval, 2- to 4-inch long leaves; it is typically green leafed but bronze, purple, and mottled yellow are available. In spring blue flowers rise 4 to 6 inches. It tolerates full sun but prefers light shade. It needs well-drained garden soil and does not tolerate drought well—watering may be required. Mow once a year, after flowers have bloomed. It is hardy to minus 10 degrees Fahrenheit.

*Maiden pink (Dianthus deltoides).* Blue-green, grass-like leaves grow about 6 inches, then stop; there are bright pink flowers on longer stems. It blooms from early to late summer. It needs full sun and good drainage. Mow after flowering to increase density. It grows in light soil and may need lime. It is hardy to minus 50 degrees Fahrenheit.

*Dichondra (D. micrantha).* It has dark green leaves, about ¾-inch across and shaped like the outline of a horseshoe; it grows 1 to 3 inches high and requires little or no mowing. Considered by some to be more beautiful than grass, it can take only light and occasional foot traffic; it is much more delicate than grass. It grows in sun or light shade. Soil must be kept moist but not soggy; the plant will not tolerate drought. Spraying against weeds sometimes may be needed. It is hardy to plus 15 degrees Fahrenheit.

*Wintercreeper (Euonymus fortunei).* This ground cover is an evergreen vine with leaves 1½ to 2 inches long. Flowers seldom occur and are not conspicuous. When grown densely, the plants may rise as high as 2 feet; the vine lengths typically are about 4 feet long. The vines often root where they touch the ground. Wintercreeper grows rapidly in good or poor soil, sun or shade. The plant tolerates drought but functions poorly in semiarid or desert areas. It is hardy to minus 20 degrees Fahrenheit.

*Blue fescue (Festuca ovina "glauca").* It grows in clumps 4 to 10 inches high and is grasslike in appearance, other than the characteristic clumps; it has a blue-gray color. It grows almost anywhere in the United States in well-drained soil and full sun, resists drought but may need some watering, and is hardy to minus 40 degrees Fahrenheit.

*Japanese spurge (Pachysandra terminalis).* An excellent ground cover alternative to grass in shady areas, individual plants of 6 to 8 inches high may be grown densely; leaves are oval, green, about 1½ to 4 inches long. It needs light shade to full shade and prefers good soil, moist and slightly acidic. It is excellent around trees and hardy to minus 30 degrees Fahrenheit.

*Ivy (Hedera).* There are many varieties of ivy. This evergreen vine is highly versatile. It lies flat, climbs, spreads for dense cover, prospers in sun or light shade, and requires minimum maintenance. It requires well-drained soil and is hardy in most areas of the United States. Consult local authorities for best local species.

*Periwinkle (Vinca major and minor).* Evergreen trailers, Vinca major reaches heights up to 2 feet, minor to about 6 inches. Except for height, both the periwinkles look about the same: dark green leaves, lilac-blue flowers in spring. It prefers light shade and well-drained, moist, rich soil.

Minor is hardy to minus 30 degrees Fahrenheit, major to minus 10 degrees Fahrenheit.

*Junipers.* The juniper is the workhorse of ground covers. There are at least two dozen varieties, each with slightly different characteristics. Rather than itemize the characteristics of each variety, the following general characteristics are given: Junipers typically range between 6 to 20 inches in height and spread 4 to 6 feet. The branches are craggy and irregular but dense, with blue-green or gray-green or silver-green needles. Some varieties, when planted over a fairly wide area, will mound up somewhat higher than usual for shrub usage. Creeper varieties stay low and will hang over retaining walls, ditches, and similar dropoffs. Other uses include steep slopes, rocky ground, and similar areas that would present problems for grass and other ground covers.

Junipers may tolerate coastal areas. They generally are rugged plants but require full sun and well-drained soil; soils with high clay content are not desirable. If spaced closely, they sometimes require thinning; otherwise little maintenance is required. Junipers are not rapid growers. They are subject to insect infestation and sometimes need spraying. Typically they are hardy to minus 25 degrees Fahrenheit. Check individual species.

It should be emphasized that all these ground covers are excellent where there will be little or no foot traffic. Thus, they are grass alternatives, not grass substitutes. This listing is merely a sampling of the dozens of ground covers that are available.

The planting plan, together with the specifications, provides a complete, detailed guide for the arrangement and installation of all lawn and lot plants and materials. The minimum objectives of the planting plan are (1) to prevent the erosion of soil and (2) to provide appropriately useful areas, as desired (Figure 8–5).

# FINAL LAND SURFACE PREPARATION AND EQUIPMENT

Topsoil may have been removed and stored on the site or it may have been brought to the site from other sources. Topsoil may be added as soon as the subgrade contours are in place. If the topsoil is not placed until after the house is complete, there is less chance of debris or undesirable organic materials being mixed in the topsoil and less danger of the topsoil becoming too compacted by heavy equipment that still may be in use on the site.

A variety of light equipment may be used to spread topsoil. A good combination is (1) a large shovel dozer (the exact size depends on the size of the project—length of hauls made, amount of soil to be carried, etc.); (2) a "toy," two-ton shovel dozer to maneuver in the smaller areas; and (3) a small farm tractor with a push blade to do the odd jobs and light finish grading.

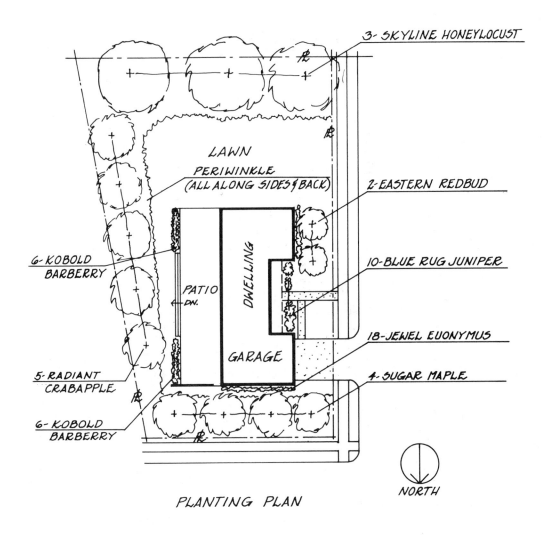

3- SKYLINE HONEYLOCUST

LAWN
PERIWINKLE
(ALL ALONG SIDES & BACK)

2-EASTERN REDBUD

6-KOBOLD
BARBERRY

DWELLING

PATIO
DN.

GARAGE

10-BLUE RUG JUNIPER

18-JEWEL EUONYMUS

5-RADIANT
CRABAPPLE

4-SUGAR MAPLE

6-KOBOLD
BARBERRY

PLANTING PLAN

NORTH

FIGURE 8–5. The planting plan. As a minimum, the planting plan shows the type, quantity, and location of plants. Small lots may have the plant labeled directly on the plan. Larger projects usually number the plants, then (on a separate plant list) identify them by common and botanical names and give quantities and plant sizes. Other information frequently required includes plant installation detail drawings and instructions; deck, patio, border treatments, etc.

Two inches of topsoil is the minimum amount for most locations. Four inches is preferred and, if budget permits, even more is desirable. Topsoil contains humus, which stores water that plants use in dry seasons. Topsoil also contains built-in fertilizer for plants, and the size and arrangement of soil particles encourage plant growth. Lawns with thin topsoil may be improved by adding fertilizer, but the plants usually do not prosper as those do with adequate topsoil.

The description concerns topsoil for grass and similar ground covers. Shrubs, flowers, gardens, and other plants have varying requirements that should be checked; 8 inches to 2 feet are typical.

## Sod

Sod is more expensive than grass, but it provides a faster finished lawn, often making sales easier and justifying the extra cost. Sod typically is available from landscape contractors in conveniently sized rectangles or may be purchased in strips up to 10 feet long by a foot to 15 inches wide. A thickness of about 2 inches usually gets enough of the roots to assure a successful growth. Some contractors locate and cut their own sod, using a tractor-towed sod cutter or cutting by hand.

In addition to providing a faster finished lawn, sod may be used where steep slopes would make seeding difficult or impossible, especially in rainy weather. After the soil surface is prepared, the sod is laid and must be tamped or otherwise pressed in firm contact with the soil to assure good root contact with the soil; otherwise the roots may not take hold. The sod should be watered after installation and requires inspection and attention until it obviously is rooted and maintaining itself.

On slopes it may be necessary to use wood stakes or pegs to hold the sod in place. Chickenwire may be spread over the sod and staked in place. Another, popular method is to use plastic mesh spread over the sod (or other low-lying ground covers) and pegged in place; when the sod or ground cover is rooted, the mesh may easily be removed.

# LAND CLEARING*     9

*The following material was rewritten from *The Clearing of Land for Development*, Copyright 1974, Caterpillar Tractor Co.)

In land clearing, several types of terrain and vegetation will be found, and these types could be subdivided into countless subtypes. Most people, however, would agree to the following classifications for land-clearing purposes.

*Desert.* Devoid of vegetation above 2 or 3 feet (0.60 or 0.90 meters) in height, it has occasional trees in low spots where water accumulates or ground springs are present.

*Bush Country 1.* It has scattered bushes, usually thorny, woody vegetation with or without scattered cactuslike plants. When not overgrazed with livestock or wildlife, it is covered with annual and perennial grasses.

*Bush Country 2.* Usually found in tropical semiarid areas, its characteristics are dense thorny brush with scattered large hardwood vegetation and undergrowth so thick that neither annual or perennial grasses can grow.

*Upland woods.* Usually with hard woods and soft woods, deciduous and coniferous, there are few, if any, vines entangling the tops. All the trees are approximately the same height and there usually is only a single canopy (i.e., the uppermost branchy layer of a forest). This vegetation is limited almost exclusively to temperate climates.

*Tropical Rain Forest.* Characterized by a mixture of hard and soft wood, two-, sometimes three-storied canopy, with or without dense underbrush, it has trees that may grow to 15 feet (4.6 meters) and over in diameter. Often the tops are heavily entwined in clinging vines. This type of vegetation requires good soil, year-round rainfall and constantly high or medium high temperatures.

# FACTORS TO CONSIDER IN DETERMINING METHODS AND EQUIPMENT

Determining exactly how certain variables increase or decrease the efficiency of individual methods and equipment is difficult. Success, however, is often a combination of being aware of the variables and applying common sense in equipping the job to meet them.

Many factors affecting production and cost are included in type and density of vegetation. Among these are the number of trees, tree size, wood density, roots, vines, and undergrowth. All of these variables can be determined by a *tree count.* To conduct this count, a straight line is measured for any convenient distance, usually 328 feet (100 meters). A tabulation is then taken along this line for a depth of approximately 16 feet (5 meters) on both sides. The tabulation should include the number of trees, their diameters, densities (hard or soft wood), and root system plus a description of any undergrowth and vines. The 328 feet × 32 feet (100 meters × 10 meters) area will produce a sample of about ¼ acre (¹⁄₁₀ hectare). This should be repeated two or three times for each area where the size and type of vegetation change significantly. The tree counts need not be parallel.

More detailed methods of analyzing vegetative cover can be found in any good forestry textbook. However, these other methods are too complex for most land-clearing purposes.

Tree counting can be done by grouping trees into categories such as

Less than 12 inches (30 cm) diameter (undergrowth)

12–24 inches (30–60 cm) diameter

25–36 inches (61–90 cm) diameter

37–48 inches (91–120 cm) diameter

49–72 inches (121–180 cm) diameter

73 inches (181 cm) and up diameter

As trees are measured, they can be counted. The diameter of the tree is found by measuring the trees at diameter-breast-height (DBH) or 4.5 feet (1.37 meters) (A) above the ground. If a buttress (B) is present, the measurement should be at the top of the buttress (C), where the trunk begins to run straight and true (Figure 9–1).

Wood density (hard or soft wood) and the root system (tap or lateral roots) should be noted when measuring. Recording the presence of vines and the type of undergrowth should also be done at this time.

Generally, wet soil encourages trees and shrubs to develop wide lateral root systems near the surface. These can be grubbed out more economically than species with deep tap roots found in dry areas.

Notations should also be made of the presence of high climbing vines binding the tree tops together. This condition complicates the felling operation, regardless of the method used.

Diameter and density affect productivity (speed of land clearing). In a case study a hardwood tree 8.8 feet (2.7 meters) in diameter took 48 minutes to fell, while a softwood tree, with a diameter twice the size, 16.1 feet (4.9 meters), required only 7 minutes to fell. The same effect can be true for other variables.

Soils play a major part in affecting the choice of methods and equipment. Included are depth of topsoil, moisture content, and presence of rocks and stones.

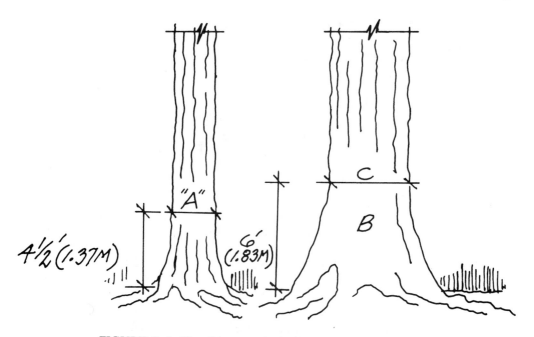

FIGURE 9–1. The diameter of trees are measured at breast height or 4.5 feet above ground. If a buttress (B) is present, the measurement should be at the top of the buttress where the trunk begins to run straight and true (C).

## Vegetation

In clearing operations the soil is often disturbed in felling and piling the vegetation. In areas where there is a shallow layer of topsoil and where planting will be done, it is imperative that this soil disturbance be kept to a minimum to ensure that the land will be conducive to planting after being cleared. The method and equipment choice will determine the degree of soil disturbance that can be expected.

## Soil Conditions

The type of soil will also play a part when tree felling production is considered. In sandy loam soils, roots often pop out of the ground when a tree is felled. At the other end of the soil scale is hard clay, which often holds roots so tightly that they have to be dug or uprooted with special tools or cut off at ground level and left.

Moisture content of the soil is another factor that affects the choice of method and equipment. In heavily wooded areas sunlight seldom is in contact with the soil for long periods of time. This frequently causes the soil to be so damp that it will not support the weight of equipment in the felling and stacking operations.

If embedded rocks or stony outcroppings are present in the area to be cleared, equipment that severs the vegetation at ground level is severely hampered in its operation, and maintenance becomes a problem. Therefore, other types of equipment could be used in these areas.

With all these factors to judge, some standard must be set so that underfoot conditions can be accurately described and understood. *Good* underfoot conditons exist when traction, flotation, and slope are not a problem for the tractor even after repeated passes in the same tracks. *Soft* conditions exist when more than one or two passes over the same track create moderate to severe impairment of machine performance. *Poor* conditions exist when the first pass is precarious and difficult.

## Topography

Grade and terrain can greatly affect the normal operation of some equipment. Such factors as steep slopes, ditches, swampy areas, and the like can decrease production, increase maintenance costs, and thus influence the choice of methods and equipment considerably.

## Rainfall and Climate

Usually all phases of land clearing from cutting to burning are concerned to some degree by temperature changes and the amount of rain that falls during a clearing project. Rainfall and the resultant water table also affect flotation. Due to heavy rain, conventional track-type tractors sometimes sink into the ground. Therefore, low ground pressure tractors should be considered.

## End Use of Land

The end use of the land is an important factor when choosing the method and equipment. For example, if the land is used for building, highway, or dam construction, total removal of vegetation is necessary. On the other hand, if the land is to be planted, cutting the trees and brush flush to the ground or 3 to 4 inches (7.5 to 10.0 cm) below ground level is all that is required. If the land will be used for grazing, certain large trees may be left on the ground along with the stumps of other trees.

# LAND-CLEARING MACHINES AND ATTACHMENTS

Machines and job conditions must be matched for each job site. What works well in one area may not be the best method in another area. Track-type tractors find application in almost every phase of land development work. The D4E, D5B, D6D, D7G, D8L, and D9L track-type tractors are well suited in the initial stages of rough clearing and pioneering. The low ground pressure D4E, D5B, and D6D can help in areas where underfoot conditions are extremely soft. Even in the final stages of land development work, track-type tractors, like the special application D4E, D5B, D6D, and D7G, are used in replanting or maintenance of vegetative growth.

Generally speaking, lower-cost clearing can be done with larger tractors if the amount of clearing involved is sufficient to merit the greater initial investment in the bigger machines. In any case, because of the need for constant shifting, a power shift transmission should be standard equipment on all tractors used in this application except in pull-type operations. In most applications a Caterpillar winch (D9L through D5B) should also be considered as standard equipment for at least one tractor per fleet.

Track-type tractors are by no means the only machines that should be considered. Imagination and resourcefulness can allow the adoption of other types of machines in specific applications. In fact, wheel loaders have been used in some areas for raking, stacking, and even grubbing operations.

In equipping land-clearing machines, consideration must be given to the various protective attachments available. For instance, the radiator, engine, and underside of the tractor should be well protected with perforated hoods, screens, crankcase guards, etc. More importantly, though, cab guards should be considered a necessity in land clearing. (It is also interesting to note that production has been estimated to increase significantly when cab guards are used.)

A familiarity with current land-clearing equipment is vital for effectively determining the proper tools for a clearing job. Substantial cost savings can be realized when the job is thoroughly planned and properly equipped. The following is a capsule description of land-clearing tools, their applications, and in some cases their advantages and disadvantages. No attempt, however, is made to compare the attachments specifically.

## Blades

*Description.* The K/G blade made by Rome Industries (Cedartown, Georgia) is designed to apply the power and weight of a track-type tractor to a sharp cutting edge.

*Rome K/G Blade*

The blade angle is 30 degrees on all models and it is constructed of special alloy steel. Its replaceable cutting edges and "stinger" can be re-sharpened with a small portable grinder. A guide bar is used to control the direction the trees fall (forward and to the right of the operator). (Figure 9–2, A–C).

*Application.* The K/G blade can be used for practically any type of land clearing, including clearing for reservoirs, lakesites, range lands, forest site preparation, agriculture, rights-of-way for pipelines or power lines, and large construction sites. It can also be used for building roads, fire-breaks, and V-type drainage ditches. Stumping and windrowing are also possible with this tool.

*Advantages.* A versatile attachment, the same tool can cut, pile, stump, and ditch. Cut trees normally fall in one direction. Given enough time, the K/G can fell any size tree.

*Fleco V Blade*

*Description.* The V-blade made by Fleco Corporation (Jacksonville, Florida) is available for Caterpillar track-type tractors through the D8H. It is equipped with a heavy-duty "splitter," angled, serrated cutting blades,

FIGURE 9–2A. CAT D8L/Medford cab guard, Rome K/G blade and protection group.

FIGURE 9–2B. CAT D8L/Medford cab guard, Rome K/G blade and protection group.

FIGURE 9–2C. Rome K/G blade on CAT D6C.

and brush rack. V-blades mount directly on the tractor trunnions and are available for cable or hydraulic control. The V is in two sections and bolts together to form the working tool. The serrated blade and splitter both are hardened steel (Figures 9–3 and 9–4).

*Application.* The V-blade is useful in high-production clearing of trees, stumps, or brush that do not require removal of subsurface roots and stumps. Applications for V-blades are for clearing dam sites, industrial sites, agricultural areas, jungles, road pioneering, and rights-of-way.

*Advantages.* When properly matched to the job, the V-blade is a highly productive tool because it can maintain a continuous path. Bolt-on design permits assembly or disassembly on the job. It also provides flexibility in moving the unit.

*Disadvantages.* Trees fall to either the right or left of the tractor (this can be a disadvantage depending on the particular job). It does not remove imbedded material such as roots and rocks. Stumps are usually not removed in one pass. The V-blade is not recommended for piling or ditching.

FIGURE 9–3. FLECO D8L V-tree cutter.

FIGURE 9–4. FLECO D8L V-tree cutter.

## Tree Pusher

*Description.* Two models of tree pushers are available from Fleco Corporation. They mount on a standard or angle bulldozer blade. One is attached with brackets to the top of the C-frame or push arms and pinned to the top of the cable or hydraulic controlled blade. It can be raised or lowered with the blade. Another method of mounting is to pin it to the C-frame or push arms so it can raise or lower independently of the dozer blade by use of a separate cable group. A double drum cable control is necessary for this unit. Both configurations are available for all track-type tractor models (Figure 9–5).

The other model of tree pusher is mounted directly on the tractor trunnions and can be operated with a cable or hydraulic control. This model is available for all tractors except the smaller track-type tractors.

*Application.* Because it removes the entire tree, the tree pusher is a highly effective tool when the land-clearing project requires that no stumps be left in the ground. The tree pusher is extremely useful in chaining operations where the chain cannot fell a large tree or when help is needed in maneuvering the chain.

FIGURE 9–5. FLECO D7G tree pusher.

*Advantages.* It provides a method for downing trees because the trees always fall away from the operator. Because the entire tree is uprooted, no stumps or roots have to be removed at a later time. It can significantly speed a chaining operation.

*Disadvantages.* The effectiveness of this tool can be impaired if trees are too large, tap roots are present, or traction is poor. Small-diameter growth usually needs to be removed by some other means. Holes left by the stumps sometimes need to be filled depending on end use of the land.

## Rakes

Fleco Corporation (Jacksonville, Florida) manufactures 12 types of rakes and all of them are specifically designed for certain jobs. All the rakes are interchangeable with standard tractor attachments unless otherwise specified. Fleco rakes are available for several models of Caterpillar equipment.

*Multiapplication Rake*    Multiapplication (MA) rakes are available from Fleco Corporation and Rome Industries. They are designed to withstand extreme shock loads under the most severe clearing conditions.

Multiapplication rakes have steel teeth equipped with replaceable wear tips. A steel center plate is located in the rake frame to protect the tractor radiator. A high brush rack is standard equipment. MA rakes interchange with the blade on a bulldozer arrangement (Figure 9–6).

*Application.* The multiapplication rake is designed for all heavy-duty land clearing including small tree and rock removal. Applications are jungle clearing, road pioneering, dam site clearing, industrial and agricultural clearing, clearing for rights-of-way, grubbing, stumping, rock work, and general-purpose clearing.

*Advantages.* A heavy-duty implement for land-clearing use in varying types of terrain. It is particularly effective in sandy soils.

*Disadvantages.* The multiapplication rake will not fell large trees.

*Description.* The rock and root rake is equipped with teeth made of manganese carbon steel castings. The teeth are curved to get under rocks, boulders, roots, etc. Replaceable wear tips are standard along with the center plate, which protects the radiator. Brush racks are available as optional equipment (Figure 9–7, A–E)

*Rock and Root Rake*

FIGURE 9–6. Rome multiapplication rake on CAT D6D.

FIGURE 9–7A. FLECO D8L rock and root rake (has optional brush rack).

FIGURE 9–7B. FLECO D3 rock and root rake (has optional brush rack).

FIGURE 9–7C. FLECO D6D rock and root rake.

FIGURE 9–7D. FLECO D3 rock and root rake (has optional brush rack).

FIGURE 9–7E. FLECO D7G rock and root rake (has optional brush rack).

*Application.* The rock and root rake should be used for general clearing, grubbing boulders, and spreading rock rip-rap. It is also useful in grubbing and piling trees, stumps, and debris.

*Blade Rake*

*Description.* The blade rake is mounted to the bulldozer blade by pinning it to the top of the blade with two pins. Models are available for both angle and straight dozers for most Caterpillar D4E track-type tractors. Installation is accomplished by welding two sets of mounting brackets to the upper edge of the blade. The rake is constructed of high-strength alloy steel and fits flush with the blade.

*Application.* Blade rakes are designed for light grubbing, piling, and raking. They are not recommended for heavy-duty clearing such as removing trees, stumps, and rocks. They are particularly suited for tractor jobs that require both raking and blading.

*Clearing and Stacker Rakes*

*Description.* The clearing and stacker rakes are available from Fleco Corporation for Caterpillar wheel and track-type loaders. Stacker rakes also are available from Rome Industries for Caterpillar track-type tractors.

FIGURE 9–8. FLECO 955L clearing rake.

The teeth of the clearing rake are shorter and less curved than those of the stacking rake. Both rakes are equipped with brush racks for greater load carry capacity. (Figures 9–8 and 9–9).

*Application.* Each style rake is designed to perform a particular function. The clearing rake is strong enough for tree pushing, grubbing, stumping, and clearing. It can also be used for boulders.

The stacker has extra height and longer curved teeth for jobs such as raking, piling, carrying, and loading downed debris. It is not, however, designed for grubbing or for raking large jungle-type trees.

*Description.* The clamp rake is available for Caterpillar track-type and wheel loaders. With the regular bucket it requires an extra hydraulic valve arrangement. The clamp rake retains all the basic features of the clearing rake for track-type loaders with the added feature of two built-in hydraulically operated clamps (Figures 9–10 and 9–11). *Clamp Rake*

*Application.* The clamp rake is designed for clearing and grubbing trees, stumps, and boulders. It also can be used for raking, carrying, loading, and piling debris.

FIGURE 9–9. FLECO 931 stacker rake.

FIGURE 9–10. FLECO 977L clamp rake.

FIGURE 9–11. FLECO 977L clamp rake.

*Description.* The pull-type wheel root rake is available from Rome Industries. It was designed specifically to follow up root plowing for the removal of unwanted roots. It leaves an area clear, ready for disk harrowing or agricultural operations.

The wheel root rake is secured to the tractor drawbar. The wheel assembly consists of two widely spaced steel-drum–type wheels for flotation and stability. Two high arches run from the wheel assembly to the rake beam to give added brush capacity.

*Application.* The wheel root rake is basically intended as a land-clearing implement for semiarid areas.

*Advantages.* With its 21-foot (6,400 mm) width, the wheel root rake rapidly combs unwanted roots out of the soil, leaving them in the windrows or piles as desired.

*Disadvantages.* The root rake cannot remove the large roots that are frequently found in rain forest areas. It must follow the root plow where soil, roots, and stumps have been loosened previously in order to avoid serious bending or breakage.

*Wheel Root Rake*

*Wake Rake*

*Description.* The pull-type wake rake has spinning wheels that literally sweep the topsoil clean of all light debris. Attached to the drawbar of a track-type tractor, it can clear the soil at speeds up to 5 miles per hour.

The wake rake is available from the Darf Corporation of Edenton, North Carolina.

*Application.* The wake rake is useful in final cleanup for picking up small loose pieces of stumps, roots, limbs, and unburned residue.

*Heavy-Duty Clearing Rake*

*Description.* The heavy-duty clearing rake is a solid weldment of high-strength, lightweight steel. Features of this rake are recessed mounting points for good balance, a high frame that carries a large load, and wear tips that can be replaced with a hammer and punch.

*Application.* The heavy-duty clearing rake is available for most Caterpillar track-type tractors. It can be used for medium- to heavy-duty land clearing, including the removal of trees and stumps. This rake is especially well suited for clearing mountainous terrain.

*Rake Summary*

Care should be taken in determining the application and the correct rake to fit that application. Picking the wrong rake can be a costly mistake because of the high wear and low production rates.

Rakes are almost universally recommended for repiling burned or burning material. Because the ash residue and soil can sift through the teeth, cleaner, hotter burns can be achieved. A summary of the rakes discussed and their application is presented next.

*Primary Rakes*

| TYPE RAKE | APPLICATION |
|---|---|
| Multiapplication rake | All heavy-duty land clearing including tree and rock removal. |
| Rock and root rake | Clearing and grubbing boulders, spreading rock rip-rap, and grubbing and piling tree stumps and debris. |
| Blade rake | Light grubbing, piling, and raking. |
| Wheel root rake | Follow-up to the root plow for removal of unwanted debris. |
| Heavy-duty clearing rake | Used in difficult land clearing conditions. |

*Utility Rakes*

| TYPE RAKE | APPLICATION |
|---|---|
| Clearing rake for track-type loader and wheel loader | Tree pushing, grubbing, stumping, and clearing trees and boulders. |
| Stacker rake for track-type loader and wheel loaders | Raking, piling, carrying, and loading downed debris. |
| Clamp rake for track-type loader and wheel loaders | Clearing and grubbing trees, stumps, and boulders; raking, carrying, loading, and piling debris. |
| Wake rake | Used in cleanup operations. |

## Fleco Skeleton Rock Bucket

*Description.* The Fleco skeleton rock bucket is designed so that small rocks and soil sift out of the load through openings in the sides, back, and bottom. This heavy-duty bucket is made entirely of alloy steel. It is equipped with Caterpillar-built tips, adaptors, and pins as standard equipment. This bucket is available for most Caterpillar wheel loaders and track-type loaders.

*Application.* The skeleton rock bucket is used to size, separate, and handle rock.

*Advantages.* By filtering fine material out of the load, this bucket eliminates the need for screening equipment. Eliminating fine material during loading provides maximum utilization of handling equipment.

*Disadvantages.* The skeleton rock bucket cannot be used to handle or load small rocks, gravel, or soil.

## Fleco Detachable Stumper with Splitter

*Description.* The Fleco detachable stumper is a one-piece manganese carbon steel casting for use on the C-frame of angle dozers. The curved face facilitates penetration in hard soil and cradles the stumps for removal. For larger stumps the detachable splitter is available as an attachment. It is welded to the left side of the standard stumper. The detachable stumper with or without splitter is available on special order for most Caterpillar track-type tractors.

*Application.* This implement is designed for use in stumping and tree removal operations. It can also be used as a utility ditcher.

*Advantages.* Power of the tractor is concentrated at one focal point. As a specialized tool, the stumper does one job well.

*Disadvantages.* The stumper is limited in its use.

## Root Plows

*Description.* Root plows made by Fleco Corporation mount on the tractor trunnions and are complete with overhead lift frame, sheaves, hydraulic group, and auxiliary trunnions. Spreader boxes are flanged in two places to speed assembly or disassembly of the unit. Both vertical standards are equipped with replaceable wear shins. Bolt-on cutting edges are reversible and hard surfaced. Optional depth of the root plow is controlled by a depth-setting arrangement with seven or more optional adjustments. This root plow is available for most track-type tractors.

Rome root plows consist of a rear trunnion-mounted frame with a horizontally mounted knife-type moldboard. This attachment moldboard is pulled through the ground by a tractor at a depth of 8 to 18 inches (203 to 457 mm). Wedge-type adjustment allows the operator to make quick and easy moldboard settings. The throat clearance from this moldboard to crossbeam allows brush and debris to flow through the plow easily. The Rome root plow is available for most track-type tractors (Figure 9–12).

FIGURE 9–12. Rome/Holt root plow with over the cab hydraulics.

*Application.* The root plow is designed for killing brush and growth by undercutting vegetation at the crown or bud ring. Large roots are forced to the surface by fins welded to the horizontal blade. Root plows also shatter hard surface crusts and hardpan, resulting in better water retention as well as preparing a good seed bed. An ideal use for root plows is in the restoration of range lands or irrigated crop land like that found in semiarid regions.

*Advantages.* It cuts roots below the bud ring. Depth is easily set and controlled.

*Disadvantages.* It will not work well in sandy or wet soils. It is not applicable to large-sized trees.

## Tool Bar Root Plow

*Description.* The root plow for a tool bar mounts on the 4½-inch × 7½-inch (114 × 190 mm) tool bar beam on the Caterpillar D4E through D6D track-type tractors. Depth of cut is controlled by adjustment of the tool bar screw jacks. This is the only difference from the standard root plow. Applications, advantages, and disadvantages are the same.

## Fleco Rolling Choppers

*Description.* Fleco rolling choppers are available as a single unit or three combinations. The drum of the chopper, which is normally filled with water to increase its weight, has welded on cutting blades that can penetrate 6 to 10 inches (152 to 254 mm) deep. Multiple drum choppers have swivel assemblies that connect the drums. Optional equipment available includes a spring-loaded tongue to reduce shock loading, a hinged tongue that swings up to reduce the overall length of the chopper for transporting, reversible blades with backup plates, and roller bearings. The choppers are available for the Caterpillar D4E through D9L track-type tractors (Figures 9–13, A–B).

*Application.* The rolling chopper offers a fast, economical method of controlling undesirable growth. While operating the tractor in second and third gear, the chopper blades can fracture and shatter growth. Soil crust is furrowed and loosened with a minimum topsoil disturbance. Applications include preparation of forest sites, brush control on right-of-way, clearing for reservoirs, preparation of seedbeds, and pasture renovation and maintenance.

*Advantage.* Properly matched to the application, this implement can be an inexpensive clearing tool.

*Disadvantage.* Large-diameter trees cannot be chopped with this tool.

FIGURE 9–13A. FLECO D7G rolling chopper.

FIGURE 9–13B. FLECO D7G rolling chopper.

# Harrows

Rome Industries manufactures two basic types of harrows: gang and offset. Many configurates are available for each type. Descriptions and applications of each harrow are given individually. (Harrows that are used primarily for some type of seedbed preparation are not discussed.) Because there are so many harrows, the advantages and disadvantages of harrows in general are given first (Figures 9–14 and 9–15).

*Rome Disc Harrows*

*Advantages of Harrows.* Harrows offer a fast and economical method of mixing organic matter with soils, leveling "stumped" areas, and speeding decomposition of embedded material.

*Disadvantages of Harrows.* They cannot be used to bring fines to the surface as does a moldboard or disk plow. Eradication of noxious grasses is difficult.

*Description.* This harrow is similar to the Rome series TRCH except that it is designed for use with lower horsepower tractors. It features extra-high gang carrier construction to prevent clogging. Models with 10, 12,

*Rome Tach Harrows*

FIGURE 9–14. Rome tach 10-32 and CAT D6D.

FIGURE 9–15. CAT D8H pulling Rome TYH 16-36.

and 16 disks are available. Hydraulic angling control may be used for all models. Boxed angle design imparts strength and rigidity to the TACH. Tapered roller bearings and overhead knife-type scrapers are standard. Rome series TACH harrows provide level clog-free plowing and thorough mixing.

*Application.* The TACH harrow provides thorough mixing and aeration to a maximum depth of 9 inches (228 mm). It is particularly useful for incorporating heavy trash and litter into the soil.

*Rome MR Harrow*

*Description.* The Rome "master," as this series is commonly called, comes with 28-inch or 30-inch (711- or 762-mm) notched disk blades, in groups of 8, 10, or 12 blades for the bush and bog configuration. A tandem model with 16 blades is available. Standard equipment includes mechanical angling control, scrapers, and weight box (bush and bog only). Tapered roller or white hard iron bearings with heavy duty gangs for severe applications are available on all models.

Heavy-duty gangs, hydraulic angling control (8-disk models only), and thicker blades are available as options. From 40 to 130 drawbar horsepower is required, depending on model desired and width of cut of that particular harrow.

*Description.* The series TRH has groups of 14 to 28 disks for a cut of 7¾ feet to 15 feet (2235–4572 mm). Standard disks are 30 inches (762 mm) in diameter and ⅜ inches (9.3 mm) thick. Optional blades are 30 inches × ½ inch (762 × 12.7 mm), 32 inches × ⅜ inch (812 × 9.3 mm), and 32 inches × 1½ inches (812 × 38 mm). Depending on the size harrow used, 65 to 175 drawbar horsepower is needed.

*Rome TRH Disc Harrow*

*Application.* This series is built for heavy service in breaking new ground and forest site preparation. It is in between the TAH and TRCH harrows in weight per disk and toughness of application.

*Description.* Rome series TRCH harrows have a high ratio of weight per disk, high clearance, and mechanical, hydraulic or cable angling controls. Width of cut ranges from 7 feet to 12 feet (2,133–3,658 mm) with 10 to 16 disks 36 inches (914 mm) in diameter and ⅜ inch (9.3 mm) thick (36 inches × ½ inch (914 × 12.7 mm) optional). Depending on the model used, 85 to 175 drawbar horsepower is required.

*Rome TRCH Harrows*

*Application.* The TRCH harrow is used for plowing, pulverizing, and mixing vegetation into the soil in one operation. It is designed especially for difficult soil conditions requiring good penetration, deep tillage up to 13 inches (330 mm), and extra-high frame clearance to prevent clogging.

*Description.* The TYMH is available in only one size, which gives a 10 foot (3 meter) wide cut with 10 disks, 50 inches (1,270 mm) in diameter and ¾ inch (19 mm) thick. It has hydraulic controls and a high clearance design. Drawbar horsepower required is 165 to 200.

*Rome TYMH Harrows*

*Application.* The design of the TYMH is for penetration down to 19 inches (482 mm) and maximum trash-handling capacity. It is ideal for deep plowing and tillage through heavy trash and crop residue.

*Description.* In one design configuration the TYH has 16 disks, 36 inches (914 mm) in diameter and ⅓ inch (8.4 mm) thick, with a cutting width of 9½ feet (2,896 mm). Standard equipment includes replaceable hardened bushings on all pivot points and weight box. Required drawbar horsepower is 150 to 180.

*Rome TYH Harrows*

*Application.* The TYH is designed for the most severe land-clearing jobs requiring equipment of maximum strength. It is built for clearing land, breaking newly cleared land, or wherever both deep penetration and maximum strength of equipment is necessary.

*Rome TRW Harrows*

*Description.* The TRW is equipped with wheels for transportation and depth control. It has an 11-foot or 13-foot (3,353- or 3,962-mm) cutting width with either 20 to 24 disks 30 inches (762 mm) in diameter and ⅜ inch (9.3 mm) thick. Required drawbar horsepower is 95 to 155.

*Application.* The TRW harrow is used for plowing, pulverizing, and mixing vegetation into the soil in one operation.

## Fleco Hydraulic Tree Shear

*Description.* The tree shear utilizes hydraulic action to shear soft wood trees up to 30 inches (762 mm) in diameter, 22 inches (558 mm) for hard wood, in less than a minute. A "kicker" mounted on the shear throws the log butt up so that the tree top hits the ground first. The shear is available on Caterpillar track-type tractors, track-type loaders, and wheel loaders (Figure 9–16, A–C).

*Application.* Primarily designed for harvesting trees for pulpwood, the tree shear could be used to cut trees in any location—as long as it is economical.

*Advantages.* It can fell trees quickly when applied correctly. It provides directional felling, which in turn speeds choker setting and skidding. The tool shears trees at ground level to provide increased wood volume.

FIGURE 9–16A. FLECO 910 tree shear.

FIGURE 9–16B. FLECO 910 tree shear.

FIGURE 9–16C. FLECO 931B tree shear.

*Disadvantages.* Capabilities are limited by tree size and composition. It cuts only trees. If underbrush must be removed, another implement must be used.

## Rome Series SS and SH Grapple Shears

*Description.* The Rome grapple shear is designed to fell, skid, and bunch with one machine. It features in-line directional felling with virtually no wood fracture. It will shear trees up to 20 inches (508 mm) in diameter, leaving stumps nearly flush with the ground. Models are available for use with either hard or soft wood.

The Rome grapple shear uses a guillotine shearing principle to provide maximum shearing speed and efficiency. The straight-line cut provides positive directional control of felling. Simple controls provide for ease of operation.

The shear is mounted on the front of Caterpillar track-type loaders and wheel loaders.

*Application.* The main purpose of the grapple shear is harvesting saleable timber.

*Advantages.* The grapple shear provides rapid felling and bunching of trees that are to be hauled off for use as lumber, plywood, or pulpwood.

*Disadvantages.* Felling capability is limited to trees of 20 inches (508 mm) in diameter.

## Ideas to Consider When Equipping Clearing Machines

After the machines and clearing tools have been selected, they must be properly equipped to handle various clearing operations effectively.

In operations such as felling large vegetation and piling where frequent direction changes occur, a power shift transmission is recommended. In constant-speed operations such as felling smaller vegetation, rootplowing, or harrowing, a direct drive transmission is desirable. If a tractor is to be used in more than one operation, its predominant use should dictate the transmission choice. Under a constant load operation, a direct drive transmission is preferable.

In large vegetation a land-clearing tractor is subject to falling trees and severe loads.

In clearing operations, tractors and operators must be well protected. A heavy-duty cab guard is essential. It should withstand any vegetation that might fall on the tractor and have support and deflector bars extending forward to protect the engine compartment.

Heavy screening should be installed around the cab to protect the operator from brush. Inside-mounted household-type screens can further protect the operator from painful and harmful insect stings. Other desirable protection includes extra-heavy radiator, crankcase, track guiding, and fuel tank guards.

Provision for adequate engine cooling is a must in any type of clearing operation. Special attachments such as perforated steel hoods and side panels have been designed with this in mind. Perforated steel side panels consisting of hinged inspection doors allow cleaning of debris around the engine and the radiator core. A reversible blower fan may be advantageous, depending on job conditions. An air breather extension running along from the hood back to the operator's compartment is recommended, especially when working in leaves or trash. Such a modification will ensure that the air breather is not plugged and that the engine is receiving an adequate supply of air.* Each machine should also be equipped with a fire extinguisher or water tank for putting out small fires, which may occur in the engine compartment (Figures 9–17 through 9–22).

FIGURE 9–17. CAT/D8K/REMCO Cab guard with optional screens.

*The hydraulic system including cylinders, lines, and tank should be well protected with guards.

FIGURE 9–18. Rome feller-buncher on CAT 930.

FIGURE 9–19. CAT 931B and Rome SJ100 shear.

FIGURE 9–20. Rome "A" frame grapple on CAT 518.

FIGURE 9–21. CAT 518 stretch frame with Rome CG-405C 118″ grapple.

FIGURE 9–22. Rome/Holt towed rake and CAT D8 tractor equipped with Rome hydraulic protection group and grille guard.

# METHODS OF LAND CLEARING

Land clearing can be divided into the following methods, each of which is discussed in this section:

- Complete removal of trees and stumps by physically uprooting and moving them to piles for disposal by burning or other means.
- Shearing the vegetation at ground level with sharp cutting blades and piling into windrows or piles for burning. The stumps and roots can also be removed, left in the soil to decay or shattered in subsequent operations by root plowing or harrowing.
- Knocking all vegetation down and crushing it to the ground for later burning in place.
- Plowing and chopping the vegetation into the top 6 to 8 inches (15 to 20 cm) of the soil in a once-over plowing operation. This allows the vegetation to decay.

For each of these general methods for land clearing, several types of equipment may be used in each particular case. This section deals with the different equipment in these specific applications and a discussion of the advantages and disadvantages of each.

The first and second methods mentioned are similar in that the woody material is not only knocked down but also removed from where it is grown and piled for burning. These two types of clearing differ in that uprooting depends on overpowering the vegetation with massive brute force, while shearing operates on the principle of shaving the material at ground level with a sharp cutting edge.

Methods three and four are similar in that the felled material is not piled. They are different in that the organic material of one is disposed of by burning and the other by decaying in the soil profile.

It should be noted that burning is not listed as an initial land-clearing method. It is difficult to get a good burn and control it in any type of vegetation without some previous preparation. Burning also removes the organic matter that might help improve some soil characteristics of fertility. Burning, nevertheless, has been used effectively in many areas as a method of disposal for knocked down brush left in place or windrowed. More discussion of burning as a method of disposal is included later in this chapter.

## Uprooting the Vegetation with a Brute Force Operation

Several types of equipment are used in this kind of clearing operation. These may include bulldozer blades, rakes, knockdown beams, or chains drawn between two or more large track-type tractors.

## Bulldozing

Early attempts to clear land mechanically involved simple modifications of earthmoving techniques using standard earthmoving equipment, i.e., the crawler tractor with its ordinary straight or angling bulldozer. Bulldozer blades are still used throughout the world even though it has been repeatedly shown that 30 to 40 percent more land can be cleared in a specified time with specialized land-clearing tools.

The bulldozer blade can be more economical in intermediate-size areas of upland woods and bush country when the small size of the area to be cleared does not warrant purchase or rental of a specialized tool. Bulldozer blades are available for all size track-type tractors and many wheel-type farm tractors. The most economical power unit size varies with the amount and type of vegetation and the amount of land to be cleared.

Generally the bulldozer blade is not an efficient land-clearing tool. When larger trees that cannot be pushed over are encountered, they must be dug out of the ground—a costly and time-consuming operation. Small trees and bushes are so limber that they bend down and the dozer blade passes over them, or else they break off, leaving stubs protruding above the soil surface that might have to be removed later. Valuable topsoil may be removed in many instances when a bulldozer blade is used to windrow brush. Because a ball of dirt is often left on the roots of the tree when it is uprooted, subsequent burning is made more difficult.

## Raking

As shown, various types of rakes are being manufactured and sold for clearing land of both trees and rocks. Rakes have the advantage of permitting the soil to pass between the teeth as it is pushed through the soil, ripping out and pushing the rocks, stumps, brush, etc. They work best in extremely sandy soil such as that encountered in northern Florida and southern Georgia. Rakes sometimes do not work well in clay soils or wet soils because of clogging between the rake teeth. When this happens, the rakes are in effect converted into a bulldozer blade. In most cases, however, a good operator can overcome this effect.

Rakes are used successfully and are almost universally recommended for repiling burned or burning material. The ash residue sifts through the teeth, and cleaner, hotter burns can be achieved.

Tractors used in the burning operation should always be equipped with a blower or reversible fan (and fire extinguishers of at least 5-gallon capacity) to prevent the ash and live sparks from the fire being sucked under and into the tractor. This is necessary from the standpoint of both safety and operator comfort. A blower fan promotes better burning by forcing large volumes of air into the fire.

## Tree Pushing

Both bulldozers and rakes depend on the brute force of the tractor to accomplish their objectives. This principle is in part applied with the tree pusher. It is a structure extending above and forward from the tractor, which gives the tractor added leverage in pushing over larger trees. The effective tree size that can be felled is dependent on size of tractor, weight, leverage, tractive conditions, soil, and root system. Tree pushers are ideal when used in combination with some device for cutting the roots around the larger trees. This allows the trees to be pushed over with greater ease. They are also used in conjunction with chaining to lift the chain higher on larger trees for increased leverage or to assist the chain against larger trees.

Even though the tree pusher may be considered a highly specialized tool with limited application, it has proven efficient in many areas when working with other felling methods.

# Chaining

The chain is dragged behind two crawler tractors. The outside tractor travels along the edge of the uncleared area. The inside tractor travels through the uncleared area, avoiding any large vegetation to be left or vegetation that it cannot knock down. The distance between the two tractors varies with the size of the tractors and the size of vegetation. The tractors should be close enough to allow travel in an almost continuous forward direction. The chaining passes should be made as long as possible to minimize tractor maneuver time.

When chaining areas of unknown terrain, a walker may be required to go in front of the inside tractor to warn of any obstructions or depressions that hinder tractor operation.

Two passes in opposite directions may be required to uproot areas of smaller vegetation as found in semiarid areas. The need for this varies with later clearing operations and the end use of the land.

Chain clearing is most economical in arid or semiarid type vegetation where only limited or no undergrowth occurs. Population of woody species of all sizes should not exceed 1,000 plants per acre (2,500 per hectare). However, experience has shown that chaining can be used in all sizes of vegetation. The upper limit in size and density varies with the size tractors used and the width of the area chained.

Chaining can be difficult when extremely heavy undergrowth conditions are present because they reduce the operator's visibility. This in turn impedes the operator's ability to maneuver the tractor around larger trees.

The terrain should be well-drained, level to gently sloping without large gullies, stone outcroppings, or other obstructions that prevent free passage and maneuverability of the tractors and chain.

# Root Plowing

The root plow is another tool for removing vegetation below the soil surface. It is designed for killing brush and growth by undercutting vegetation at the crown or bud ring. Large roots are forced to the surface by fins welded to the horizontal blade. Root plows also shatter hard surface crusts and hardpan, which results in better water retention and prepares a good seedbed.

Root plows are available for mounting on tractor trunnions or tool bars. The vertical standards are equipped with replaceable wear shins, and bolt-on cutting edges are reversible. The root plow is normally operated in the "float" position, and depth is controlled by a depth-setting arrangement with several adjustments. It operates at depths from 8 to 20 inches (20 to 50 cm) and is available in a number of sizes from several manufacturers.

One advantage of the root plow is that it cuts the vegetation below the bud ring, killing brush that would normally resprout if cut at ground level. Because depth is easily set and controlled, it is easy to operate and does an effective job. The main disadvantages of the root plow are that size of vegetation is limited and it does not work well in sandy soils.

## Grubbing

A variation of the root plow, but generally smaller and mounted on track-type or wheel tractors, is the grubber. The application of the grubber is for use in medium to light brush of average density, where the tractor can move from one plant to another. The grubber can be a highly efficient tool in areas suitable for its application.

## Cutting the Vegetation at Ground Level

This method varies from those previously discussed in that the vegetation is cut off at or slightly above ground level, leaving the stumps in the ground to decay or to be removed later. The tools and their use for this type of clearing probably vary more than any other method. They range from the use of a band ax or machete on one end, to the use of a large tractor with a cutting blade on the other.

The main advantage of this method is that if the stumps can be left in the ground, the initial clearing cost is decreased considerably. It is especially effective in larger vegetation where the brute force of the tractor is not enough to uproot the vegetation without digging around it. The topsoil is left undisturbed (important in areas where it is thin), and the stumps will rot in place. This method is not, of course, suitable for areas under buildings or elsewhere where firm bearing soil is required.

## Hand Clearing

Clearing with hand tools is probably the oldest and most widely used method of clearing. Hand tools are adequate for small areas that do not warrant investment in mechanical equipment. Their economical use in larger areas is affected by the availability of labor versus capital and the degree of clearing desired.

Single or double-bitted axes can be used to cut most top growth. They become less efficient in small or large growth. Axes can also be used as an aid in grubbing roots. They must, of course, be properly sharpened to be used effectively.

Machetes can be used on smaller stems and branches that are commonly cut with an ax. They are especially effective in the underbrushing that precedes tree felling when hand clearing jungle areas. Machetes can be sharpened with a whetstone or file.

Brush hooks are useful in cutting small vegetative growth. The brush hook is swung like a scythe. It is sharpened by grinding with an abrasive wheel or emery.

Grub hoes and mattocks can be used to chop off small brush near ground level or to dig out small roots. They are not effective in large vegetation.

## Power Sawing

In larger-size vegetation, power chain saws are more efficient than axes or similar hand tools. Most chain saws are available in lengths from 1 to 5 feet (0.3 to 1.5 m). They are generally powered by two-stroke-cycle gasoline engines. They leave a stump about ground level, which hinders later clearing and land use operations. Chain saws are most economical in intermediate to large-size vegetation in small- to medium-size areas or in pruning felled material.

## Sickle Mowing

Light brush, with a stem diameter of less than 1.5 inches (3.8 cm), can be cut with regular farm tractor mowers adapted for heavy-duty operation. These mowers have short and heavier sickle bars equipped with stub guards and extra hold-down clips. The tractor is run in low gear to give a high sickle speed in comparison to the forward speed. Larger diameter brush can be cut, but continuous forward direction is not usually possible. This equipment is usually most economical in intermediate size areas.

## Blade Shearing

Perhaps the most efficient land-clearing tool for medium and large vegetation in intermediate to large areas is a shearing blade on a track-type tractor. The shearing blade principle differs from the bulldozer principle of land clearing in that the total horsepower of the tractor is applied to a sharp cutting edge. The shearing blades are usually equipped with a stinger or wedgelike projection. This allows larger trees to be split in one or more successive passes before actually felling the trees with the cutting edge. By cutting and splitting the trees, much larger trees may be felled with a given size tractor. Later, burning is also faster and cleaner because the tree has been split and there is no rootball on the butt of the logs.

Another advantage of shearing blades over bulldozer blades in land clearing is ease of operation. Clearing blades are equipped with a flat sole at the bottom of the ground to prevent digging in. This permits faster operation and less operator fatigue since he is not constantly manipulating the controls to keep the blade from digging into the ground.

Two types of shearing blades exist: the angle blades, like the K/G manufactured by Rome Industries, Cedartown, Georgia, and the V-type blade manufactured by the Fleco Corporation, Jacksonville, Florida.

The K/G blade is available for most track-type tractors. The blade angle is 30 degrees, and the blade can be operated either by cable or hydraulic control. The replaceable cutting edges and stinger should be resharpened with a portable grinder daily. A guide bar is used to control the direction the trees fall—forward and to the right of the operator.

This type blade is a versatile attachment in that it can cut, pile, stump, and ditch. Cut growth normally falls in one direction; given enough time, the K/G blade can fell any size tree.

The disadvantage of the K/G blade is that it does not remove embedded material such as roots, rocks, etc. in one pass. When stumps are to be removed, the blade requires another pass over the area with the blade tilted. Rocks and stony outcroppings can severely damage the cutting edge of the blade and should be avoided.

The V blade is available for track-type tractors through the D8H size. It is equipped with a heavy-duty splitter; angled, serrated cutting edge; and brush rack. This blade mounts directly on the tractor trunnions and is available for cable or hydraulic control. The V is in two sections and bolts together to form the working tool.

When properly matched to the job, the V blade is a high-production tool, which maintains a continuous path. The bolt-together design permits assembly or disassembly on the job and provides flexibility in moving the unit.

In some jobs with the V blade, it is a disadvantage to have trees fall to both the right and left of the tractor. The V blade, like the angle blade, does not remove embedded material such as roots, rocks, etc., and it does not usually remove stumps in one pass. Unlike the angle blade the V blade cannot pile or ditch. This is especially important in smaller jobs where only one tractor is used for the entire clearing operation.

Where land use requires the immediate removal of the stumps left in the ground by shearing blades, a second operation is performed. The stumps may be shattered with heavy-duty offset disk plows, removed with the stinger of the Rome K/G blade, or grubbed out with a rake or stumper.

The use of shearing blades of whatever type should be limited to heavier clay and loam soils relatively free of stones. Under extremely sandy conditions the clearing can best be done with rakes or other clearing tools.

All tractors with shearing blades should be equipped with heavily constructed cab guards for protection against falling trees. In certain areas an insect-proof compartment should be provided to protect the operator.

## Tree Shearing

Another land-clearing tool, which is primarily designed for harvesting trees for pulpwood, is the tree shear. This tool utilizes hydraulic action to shear softwood trees up to 30 inches (760 mm) in diameter or hardwood trees up to 22 inches (558 mm) in less than a minute. A kicker mounted on the shear throws the log butt up so that the tree tops hit the ground first.

The tree shear can fell trees quickly at ground level and provides directional felling. The disadvantages of the tree shear are that its capabilities are limited by tree size and composition and it cuts only trees. If underbrush must be removed, another implement must be used.

## Knocking the Vegetation to the Ground

Knocking the vegetation to the ground is an inexpensive way of clearing land, but unfortunately its successful application is limited to specific situations. It is highly effective in clearing bush-type vegetation and smaller upland woods where the diameter of the woody vegetation does not exceed 6 to 8 inches (15 to 20 cm). In rain forest areas the smaller vegetation may be knocked down while larger vegetation is uprooted.

Because much of the vegetation is not uprooted and is sometimes chopped up, it is normally not piled. It may be burned in place at a later time, left in place to decay, or incorporated into the soil. If it is to be burned in place, the vegetation must be sparse enough to allow native grasses to grow intermittently because the grasses are required to provide fuel for the burn.

Several types of equipment are used to knock the vegetation down and leave it or chop it up into smaller pieces.

## Rotary Mowing

Rotary mowers pulled by farm tractors can be used in vegetation up to 4 inches (10 cm) in diameter. They have one or more revolving blades, rotating around a vertical shaft and powered by tractor power takeoff. These blades sever the vegetation at or near ground level and shred it into small pieces. Rotary mowers are available in several sizes and are most efficient in small- to medium-size brush in intermediate-size areas. Their use is not recommended in hilly terrain or where rocks and stones are present. Extreme tractor tire damage can be expected when recrossing areas mowed if vegetation is the type that leaves spikes in the ground.

## Flail-Type Cutting

Flail-type rotary cutters, which are also tractor-drawn, have cutting knives that rotate around a horizontal shaft to knock down and shred small brush at or near ground level. These cutters are also available in a wide range of sizes as power takeoff units for both wheel-type and track-type tractors. They are most efficient in small- to medium-size brush in intermediate-size areas.

## Chopping

In larger size areas, this type of clearing is generally done with rolling choppers. The drum of the chopper, which can normally be filled with water to increase its weight, has welded on cutting blades that can penetrate 6 to 10 inches (15 to 25 cm) deep. These blades cut, fracture, and shatter growth. Soil crust is furrowed and loosened with minimum topsoil disturbance. The woody vegetation is left in a thick flattened mat.

Rolling choppers are available in a number of combinations, both self-propelled and pulled by track-type tractors. They come in several weights per length of cut. The tractor-drawn models are available in single, tandem, and dual combinations in a wide range of sizes.

The main disadvantage of this tool is that large diameter trees cannot be chopped. Another problem is that in order for the vegetation to be burned in place, it must be left for a long time to dry thoroughly.

Many thousands of acres are cleared every year simply by the use of a tillage implement pulled behind a tractor. The implement cuts and chops the material into the upper 6 to 10 inches (15 to 25 cm) of the soil profile. This method is limited to situations where the vegetation does not exceed 3 or 4 inches (7.5 to 10 cm) in diameter. There should be adequate rainfall to promote rapid decomposition of the material chopped into the ground. The soil surface should be free of large protruding stumps and free of stones or stone outcroppings that would limit the effectiveness of the disks in chopping the woody vegetation.

## Incorporating the Vegetation into the Soil

*Moldboard Plowing.* Pull-type, semimounted or full-mounted mold-board plows drawn by wheel or track-type tractors can be used to turn and cover small brush if the soil is not excessively hard, sticky, or rocky.

For all but the lightest plowing, plows with heavy-duty frames should be used.

Jointers and coulters should be removed, and covering wires may be added to help cover the trash. Plowshares should be kept sharpened for best performance. Plows are available in a wide range of sizes from many farm equipment manufacturers.

*Disk Plowing.* Tractor-drawn disk plows can also be used effectively in covering small brush. They can be used on soil that is dry, hard, sticky, or rocky, where moldboard plows are generally not recommended. However, disk plows do not normally cover brush as thoroughly as moldboard plows. Variations of the standard disk plows have been developed to incorporate a "stump jump action," where each disk is independently adjustable and spring loaded to permit it to ride over any fixed obstruction which may be encountered. They are available in sizes that can be pulled by track-type or wheel tractors.

## Offset Harrowing and Gang Harrowing

For slightly larger brush, heavy-duty offset and gang harrows pulled by track-type tractors equipped with bulldozer blades can be effective land-clearing tools. The vegetation is bent over with the dozer blade and then cut and chopped into the soil profile by the harrow. In smaller brush the dozer blade is not needed.

Offset harrows are available in many types and sizes. Care should be taken to select the type and size most suitable to the application for which it is intended.

Heavy-duty offset and gang harrows do not invert the soil layer and vegetative matter but chop up this material and mix it throughout the soil profile, unlike the moldboard or disk plow.

All of these harrows and plows can be used to incorporate previously shredded or uncut vegetation into the soil. Larger stumps may damage conventional moldboard plows. Newer moldboard plows, with protection devices that allow each bottom to swing back when it hits an obstruction, can be used in areas with larger stumps. Under these conditions, the heavy-duty harrows are usually more effective because of their chopping action.

Once the vegetation has been felled, it must usually be disposed of in some manner. The method of disposal is determined by a number of variables including type and size of vegetation, end use of land, rainfall, and terrain. Because disposal is often an expensive operation, care should be taken to select the more economical method.

## Disposal of Vegetation after Initial Clearing

*Leaving in Place.* If the variables affecting disposal permit elimination in place, this may be the most economical method available. With small vegetation that is chopped up during initial clearing, the vegetation may be left to decay or be incorporated into the topsoil. With larger vegetation the end use of the land may permit scattered vegetation to be left in place. However, larger vegetation that cannot be incorporated into the soil must usually be disposed of in some other manner.

*Burning in Place.* Burning vegetation in place after it has been knocked down can be an effective means of disposal when conditions permit. These conditions include fuel for burning in the form of grasses or small brush, a dry enough climate to allow burning, and an end use of the land where some larger trees can be left on the ground.

All brush can be burned more cleanly if a high proportion of the fuel is dry. For this reason all brush should be prepared in some manner before it is burned. Crushing of light or medium material usually causes it to dry enough during clear weather. A few weeks may be necessary for proper drying.

Heavy jungle brush with many large trunks should often be left to dry 1½ to 2 months or longer before burning. Indicators of dryness are (a) bark on the larger trees cracking and (b) dried foliage beginning to fall. Dry foliage is, however, an excellent fuel and should be utilized. It is sometimes necessary to plant grass in the felled areas and to delay burning until this grass has grown and dried sufficiently to serve as a fuel.

In small vegetation, chemical spraying can sometimes effectively prepare the vegetation for an efficient burn. Two chemical treatments can be used to prepare brush for burning: (1) contact herbicides that kill only leaves and twigs and (2) systematic herbicides that kill part of the stems as well as the leaves and twigs.

Contact herbicides should be used when the interval between spraying and burning is brief. The contact chemicals can be applied during clear weather only a few days before burning. Systematic herbicides can be applied at the height of plant growth in the spring to prepare the brush for burning the next fall or following spring.

If weather conditions are suitable, burning can normally be accomplished during any season of the year. However, the season can affect the efficiency of the burn and the condition of the seedbed afterward. In areas with wet and dry periods, burning may be possible only during the dry season after the vegetation has had an opportunity to dry out. Care must be taken to ensure that surrounding areas are not so dry that the burn cannot be controlled. In areas with four seasons, where control is a problem, late spring and late fall are generally the best burning periods because the surrounding areas are higher in moisture content.

*Weather Conditions.* The most important factor affecting the burn is the weather. The burn should take place only after a reliable forecast of favorable weather. Unstable weather conditions should be avoided. In jungle areas at least one week's continuously dry weather is desirable before the actual burn. In bush areas it is important to burn only in weather under which spot fires will not start from embers flying across the control lines. Extreme caution should be exercised in setting burns in heavy winds.

*Control Lines.* In order to control the in-place burn effectively, it is desirable to locate fire lines or belts around the boundaries of the area to be burned. In rain forest areas these belts may be of unfelled vegetation. In bush areas they are previously cleared land. It is also necessary to have escape roads cut in the area to be burned for safety of the burners.

Lines may divide the area into units as small as 10 to 20 acres (4 to 8 hectares) for difficult control conditions to as large as 2,000 acres (800 hectares) where control is not a problem. If possible, each unit should be a natural burning unit within which topographic features aid the effectiveness of burning and control of fire. If the units cannot be determined by terrain, they should be nearly square or rectangular, with the long axis parallel to upslope drafts or to the prevailing wind.

The units may be burned in a way to aid in effective burning of the entire area. The choice of units may be determined in conjunction with the felling procedure.

*Ignition Techniques.* In-place firing is normally carried out by burners, who go through the area on foot with kerosene-soaked strips, which are thrown into the felled brush. Closely spaced ignition points help build up the intense heat needed to obtain a clean burn.

To ignite an area, the firing crew starts at the upslope or downwind side of the area and sets closely spaced fires along the line. When the line can be held, the firing is speeded until the many small fires pull together and burn as a single intense fire over a few acres. The firing progresses downslope, or against the wind, at the speed required to keep a small acreage burning until the entire burning unit has been covered.

The spacing of ignition points and the number of burners required to burn an area depend on vegetation and burning conditions. In jungle areas it has been found that the maximum area that one person can cover in one burn is about 10 acres (4 hectares). Ignition points may vary from a few feet (meters) apart to 100 feet (30 meters) apart, depending on conditions.

In areas of larger vegetation, it may be necessary to prune, stack, and reburn according to clearing specifications all timbers that are to be removed. This should begin as soon as it is possible to reenter the area. Front-mounted rakes can be used or the vegetation can be cut into lengths suitable for carrying and stacking around large buttresses.

*Safety Recommendations.* It should be remembered that burning can be safely conducted only by people who thoroughly understand fire behavior. They should observe the following recommendations:

1. Make sure the brush within the area to be burned is more burnable than the woody fuels outside the area.

2. Determine what weather conditions will allow efficient burning of the prepared area and yet will assure continuous control of the fire.

3. Burn areas large enough for an efficient burn but small enough that the burn is under control at all times.

4. Prepare a complete plan for the burn, have it approved, and follow it rigidly.

5. Delay burning until all desired conditions are met, regardless of the cost of rescheduling.

6. Provide for the safety of the crews at all times.

## Piling

If vegetation is not disposed of in place, it is normally piled, then burned or left to decay. The equipment used for piling is often determined by what equipment is used for felling. The angled shearing blades and clearing rakes discussed previously are quite suitable for piling. In small areas, piling of light material may be done by hand.

As mentioned, one advantage of the K/G blade for clearing is its multiple application as both a felling and piling tool. The cutting blade is equipped with a flat sole, which allows it to float on top of the ground without disturbing the topsoil. The stinger on most cutting blades can be used to lift the vegetation partially, making it easier to push. Because of the floating and lifting action of the blade, little dirt is carried to the pile with the vegetation. This facilitates burning.

Clearing rakes also can be used for felling and piling. Because their principal felling application is in sandy or rocky type soils, they are often used for piling in those conditions. They are especially effective in removing some surface roots as they pile. Again, rakes are not recommended for wet or clay-type soils that tend to build up between the teeth, causing a bulldozing effect. The resulting soil mixed with the vegetation may hinder later burning. A discussion of types and sizes of rakes is included in the section on machines and attachments.

# Disposal of Piles

The method for disposal of piled brush and the location of piles are determined by the size, type, and density of the brush, climate, rainfall, and size and type of equipment used.

*Leaving in Low-Lying Areas.* When swamps or other low-lying areas are present, it is sometimes desirable to pile brush in these areas. By leaving the brush to decay, further disposal is eliminated.

The main problem with this method of disposal is that drainage is often adversely affected. Insect and rodent breeding and the threat of disease may also be problems if such methods are used.

*Piling in Well-Placed Windrows.* When no suitable low-lying areas are available and burning is not practical, vegetation is sometimes piled in well-placed windrows and left to decay. In areas of level terrain the windrows may be parallel, facilitating piling and later operations. In hilly areas the windrows may be left on the contour to facilitate piling and to help control erosion. The distance between windrows may be 100 to 200 feet. It varies with size and density of vegetation and size of equipment used.

*Piling in Windrows for Burning.* In many situations the best way to dispose of the vegetation is by burning. A clean and economical burn requires careful planning and close supervision. The windrows must be piled as compactly as possible, parallel to the prevailing winds, with a minimum of soil mixed with the vegetation.

Weather is the most important factor affecting the burning of piled brush just as it is when burning in place. Unstable weather conditions should be avoided, and at least one week's continuously dry weather is necessary before the actual burn.

The vegetation should be allowed to dry until the bark on the larger trees cracks and the foliage has dried and begins to fall. When vegetation dries in a pile, it will go through a period of heating. This is often a good time to burn the material, if other conditions permit, due to the added internal heat.

The number and timing of the ignition sets vary with the type and size of vegetation, the size of pile, and the moisture content. Because the brush will be repiled to complete the burning, ignition timing is not so critical as with in-place burning. However, it is important that sets be close enough to ensure a complete initial burn in order to minimize repiling costs.

In certain clearing conditions, if the vegetation is difficult to burn, it may be necessary to aid the burning with forced air and fuel or a combination of the two. The combination of air and diesel fuel allows burning of green material even during inclement weather. It should be remembered that the use of a burner is no substitute for adequate drying time. Costs will be increased, and the burn may be less complete if conditions require the use of a burner.

Brush burners equipped with four-cycle engines, airplane-type propellers, and self-priming fuel pumps supply air at a high velocity and a continuous fuel spray for starting and maintaining fires. They are highly mobile and are a safe method of promoting a more complete burn of materials.

*Repiling.* After the initial burn, repiling should start as soon as the heat has subsided enough to permit a crawler tractor with a blower-type fan to approach the fire without damage. The piles should be stoked and the fire kept alive until the woody material is completely consumed by the flames. The initial heat should be used to get larger logs burning while the smaller material is piled on to keep them burning.

Windrows should be cut into segments as soon as possible, making round piles of burning debris. When one pile has lost most of its heat, it should be pushed to another pile to maintain the greatest possible concentration of heat and burning material and achieve quicker and more complete burns.

The best tools for repiling are tractor-mounted rakes, which allow the dirt and ashes to sift through the teeth. Shaking the rake up and down with the controls while moving forward with a load helps remove dirt. Dropping the load and picking it up again just before pushing it into the windrow also helps to sift the dirt and ashes through the teeth.

## Other Methods of Disposal

Other methods of disposal include utilizing cut material for firewood and charcoal, hauling to other areas for disposal, and burying. All three methods are generally limited to small localized areas where only a small amount of vegetation is involved. The demand for firewood and charcoal is small in most areas. Burying or hauling the vegetation away is too costly for most land-clearing operations. A more economical method can usually be found.

## Final Cleanup

Regardless of the method of felling and disposal used in clearing the land, loose pieces of stumps, roots, and limbs will be left on the ground.

Some unburned debris will be left after even the most efficient burns.

This material can be disposed of in many ways. In many areas the cheapest and most practical method is to pick up this residue by hand, then pile, burn, or haul it away in carts or trucks.

Mechanical tools used for final cleanup include rakes and spring tooth chisels or tines mounted on wheel or track-type tractors. Rakes can be used in sandy soils to pick up the debris and allow the soil to sift through the teeth. A recent innovation for this type of operation has been the Wake rake developed in Australia. The principle of this tool is literally to sweep the topsoil clean of all light debris at speeds up to 5 miles per hour. The final windrows in heavy material can be up to 5 feet high. Most mechanical tools are not recommended in wet clay soils because of their bulldozing effect. The debris is piled, buried, hauled away, or burned.

## Other Operations

Some land-clearing jobs may include further operations as a part of the specifications or contract. In areas with vegetation left in place, this may be no more than hand seeding the area with grasses or legumes. In other areas it may include leveling, plowing, and seeding.

Minor leveling operations can be done with bulldozers, shearing blades, disk harrows, or even chains. It is recommended that more extensive leveling be carried out under a separate operation because it is not generally considered land clearing as such and requires different types of equipment.

Plowing may be considered a part of the complete land-clearing job. Disk harrows are used to mix organic material into the soil. They split and chop embedded roots and stumps, speeding decomposition of these materials. They are also used to help prepare a seedbed for planting. A number of disk harrow types and sizes are available from various manufacturers. They should be consulted to determine the size and type for a particular application. It is, however, imperative that the selected tool be of extra heavy design and quality to withstand the loads and shock treatment that it will receive.

After the first plowing it is often desirable to plant a leguminous crop such as soybeans, velvet beans, or alfalfa on the newly cleared land. The legume plants fix nitrogen from the air, making it available in the soil for use by the bacteria in the decomposition of the roots. Legumes also shade the ground and inhibit resprouting of the chopped roots while decomposition takes place.

The need for any or all of these operations is determined by each specific clearing situation. No attempt is made to recommend which, if any, should be carried out.

## Rocks

Perhaps the most universal method of mechanical rock clearing is a crawler tractor with front mounted heavy-duty rakes. Another type of rake is available on a track-type loader. The latter has the advantage of being able to pry out boulders and to load into some type of conveyance.

# DETERMINATION OF COST AND PRODUCTION

As stated, it is extremely difficult to establish specific rules of thumb for selecting land clearing equipment. Too many variables are involved. Such factors as the end use of land, underfoot conditions, type of vegetation, and specifications directly influence the selection of equipment for any specific clearing job. The final decision must be based on good judgment and common sense.

It is equally difficult to estimate with a reasonable degree of accuracy the total production, per unit production, and cost per acre (hectare) for a land-clearing operation. One excellent source of cost information both for machine costs (depreciation, repairs, etc.) and local costs (labor, fuel, etc.) is the equipment dealer servicing the project.

In addition to job cruise samples, all possible data should be gathered from aids such as

Aerial photo maps

General topography maps

Water table maps

Yearly rainfall figures

Before beginning production and cost calculations, all pertinent information should be acquired and tabulated as follows:

1. Total acres to be cleared.
2. Time available for job (in years).
3. Time available in hours per year per tractor.*
4. Acquire all information possible from each job cruise. Tabulate each one separately for later use. Use the following table for a guide.

*Machine availability:

% × hours worked/day × working days per year = hours/year/tractor

This is efficiency due to weather, transportation, repairs, etc., expressed in percentage. These figures may be obtained from an equipment dealer.

Tree Diameter          1'–2'    2'–3'    3'–4'    4'–6'    Above 6'

Number of Trees/Acre

% Hardwoods

Vines present?
  Yes or no

Description of root system

Description of undergrowth

Description of soil

End use of land

Debris disposal method

Soil conservation to be practiced

Grade and terrain

Water table conditions

Rainfall

Underfoot conditions

Follow the next steps:

1. Select general method for clearing land.
2. Decide on machines to be used.

    _____

    _____

    _____

3. Calculate local owning and operating (O&O) cost for each machine.

    Machine               O & O Cost

    _____

    _____

    _____

    _____

4. Determine implements or attachments to be used and calculate local owning and operating cost for each.

    Attachment           O & O Cost

    _____

    _____

    _____

    _____

5. Estimate working speed (mph) for these operations:

| Machine | Speed (mph) |
|---|---|
| | |
| Harrowing | |
| Root plowing | |
| Rolling chopper | |
| Chaining | |

## Calculating Production and Cost

Now that the preliminary material has been gathered, it is possible to proceed with the calculations necessary to arrive at an estimate of production and costs. (They are estimates because much of the material that goes into the calculations is estimates. Consequently the final figure is only as accurate as the numbers used.)

To eliminate confusion, the following section has been organized in this manner:

| | |
|---|---|
| Cutting | Production |
| | Costs |
| | Additional calculations |
| Piling | Production |
| | Costs |
| | Additional calculations |
| Harrowing | American Society of Agricultural Engineers (ASAE) formula for production |
| | Fleco formula for production |
| | Cost |
| Root plowing— rolling chopper | Short paragraph stating procedures to follow |
| Burning | Production |
| | Costs |
| Chaining | Production |
| | Costs |
| Conclusion | Figuring total costs |

Each step under production and costs that is used to determine a final figure has a letter designation (double letters—AA—are used when the complete alphabet has been utilized). Some steps may be eliminated or used as necessary. For example, if root plowing, raking, and burning are to be done, the cutting, chaining, and harrowing calculations can be eliminated. When numbers are used as a reference, they indicate acquired information and when letters are used, they refer to the actual calculations.

## Cutting

### Production

A. Using Rome's formula for cutting, calculate total time (minutes) for cutting per acre:

$$\overline{\hspace{6cm}}$$
(minute/acre)

B. Divide 60 minutes by A, (minutes/acre):

$$\overline{\hspace{6cm}}$$
acre/hours

C. Divide number of acres by B, (acres/hours)—see $E_1$, total acres to be cleared:

$$\overline{\hspace{6cm}}$$
(hours required for cutting)

D. Divide C (hours required for cutting) by number of years for job:

$$\overline{\hspace{6cm}}$$
(hours/year)

E. Divide D (hours/year) by number of hours per year per tractor:

$$\overline{\hspace{6cm}}$$
(number of tractors required)

$E_1$. If more than one tractor is required (E), divide C by number of tractors to get actual hours required for cutting per machine:

$C_1$ $\overline{\hspace{6cm}}$
(hours required for cutting)

### Costs

F. Machine O & O (O & O cost × number of machines):

$\$\underline{\hspace{3cm}}$/per hour

G. Attachment O & O (O & O cost × number of attachments):

$\$\underline{\hspace{3cm}}$/per hour

H. Add F and G:

$\$\underline{\hspace{3cm}}$/per hour

I. Multiply H by C (hours required for cutting) for the total cost of the cutting operation:

$\$\underline{\hspace{6cm}}$

Additional Calculations
Divide I (total cost of the cutting operation) by

Total number of acres to find _____$/acre

Total number of hours to find _____$/hour

Total number of weeks to find _____$/week

Or any other cumulative total such as months, years, etc.

*Harrowing*
*Production—ASAE formula*
S.     Speed (mph) of machine-pulling implement:

_____
(mph)

T.     Multiply S (speed) by width of cut (feet) of the implement:

_____
(acres/per 10 hours)

U.     Divide T by 10:

_____
(acres/hour)

V.     For metric system only, multiply U by 0.405:

_____
(hectares/hour)

W.     Divide number of acres by U to determine hours required for one complete harrowing:

_____
(hours)

X.     Multiply W by number of harrowings for total hours required for harrowing:

_____
(hours)

*Production—Fleco's formula*
Y.     Working width (feet) of implement:

_____
(feet)

Z.     Multiply Y by 10 percent and add this to Y:

_____

AA. Multiply Z by speed (mph) of machine with implement:

_____

BB. Divide AA by 10:

_____
(acres/hour)

CC. For metric system only, multiply BB × 0.405:

_____
(hectares/hour)

DD. Divide number of acres by BB to determine hours required for one complete harrowing:

_____
(hours)

EE. Multiply DD by number of harrowings for total hours required for harrowing:

_____
(hours)

## Piling

### Production

J. Using Rome's formula for piling, calculate total time (minutes) per piling per acre:

_____
(minutes/acre)

K. Divide 60 minutes by J (minutes/acre):

_____
(acre/hours)

L. Divide number of acres by K (acre/hours)—see $N_1$, total acres to be cleared):

_____
(hours required for piling)

M. Divide L (hours required for piling) by number of years for job:

_____
(hours/year)

N. Divide M (hours/year) by number of hours per year per tractor:

_____
(number of tractors required)

$N_1$. If more than one tractor is required (N), divide L by number of tractors to get actual hours required for piling per machine:

$$L_1 \underline{\hspace{6cm}}$$
(hours required for piling)

*Costs*

O. Machine O & O (O & O cost × number of machines):

$\underline{\hspace{3cm}}$/per hour

P. Attachment O & O (O & O cost × number of machines):

$\underline{\hspace{3cm}}$/per hour

Q. Add O and P:

$\underline{\hspace{3cm}}$/per hour

R. Multiply Q by L (hours required for piling) for the total cost of the piling operation:

$\underline{\hspace{5cm}}$

Additional Calculations

Divide R (total cost of the piling operation) by

Total number of acres to find $\underline{\hspace{4cm}}$/acre

Total number of hours to find $\underline{\hspace{4cm}}$/hour

Total number of weeks to find $\underline{\hspace{4cm}}$/week

Or any other cumulative total such as months, years, etc.


*Costs*

FF. Machine O & O (O & O cost × number of machines):

$\underline{\hspace{6cm}}$/per hour

GG. Implement O & O (O & O cost × number of implements):

$\underline{\hspace{6cm}}$/per hour

HH. Add FF and GG:

$\underline{\hspace{6cm}}$/per hour

II. Multiply HH times EE or X for the total cost of harrowing:

$\underline{\hspace{6cm}}$

Again, any cumulative total can be divided into II to arrive at a per-unit cost.

For calculating production or cost for either of these operations, use ASAE's or Fleco's production formula for harrowing and the cost calculations immediately following them.

*Root Plowing—*
*Rolling*
*Chopper*

*Burning*

> *Production*

JJ.   Estimate production of machine* with implement in hours/acre:

_____
(hours/acre)

KK.   Estimate acres to be burned:

_____
(acres)

LL.   Multiply JJ times KK to get approximate hours required for burning:

_____
(hours)

> *Costs*

MM.   Machine O & O (O & O cost × number of machines):

$_____/per hour

NN.   Attachment O & O (O & O cost × number of attachments):

$_____/per hour

OO.   Add MM and NN:

$_____/per hour

PP.   Multiply OO times LL for subtotal cost of burning:

$_____

QQ.   Multiply gallons of fuel to be used times $/gallon and add to PP for total cost of burning:

$_____

Any cumulative total can be divided into QQ to arrive at a per-unit cost.

---

*This is the machine that will be tending the fire; production will usually be 0.5 to 1 hour/acre.

*Chaining*                (Note: No analyses have been given for the tree pusher, stumper, tree shear, and chaining. No known method allows the computation of production and costs for these methods. However, for a rough estimation of production and costs when chaining, the following analysis is possible.)

*Production*

RR.   Machine mph:

_____
                         (mph)

SS.   Multiply RR by working width of chain:

_____

TT.   Divide SS by 10 for total acres chained per hour:

_____
                      (acres/hour)

UU.   Divide number of acres by TT to determine total number of hours required for chaining:

_____
                         (hours)

*Costs*

VV.   Machine O & O (O & O cost × number of machines):

       $_____/per hour

WW.   Chain O & O (O & O cost × number of chains):

       $_____/per hour

XX.   Add VV and WW:

       $_____/per hour

YY.   Multiply XX by UU for the total cost of chaining:

       $_____

## Conclusion

Now that the individual production and cost phases have been estimated, the complete expenses incurred for clearing land can be tabulated. The cost for each operation chosen is entered on its respective line and a total is taken. This is the total estimated cost for the clearing operations used.

| REFERENCE LETTER | OPERATION | COST |
|:---:|:---|:---|
| I | Cutting | $_____ |
| R | Piling | $_____ |
| II | Harrowing | $_____ |
| | Root plowing | $_____ |
| | Chopping | $_____ |
| QQ | Burning | $_____ |
| YY | Chaining | $_____ |
| | Total cost | $_____ |

Any cumulative total can be divided into the total cost to arrive at a per-unit cost. For example,

Total cost divided by number of acres = $_____ /acre

Total cost divided by number of hours = $_____ /hour

No road construction, drainage, leveling, etc., operations were considered because this discussion is centered on land clearing.

# SPECIFICATIONS

The manner in which specifications are written greatly affects the outcome of a land-clearing project. Poorly written specifications can mean the difference between success and failure.

All specifications and supplementary information must be written in such a way that the contractor or governmental project engineers can clearly understand exactly what the job requirements are, what the job limitations are, and what is expected by the contracting agency or owner. If specifications are not written clearly and concisely, the contracting agency should expect to pay more per acre. If the job is not understood, the contractor will understandably bid high to protect against loss.

Points to remember when writing specifications follow:

1. State all terms clearly and concisely.
2. Specify job requirements exactly. Use dimensions, examples, comparisons, etc., to illustrate what is desired.
3. Define the end use of land clearly and exactly.

4. Knowing that all variables mentioned affect the total time requirement, specify a job's completion date realistically.

5. Avoid writing specifications so rigidly that they force the contractor to use a less efficient method.

6. Specifications should be written for each operation required and with as few "as directed" as possible.

7. Job requirements should not call for more work to be done than is absolutely necessary.

8. If total clearing is necessary, ensure that the work to be done is really land clearing and not earthmoving. For example, if gullies, streams, and ditches are to be made usable, a major earthmoving project (rather than land clearing) might have to be done.

9. When determining disposable methods or requirements, remember that tree size and rainfall may limit burning. Thus, disposal may be done correctly and economically by just piling the refuse on unusable land.

10. If logging of saleable wood is to be done, it should be done before or after the actual clearing.

Some materials can be helpful to the contractor:

Aerial photo maps of the entire area to be cleared

General topography map

Water table map

Yearly rainfall figures

Map showing access routes to and throughout area

Average tree count per acre, including the number of trees/acre, percentage of hardwoods, soil conditions, root systems present, and the size ranges of the trees, tabulated in a clear and concise manner.

# LAND-CLEARING FORMULAS

## Cutting and Windrowing

The following is Rome Plow Company's formula for determining either cutting or windrowing time per acre (in minutes) for a tractor equipped with a shearing blade such as the K/G.

To estimate tractor hours per acre on a specific land-clearing job, apply the factors shown in Tables 9–1 and 9–2, together with data obtained from the job cruise in the field, in the formula:

Table 9–1. Cutting Production Table (K/G Blade)

| CATERPIL-LAR TRACK-TYPE TRACTOR* | BASE MINUTES, $B$** | DIAMETER RANGE 1'–2' (30–60 CM), $M_1$† | DIAMETER RANGE 2'–3' (60–90 CM), $M_2$ | DIAMETER RANGE 3'–4' (90–120 CM), $M_3$ | DIAMETER RANGE 4'–6' (120–180 CM), $M_4$ | DIAMETER OVER 6' (180 CM) PER FOOT (30 CM), $F$‡ |
|---|---|---|---|---|---|---|
| D9L | 39 | 0.1 | 0.4 | 1.3 | 3 | 1.0 |
| D8L | 45 | 0.2 | 1.3 | 2.2 | 6 | 1.8 |
| D7G | 62 | 0.5 | 1.8 | 3.6 | 11 | 3.6 |
| D6G | 100 | 0.8 | 4.0 | 8.0 | — | — |

*Current models (power shift when applicable) working terrain under 10 percent grade with good footing and no stones, in average hard-soft wood mix. Tractor and tools in proper operating condition.

**Minutes required to cover acre of light material where no trees need splitting or individual treatment.

†$M_1$ is minutes required to cut or pile trees 1' to 2' (30–60 cm) diameter at ground level; $M_2$ same for 2'–3' (60–90 cm) trees; $M_3$ same for 3'–4' (90–120 cm) trees; $M_4$ same for 4'–6' (120–180 cm) trees.

‡Number of minutes needed per foot of diameter to cut or pile trees over 6' (180 cm) diameter. Thus, a D9L cutting an 8' tree needs 8 × 1.0 or about 8 minutes; piling, it needs 8 × 0.3 or about 2.4 minutes.

Table 9–2. Windrowing Production Table Caterpillar Track-Type Tractor

| CATERPIL-LAR TRACK-TYPE TRACTOR* | BASE MINUTES, $B$** | DIAMETER RANGE 1'–2' (30–60 CM), $M_1$† | DIAMETER RANGE 2'–3' (60–90 CM), $M_2$ | DIAMETER RANGE 3'–4' (90–120 CM), $M_3$ | DIAMETER RANGE 4'–6' (120–180 CM), $M_4$ | DIAMETER OVER 6' (180 CM) PER FOOT (30 CM), $F$‡ |
|---|---|---|---|---|---|---|
| D9L | 97 | 0.08 | 0.1 | 1.2 | 2.1 | 0.3 |
| D8L | 111 | 0.1 | 0.5 | 1.8 | 3.6 | 0.9 |
| D7G | 135 | 0.4 | 0.7 | 2.7 | 5.4 | — |
| D6D | 185 | 0.6 | 1.2 | 5.0 | — | — |

(200' spacing between windrows)

$$T = B + M_1N_1 + M_2N_2 + M_3N_3 + M_4N_4 + DF$$

where

$T$ = time per acre in minutes

$B$ = base time for each tractor per acre

$M$ = minutes per tree in each diameter range

$N$ = number of trees per acre in each diameter range obtained from field cruise

$D$ = sum of diameter in feet of all trees per acre above 6 feet (180 cm) in diameter at ground level obtained from field cruise

$F$ = minutes per foot of diameter for trees above 6 feet (180 cm) in diameter

In cutting, some factors affect the production time:

Add 50 percent to diameter range times if stumps are dug out after cutting to ground level.
Add 25 percent to diameter range times if trees and stumps are taken out in one operation.
With the presence of hardwoods at
      75 to 100 percent, add 30 percent to total time (T).
      25 to 75 percent, there is no change.
      0 to 25 percent, subtract 30 percent from total time (T).
With density of vegetation less than 12-inch (304 mm) diameter, for
      Dense—600 trees/acre—add 100 percent to base time (B).
      Medium—400 to 600 trees/acre—there is no change.
      Light—less than 400 trees/acre, subtract 30 percent from total time (T).
With the presence of heavy vines, add 100% to base time (B).

The formula for windrowing is the same as piling. The base times are shown in Table 9–2.

In windrowing, other factors affect production time:

Add 25 percent to total time when piling grubbed vegetation.
Subtract 25 to 50 percent from total time per tractor when using three or more tractors in combination.
For burning, allow 30 minutes to 1 hour tractor time per acre.
In dense, small-diameter brush with few or no large trees and when vines are entangled within the felled material, reduce piling base by 30 percent.

## Estimating Hourly Production (Constant Speed Operation)

The American Society of Agricultural Engineers formula for estimating hourly production of a constant speed operation is

$$\frac{\text{Speed (mph)} \times \text{width of cut (feet)}}{10} = \text{acres/hour}$$

When production calculations are required for cutting, piling, and stumping, the production tables (with formula) can be used. When harrowing, root plowing, etc., production can be estimated with the preceding formula. This formula allows for 82.5 percent efficiency.

Graphs 1 and 2 show the speeds, production per hour, and width of cut that can be accomplished in a constant-speed operation.

Fleco Corporation has a formula to figure approximate acreage covered by an agricultural implement in an hour. This formula is the same as the ASAE formula except that it adds 10 percent to the working width of the implement in feet, then multiplies this figure by the speed of the tractor in miles per hour. This figure is in turn divided by 10 to obtain acres per hour in a 10-hour day.

This formula is used for Fleco's rolling choppers and root plows. The 10 percent factor is an allowance for losses due to turning, etc. The efficiency of this formula is approximately 90 percent.

Note: Neither Fleco Corporation nor Rome Industries claims absolute accuracy in these formulas because of the many variables that increase or decrease production.

## Estimating the Number of Machines Needed

To find the number of machines required for each phase of land clearing, use this formula:

Number of machines needed

$$= \frac{\text{*hours/acre} \times \text{number of acres}}{\text{time scheduled to complete job (hours)}}$$

## EQUIPMENT SELECTION BY SIZE OF AREA, VEGETATION, AND METHOD

Table 9–3. Light Clearing Vegetation up to 2 in. (5 cm) Diameter

|  | UPROOTING VEGETATION | CUTTING VEGETA-TION AT OR ABOVE GROUND LEVEL | KNOCKING THE VEGETATION TO THE GROUND | INCORPORATION OF VEGETATION INTO THE SOIL |
|---|---|---|---|---|
| Small areas 10 acres (4.0 hectares) | Bulldozer Blade Axes, Grub hoes and Mattocks | Axes, Machetes, Brush Hooks, Grub Hoes and Mattocks, Wheel-mounted Circular Saws | Bulldozer Blade | Moldboard Plows Disc Plows Disc Harrows |

*Average machine production for all operations in hours/acre.

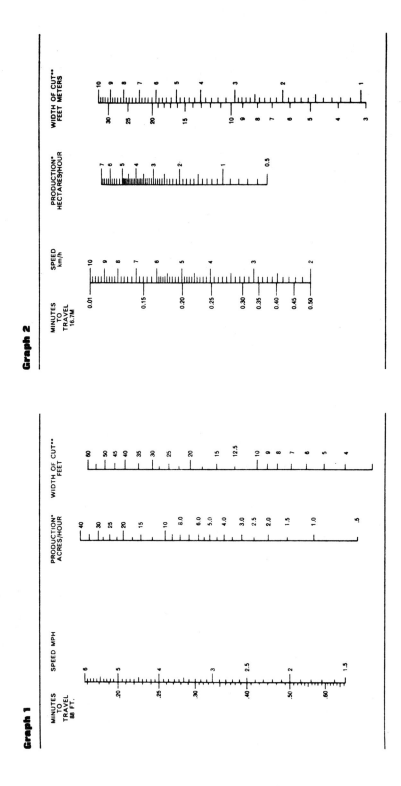

*Based on 82.5% efficiency.
**When width of cut exceeds 60 feet (10 meters) use a multiple of the width of cut and increase production proportionately.

254

| | UPROOTING VEGETATION | CUTTING VEGETATION AT OR ABOVE GROUND LEVEL | KNOCKING THE VEGETATION TO THE GROUND | INCORPORATION OF VEGETATION INTO THE SOIL |
|---|---|---|---|---|
| Medium areas 100 acres (40 hectares) | Bulldozer Blade | Heavy-duty Sickle Mowers (up to 1½"– 3.7 cm diameter) Tractor-mounted Circular Saws; Suspended rotary mowers | Bulldozer Blade, Rotary Mowers; Flail-type Rotary Cutters; Rolling Brush Cutters | Moldboard Plows; Disc Plows Disc Harrows |
| Large areas 1,000 acres (400 hectares) | Bulldozer Blade Root Rake, Grubber, Root Plow, Anchor Chain drawn between two crawler tractors, rails | | Rolling Brush Cutter; Flail-type Cutter; Anchor Chain drawn between two crawler tractors; rails | Undercutter with Disc; Moldboard Plows; Disc Plows; Disc Harrows |

The most economical size area for each type of equipment will vary with the relative cost of capital equipment versus labor. It is also affected by whether there are alternate uses for equipment such as using tractors for tillage.

Table 9–4. Intermediate Clearing Vegetation 2 to 8 in. (5–20 cm) Diameter

| | UPROOTING VEGETATION | CUTTING VEGETATION AT OR ABOVE GROUND LEVEL | KNOCKING THE VEGETATION TO THE GROUND | INCORPORATION OF VEGETATION INTO THE SOIL |
|---|---|---|---|---|
| Small areas 10 acres (4.0 hectares) | Bulldozer Blade | Axes, Crosscut Saws, Power Chain Saws, Wheel-mounted Circular Saws | Bulldozer Blade | Heavy-duty Disc Plow; Disc Harrow |
| Medium areas 100 acres (40 hectares) | Bulldozer Blade | Power Chain Saws, Tractor-mounted Circular Saws | Bulldozer Blade Rolling Brush Cutter (up to 5 in-12 cm Diameter), Rotary Mower (up to 4 in.-10 cm dia.) | Heavy-duty Disc Plow; Disc Harrow |
| Large areas 1,000 acres (400 hectares) | Shearing Blade Angling (Tilted) Bulldozer Blade, Rakes, Anchor Chain drawn between two crawler tractors Root Plow | Shearing Blade (Angling or V-type) | Bulldozer Blade Flail-type Rotary Cutter, Anchor Chain | Bulldozer Blade with Heavy-duty Harrow |

Table 9–5. Large Clearing Vegetation 8 in. (20 cm) Diameter or Larger

| | UPROOTING VEGETATION | CUTTING VEGETATION AT OR ABOVE GROUND LEVEL | KNOCKING THE VEGE-TATION TO THE GROUND |
|---|---|---|---|
| Small areas 10 acres (4.0 hectares) | Bulldozer Blade | Axes, Crosscut Saws, Power Chain Saws | Bulldozer Blade |
| Medium areas 100 acres (40 hectares) | Shearing Blade Angling (Tilted), Knockdown Beam, Rakes, Tree Stumper | Shearing Blade (Angling or V-type), Tree Shear (up to 26 in. (65 cm) softwood; 14 in. (35 cm) hardwood), Shearing Blade—Power Saw Combination | Bulldozer Blade |
| Large areas 1,000 acres (400 hectares) | Shearing Blade Angling (Tilted), Knockdown Beam, Rakes, Tree Stumper, Anchor Chain with Ball drawn between two crawler tractors | Shearing Blade (Angling or V-type), Shearing Blade—Power Saw Combination | Anchor Chain with Ball drawn between two crawler tractors |

# CONVERSION TABLES

Table 9–6. Number of Trees Per Acre (hectares)
(Square and Rectangular Spacing)

| TREE SPACING, FEET (METERS) | | NUMBER TREES PER ACRE (HECTARES) | | TREE SPACING, FEET (METERS) | | NUMBER TREES PER ACRE (HECTARES) | |
|---|---|---|---|---|---|---|---|
| 2 × 2 | (.6 × .6) | 10,890 | (26,909) | 8 × 10 | (2.4 × 3.0) | 544 | (1,344) |
| 3 × 3 | (.91 × .91) | 4,840 | (11,959) | 8 × 12 | (2.4 × 3.7) | 454 | (1,122) |
| 4 × 4 | (1.2 × 1.2) | 2,722 | (6,726) | 8 × 25 | (2.4 × 7.6) | 218 | (539) |
| 4 × 5 | (1.2 × 1.5) | 2,178 | (5,382) | 9 × 9 | (2.7 × 2.7) | 538 | (1,329) |
| 4 × 6 | (1.2 × 1.8) | 1,815 | (4,485) | 9 × 12 | (2.7 × 3.7) | 403 | (996) |
| 4 × 8 | (1.2 × 2.4) | 1,362 | (3,365) | 10 × 10 | (3.0 × 3.0) | 436 | (1,077) |
| 4 × 10 | (1.2 × 3.0) | 1,089 | (2,691) | 10 × 12 | (3.0 × 3.7) | 363 | (897) |
| 5 × 5 | (1.5 × 1.5) | 1,742 | (4.304) | 11 × 11 | (3.4 × 3.4) | 360 | (890) |
| 5 × 6 | (1.5 × 1.8) | 1,452 | (3,588) | 12 × 12 | (3.7 × 3.7) | 302 | (746) |
| 5 × 8 | (1.5 × 2.4) | 1,089 | (2,691) | 12 × 18 | (3.7 × 5.5) | 202 | (499) |
| 5 × 10 | (1.5 × 3.0) | 871 | (2,152) | 13 × 13 | (4.0 × 4.0) | 258 | (638) |
| 6 × 6 | (1.8 × 1.8) | 1,210 | (2,990) | 14 × 14 | (4.3 × 4.3) | 222 | (549) |
| 6 × 8 | (1.8 × 2.4) | 908 | (2,244) | 15 × 15 | (4.6 × 4.6) | 194 | (479) |
| 6 × 10 | (1.8 × 3.0) | 726 | (1,794) | 16 × 16 | (4.9 × 4.6) | 170 | (420) |
| 6 × 12 | (1.8 × 3.7) | 605 | (1,495) | 18 × 18 | (5.5 × 5.5) | 134 | (331) |
| 7 × 7 | (2.1 × 2.1) | 889 | (2,197) | 18 × 20 | (5.5 × 6.0) | 121 | (299) |
| 7 × 10 | (2.1 × 3.0) | 622 | (1,537) | 20 × 20 | (6.0 × 6.0) | 109 | (269) |
| 8 × 8 | (2.4 × 2.4) | 681 | (1,683) | 25 × 25 | (7.6 × 7.6) | 70 | (173) |

Table 9–7. Linear Conversion Factor Table

| INCHES | FEET | YARDS | RODS | MILES | CENTI-METERS | METERS | KILO-METERS |
|---|---|---|---|---|---|---|---|
| ① | 0.083 | 0.028 | 0.005 | | 2.540 | 0.0254 | |
| 12 | ① | 0.333 | 0.061 | 0.0002 | 30.480 | 0.305 | 0.0003 |
| 36 | 3 | ① | 0.182 | 0.0006 | 91.440 | 0.914 | 0.0009 |
| 0.3937 | 0.033 | 0.011 | | | ① | 0.01 | |
| 39.37 | 3.281 | 1.094 | 0.199 | 0.0006 | 100 | ① | 0.001 |
| | | | | FURLONGS | | | |
| 198 | 16.5 | 5.5 | ① | 0.003 | 0.025 | 5.029 | 0.005 |
| | 5,280 | 1,760 | 320 | ① | 8 | 1,609,347 | 1.609 |
| | 660 | 220 | 40 | 0.125 | ① | 201.168 | 0.201 |
| | 3,280.83 | 1,093.61 | 198.838 | 0.621 | 4.971 | 1,000 | ① |

Table 9–8. Area Conversion Factor Table

| SQUARE INCHES | SQUARE FEET | SQUARE YARDS | ACRES | SQUARE CENTI-METERS | SQUARE METERS | HECTARES | SQUARE KILO-METERS |
|---|---|---|---|---|---|---|---|
| ① | 0.007 | | | 6.452 | 0.0006 | | |
| 144 | ① | 0.111 | 0.00002 | 929.034 | 0.093 | | |
| 1,296 | 9 | ① | 0.0002 | 8,361.31 | 0.836 | | |
| 0.155 | 0.001 | | | ① | 0.0001 | | |
| 1,549.997 | 10.764 | 1.196 | 0.0002 | 10,000 | ① | 0.0001 | |
| | | | | SQUARE MILES | | | |
| | 43,560 | 4,840 | ① | 0.002 | 4,046.87 | 0.405 | 0.004 |
| | 27,878,400 | 3,097,600 | 640 | ① | 2,589,998 | 258.999 | 2.590 |
| | 107,638.7 | 11,959.9 | 2.471 | 0.004 | 10,000 | ① | 0.01 |
| | 10,763,867 | 1,195,985 | 247.104 | 0.386 | 1,000,000 | 100 | ① |

In converting, note the constant ① in the unit you are working with and its relationship to the unit of measure needed.

# GRAPHICS AND MODELS 10

Graphic art first is a tool that helps designers select the best of available alternatives; this is perhaps the highest and most creative use of graphics. Next, graphic art is used to convey to others basic ideas, to promote concepts and plans, to reflect objectives and priorities, to illustrate design features, and to gather support for planning proposals. Planning, architectural, engineering, and related fields all use graphic art similarly. Let us examine, by example, some of the uses of graphic art.

1. *A Mining Operation.* Providing plans for the protection and restoration of natural and man-made resources (such as streets, buildings, and communities) is a vital function of the site planner. Mining operations of the past typically left the land barren and desolate. Today planning is more an integral part of mining operations, providing concepts that assure positive environmental ends as well as efficient approaches to extracting raw materials. Figure 10–1, A–E suggests approaches to mining and restoring a mountainous area near Middlesboro, Tennessee.

2. *A Public Recreation Park.* Public parks often must serve a wide variety of age groups and interests. The final development plan is the graphic result of much research, study, and discussion with community members and their representatives. The development plan must be presented in a form that can be understood by the public as well as professionals (Figure 10–2).

3. *Special Design Features and Amenities.* Certain design features and amenities, such as lakes, sitting areas, meeting places, and wildlife sanctuaries, can give a development a human element that it otherwise would not have. Such features raise the quality of life in a development. But they can be expensive. Thus, these features and amenities must be "sold" to those who pay for them. Graphics, more than words could hope to do, speak for the importance of including such amenities and special features (Figure 10–3, A–D).

4. *Renderings.* Renderings are presentation drawings of a site, buildings, or special features of a site, done in an illustrative style. Renderings are often done by artists who specialize in such work. They may be done in a variety of media, including pen and ink, pencil, transparent and opaque watercolor, or some combination of these materials (Figure 10–4, A–D).

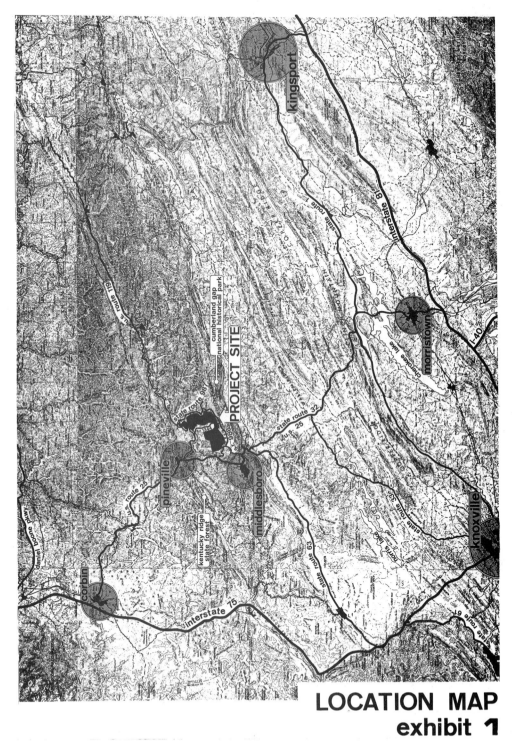

**LOCATION MAP**
**exhibit 1**

FIGURE 10–1A. Planning mining approaches with an eye to restoration should be an integral part of all mining operations. (Continued)

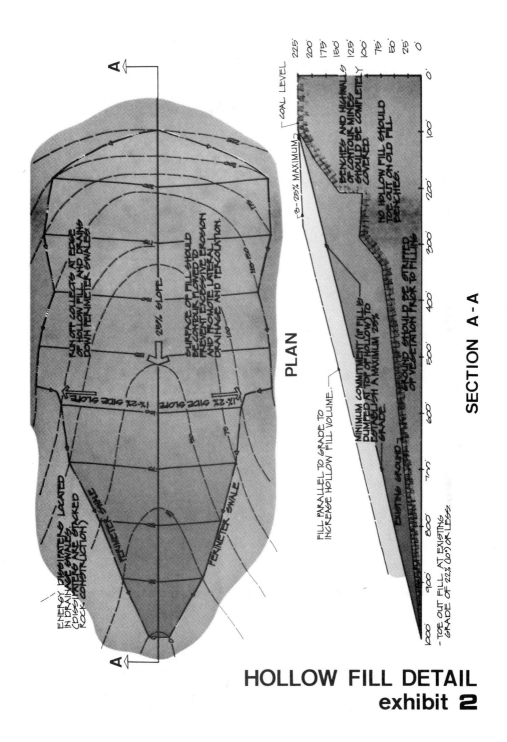

PLAN

SECTION A-A

**HOLLOW FILL DETAIL**
exhibit **2**

FIGURE 10–1B.

263

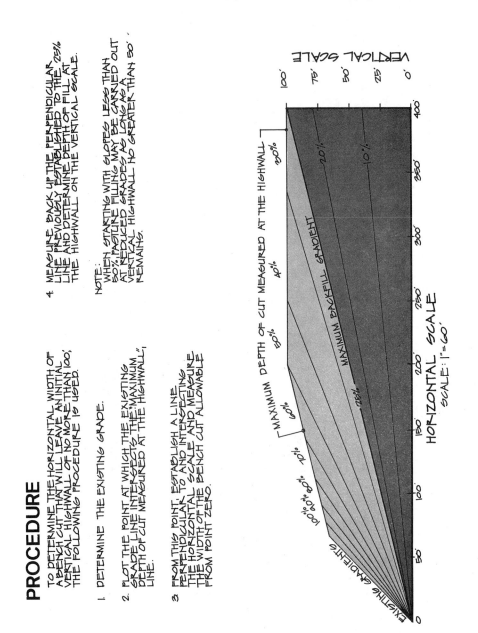

## PROCEDURE

TO DETERMINE THE HORIZONTAL WIDTH OF A BENCH CUT THAT WILL LEAVE AN INITIAL VERTICAL HIGHWALL OF NO MORE THAN 100', THE FOLLOWING PROCEDURE IS USED.

1. DETERMINE THE EXISTING GRADE.

2. PLOT THE POINT AT WHICH THE EXISTING GRADE LINE INTERSECTS THE "MAXIMUM DEPTH OF CUT MEASURED AT THE HIGHWALL" LINE.

3. FROM THIS POINT, ESTABLISH A LINE PERPENDICULAR TO AND INTERSECTING THE HORIZONTAL SCALE AND MEASURE THE WIDTH OF THE BENCH CUT ALLOWABLE FROM POINT ZERO.

4. MEASURE BACK UP THE PERPENDICULAR LINE PREVIOUSLY ESTABLISHED TO THE 25% VERTICAL HIGHWALL OF NO MORE THAN 100; AND DETERMINE DEPTH OF FILL AT THE HIGHWALL ON THE VERTICAL SCALE.

NOTE:
WHEN STARTING WITH SLOPES LESS THAN 50%, PASTURE FILLING MAY BE CARRIED OUT AT REDUCED GRADES AS LONG AS A VERTICAL HIGHWALL NO GREATER THAN 50' REMAINS.

# CONTROLLED RELATIONSHIPS
# OF CONTOUR MINING
## exhibit 3

FIGURE 10–1C.

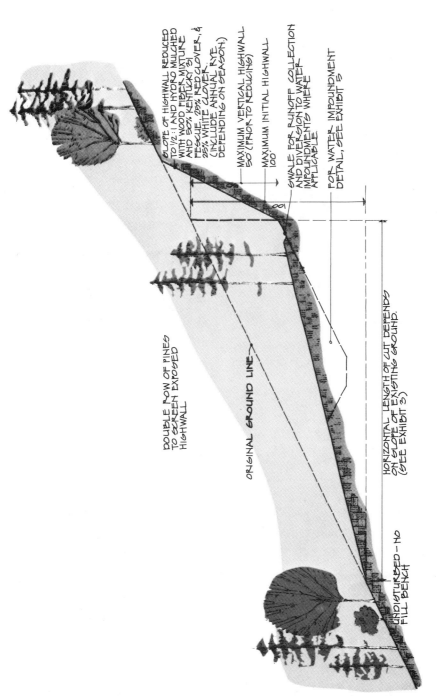

SLOPE OF HIGHWALL REDUCED TO 1/2:1 AND HYDRO MULCHED WITH WOOD FIBER MIXTURE AND 50% KENTUCKY 31 FESCUE, 12% RED CLOVER, & 25% WHITE CLOVER. (INCLUDE ANNUAL RYE DEPENDING ON SEASON.)

MAXIMUM VERTICAL HIGHWALL 50' (PRIOR TO REDUCING)

MAXIMUM INITIAL HIGHWALL 100'

SWALE FOR RUNOFF COLLECTION AND DIVERSION TO WATER IMPOUNDMENTS WHERE APPLICABLE.

FOR WATER IMPOUNDMENT DETAIL, SEE EXHIBIT 5

100:1

DOUBLE ROW OF PINES TO SCREEN EXPOSED HIGHWALL

ORIGINAL GROUND LINE

HORIZONTAL LENGTH OF CUT DEPENDS ON SLOPE OF EXISTING GROUND. (SEE EXHIBIT 3)

UNDISTURBED - NO FILL BENCH

# PASTURE FILL DETAIL
## exhibit 4

FIGURE 10–1D.

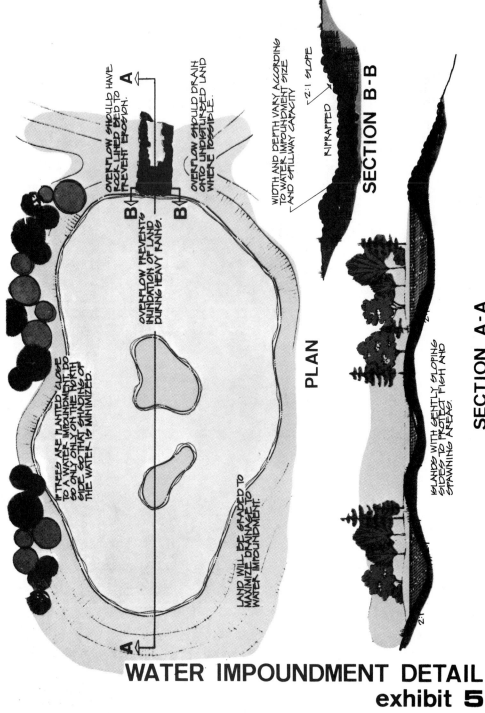

Overflow should have rock-lined bed to prevent erosion.

Overflow prevents inundation of land during heavy rains.

Overflow should drain onto undisturbed land where possible.

If trees are planted close to a water impoundment, do so only on the north side so that shading of the water is minimized.

Land will be graded to maximize drainage to water impoundment.

Width and depth vary according to water impoundment size and spillway capacity.

Riprapped

2:1 Slope

SECTION B-B

PLAN

Islands with gently sloping sides to protect fish and spawning areas.

SECTION A-A

# WATER IMPOUNDMENT DETAIL
## exhibit 5

FIGURE 10–1E.

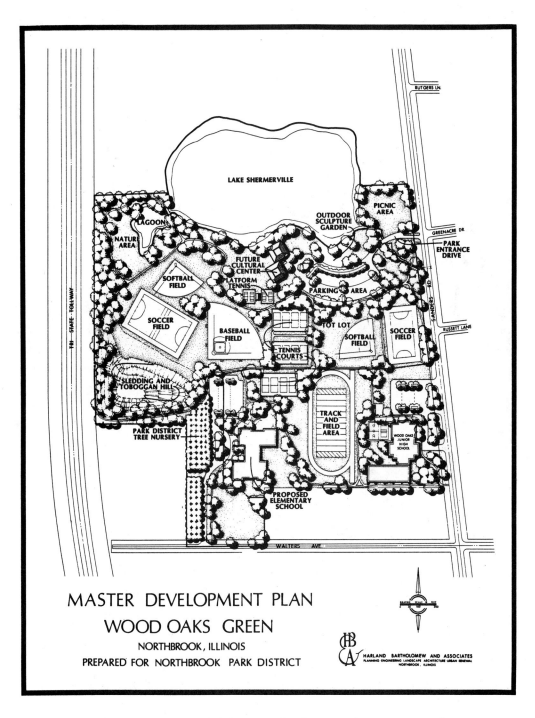

FIGURE 10–2. In the early stages, development plans are prepared in a graphic sketch and/or schematic format which can be understood by all interested parties whether or not they have planning expertise.

FIGURE 10–3A. Lakes, public areas, community buildings, sports and wildlife areas and other amenities and special site features are presented in an illustrative format.

FIGURE 10–3B.

FIGURE 10–3C.

FIGURE 10–3D.

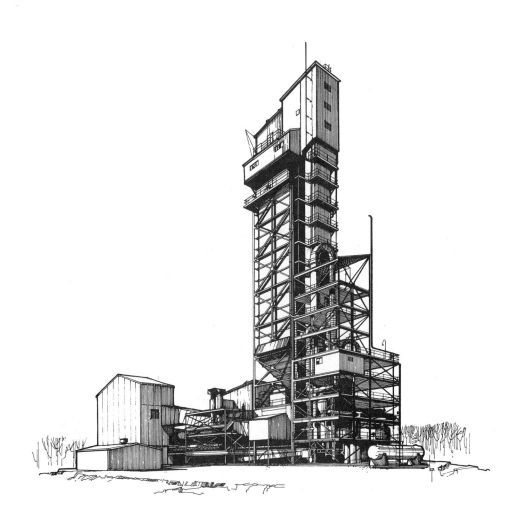

FIGURE 10–4A. Pen and ink rendering.

FIGURE 10–4B. Pen and ink rendering.

FIGURE 10–4C. Watercolor rendering.

FIGURE 10–4D. Watercolor rendering.

# MODELS

Some projects or portions of projects are so complex that, regardless of how explicit the graphics, the project cannot be visualized adequately. In such cases models may be needed. There are different models for different purposes and users.

A clay model, for example, is a quick and inexpensive method for designers to gain an accurate three-dimensional sense of scale, massing, proportion, and similar site considerations. Clients, financial institutions, federal agencies, and others who may be unskilled in visualizing built components from two-dimensional drawings may need more detail than a clay model offers.

Thus, the degree of realistic detail needed depends on its purpose and on the skill of its viewers. Finished, highly detailed presentation models can be quite expensive, especially for large projects. Balsa wood and poster board models with limited detail can be effective for both professional and nonprofessional viewers (Figure 10–5, A–B).

FIGURE 10–5A. Models are used when two-dimensional graphics are not considered adequate to properly present all or portions of the site. The type material and the amount of detail used on models depends on the needs of the user.

FIGURE 10–5B.

COST  11

Every site has objectives, goals, functions—that is, a site program. The site planner strives to accomplish these goals as cheaply as possible, while maintaining acceptable levels of quality; the task is not a simple one. It is not a simple task because site costs and quality are not the straightforward terms they might at first appear.

First on the cost list is the environment. No project can be built without alteration of the land; that alteration is a cost to us all and must be weighed against the value gained.

The client, if the client is a developer, is usually one of two types: a developer who builds to sell or a developer who builds to own and operate. The developer who builds to sell may be uninterested in spending money beyond the absolute minimum standards of market demand, safety, and health. The developer who builds to own, on the other hand, may want more quality than the budget provides.

Every development has a monetary impact on the surrounding social environment. The development may benefit and improve the surrounding community, or the development may be a disruptive force that diminishes the quality of life and thus reduces the monetary value of the surrounding community.

There are many costs to development and to understand more fully the eventual total cost of the development, the site planner must first think of cost in a broad sense, because the site planner must orchestrate, as much as possible, all the varied interests and definitions of cost and quality into a harmonious site plan; this is a difficult task. It would be misleading to say that it is always a possible task; it simply is not. And thus the site planner must sometimes decide between trying to make the best of poor possibilities and refusing the job.

Fortunately skill and planning and design often turn marginal projects into good projects. An important part of the skill involved is knowing site construction costs, which are considerably simpler than the broad implications of cost.

# COST ESTIMATING

The cost estimate of a project usually determines whether the project will be built. Thus, cost estimating is an essential skill of site planning. As with every phase of the site planning process, the initial data gathered are not as refined as the final data; this saves the client consultation time on projects that obviously (by studying the initial data) are not economically feasible. Preliminary cost data must, however, be accurate enough so that the site planner can determine whether more data should be gathered. Generally speaking, early estimates should be 80 to 85 percent accurate. Final cost estimates should strive to be more than 90 percent accurate.

The physical components of the project are estimated using two basic sheets: the workup sheet and the summary sheet. The workup sheet describes and itemizes the work proposed, for example, 10,000 cubic yards of slab-on-grade concrete, 2,500 pounds per square inch, machine troweled—this is a fairly typical item. Every item of work on the project, from start to finish, must be accounted for and itemized into appropriate quantities that can be cost-checked; the concrete, for example, is given in cubic yards because concrete usually is ordered in cubic yards. The workup sheet is produced from the project plans and specifications (and thus is no better than—or more accurate—than the plans and specifications) and may contain sketches, detailed calculations, notes, and other information needed to describe and itemize the work to be done. All the sheets should be numbered and the total number of sheets noted on each sheet (sheet 1 of 25, etc.). The participants in the project are also identified, and each sheet is dated.

The summary sheet is a refined and condensed version of the workup sheet. The summary sheet does not, for example, contain sketches or rough calculations, notes, etc.

To help simplify and standardize the estimating process, certain organizations have evolved standard formats for job specifications, data filing, cost analysis, and filing. The Construction Specifications Institute (CSI) is such an organization. CSI's Uniform Construction Index is a well-known system of formats for the whole range of construction activities (Figure 11–1, A–B).

Labor costs vary from skill to skill and in different areas of the country. Figure 11-2 gives wage rates and other data for various labor skills in the Atlanta area; these figures are available from the Department of Labor for the entire United States and are updated periodically. To determine how much time is required to do particular jobs—laying concrete slabs, for example—the site planners usually refer to past jobs of their own and other firms. As with all phases of site planning, it is wise to keep close contact with subcontractors, as they are one of the best sources of current information on the building scene.

What does a site planner do with cost data? If the site planner can provide reliable cost information, project owners—whether private developers as in the case study that follows or some agency in the public domain—can determine whether the project is economically feasible for their needs and can determine how best to proceed with building the project (project phasing).

DIVISION 1 - GENERAL
REQUIREMENTS
   SUMMARY OF WORK
   ALTERNATIVES
   PROJECT MEETINGS
   SUBMITTALS
   QUALITY CONTROL
   TEMPORARY FACILITIES &
      CONTROLS
   MATERIAL & EQUIPMENT
   PROJECT CLOSEOUT

DIVISION 2 - SITE WORK
   SUBSURFACE EXPLORATION
   CLEARING
   DEMOLITION
   EARTHWORK
   SOIL TREATMENT
   PILE FOUNDATIONS
   CAISSONS
   SHORING
   SITE DRAINAGE
   SITE UTILITIES
   PAVING & SURFACING
   SITE IMPROVEMENTS
   LANDSCAPING
   RAILROAD WORK
   MARINE WORK
   TUNNELING

DIVISION 3 - CONCRETE
   CONCRETE FORMWORK
   EXPANSION & CONTRACTION
      JOINTS
   CONCRETE REINFORCEMENT
   CAST-IN-PLACE CONCRETE
   SPECIALLY FINISHED
      CONCRETE
   SPECIALLY PLACED
      CONCRETE
   PRECAST CONCRETE
   CEMENTITIOUS DECKS

DIVISION 4 - MASONRY
   MORTAR
   MASONRY ACCESSORIES
   UNIT MASONRY
   STONE
   MASONRY RESTORATION &
      CLEANING
   REFRACTORIES

DIVISION 5 - METALS
   STRUCTURAL METAL
      FRAMING
   METAL JOISTS
   METAL DECKING
   LIGHTGAGE METAL FRAMING
   METAL FABRICATIONS
   ORNAMENTAL METAL
   EXPANSION CONTROL

DIVISION 6 - WOOD & PLASTICS
   ROUGH CARPENTRY

HEAVY TIMBER
   CONSTRUCTION
TRESTLES
PREFABRICATED
   STRUCTURAL WOOD
FINISH CARPENTRY
WOOD TREATMENT
ARCHITECTURAL
   WOODWORK
PREFABRICATED
STRUCTURAL PLASTICS
PLASTIC FABRICATIONS

DIVISION 7 - THERMAL &
MOISTURE PROTECTION
   WATERPROOFING
   DAMPPROOFING
   INSULATION
   SHINGLES & ROOFING TILES
   PREFORMED ROOFING &
      SIDING
   MEMBRANE ROOFING
   TRAFFIC TOPPING
   FLASHING & SHEET METAL
   ROOF ACCESSORIES
   SEALANTS

DIVISION 8 - DOORS & WINDOWS
   METAL DOORS & FRAMES
   WOOD & PLASTIC DOORS
   SPECIAL DOORS
   ENTRANCES & STOREFRONTS
   METAL WINDOWS
   WOOD & PLASTIC WINDOWS
   SPECIAL WINDOWS
   HARDWARE & SPECIALTIES
   GLAZING
   WINDOW WALLS/
      CURTAINWALLS

DIVISION 9 - FINISHES
   LATH & PLASTER
   GYPSUM WALLBOARD
   TILE
   TERRAZZO
   ACOUSTICAL TREATMENTS
   SUSPENSION SYSTEMS
   WOOD FLOORING
   RESILIENT FLOORING
   CARPETING
   SPECIAL FLOORING
   FLOOR TREATMENT
   SPECIAL COATINGS
   PAINTING
   WALL COVERING

DIVISION 10 - SPECIALTIES
   CHALKBOARDS &
      TACKBOARDS
   COMPARTMENTS & CUBICLES
   LOUVERS & VENTS
   GRILLES & SCREENS
   WALL & CORNER GUARDS
   ACCESS FLOORING

SPECIALTY MODULES
PEST CONTROL
FIREPLACES
FLAGPOLES
IDENTIFYING DEVICES
PEDESTRIAN CONTROL
   DEVICES
LOCKERS
PROTECTIVE COVERS
POSTAL SPECIALTIES
PARTITIONS
SCALES
STORAGE SHELVING
SUN CONTROL DEVICES
   (EXTERIOR)
TELEPHONE ENCLOSURES
TOILET & BATH ACCESSORIES
WARDROBE SPECIALTIES

DIVISION 11 - EQUIPMENT
   BUILT-IN MAINTENANCE
      EQUIPMENT
   BANK & VAULT EQUIPMENT
   COMMERCIAL EQUIPMENT
   CHECKROOM EQUIPMENT
   DARKROOM EQUIPMENT
   ECCLESIASTICAL EQUIPMENT
   EDUCATIONAL EQUIPMENT
   FOOD SERVICE EQUIPMENT
   VENDING EQUIPMENT
   ATHLETIC EQUIPMENT
   INDUSTRIAL EQUIPMENT
   LABORATORY EQUIPMENT
   LAUNDRY EQUIPMENT
   LIBRARY EQUIPMENT
   MEDICAL EQUIPMENT
   MORTUARY EQUIPMENT
   MUSICAL EQUIPMENT
   PARKING EQUIPMENT
   WASTE HANDLING
      EQUIPMENT
   LOADING DOCK EQUIPMENT
   DETENTION EQUIPMENT
   RESIDENTIAL EQUIPMENT
   THEATER EQUIPMENT
   REGISTRATION EQUIPMENT

DIVISION 12 - FURNISHINGS
   ARTWORK
   CABINETS & STORAGE
   WINDOW TREATMENT
   FABRICS
   FURNITURE
   RUGS & MATS
   SEATING
   FURNISHING ACCESSORIES

DIVISION 13 - SPECIAL
CONSTRUCTION
   AIR SUPPORTED STRUCTURES
   INTEGRATED ASSEMBLIES
   AUDIOMETRIC ROOM
   CLEAN ROOM
   HYPERBARIC ROOM

FIGURE 11–1A. Organizations such as the Construction Specification Institute have categorized and numbered the typical construction activities. This standardization helps in planning, estimating costs, scheduling and using personnel effectively.

INCINERATORS
INSTRUMENTATION
INSULATED ROOM
INTEGRATED CEILING
NUCLEAR REACTORS
OBSERVATORY
PREFABRICATED BUILDINGS
SPECIAL PURPOSE ROOMS &
  BUILDINGS
RADIATION PROTECTION
SOUND & VIBRATION
  CONTROL
VAULTS
SWIMMING POOL

**DIVISION 14 - CONVEYING**
**SYSTEMS**

DUMBWAITERS
ELEVATORS
HOISTS & CRANES

LIFTS
MATERIAL HANDLING
  SYSTEMS
TURNTABLES
MOVING STAIRS & WALKS
PNEUMATIC TUBE SYSTEMS
POWERED SCAFFOLDING

**DIVISION 15 - MECHANICAL**

GENERAL PROVISIONS
BASIC MATERIALS &
  METHODS
INSULATION
WATER SUPPLY &
  TREATMENT
WASTE WATER DISPOSAL &
  TREATMENT
PLUMBING
FIRE PROTECTION
POWER OR HEAT

GENERATION
REFRIGERATION
LIQUID HEAT TRANSFER
AIR DISTRIBUTION
CONTROLS &
  INSTRUMENTATION

**DIVISION 16 - ELECTRICAL**

GENERAL PROVISIONS
BASIC MATERIALS &
  METHODS
POWER GENERATION
POWER TRANSMISSION
SERVICE & DISTRIBUTION
LIGHTING
SPECIAL SYSTEMS
COMMUNICATIONS
HEATING & COOLING
CONTROLS &
  INSTRUMENTATION

FIGURE 11–1A. (Continued)

## SITE WORK

02000. ALTERNATIVES
02001. -02009. unassigned
02010. SUBSURFACE EXPLORATION
02011. Borings
02012. Core Drilling
02013. Standard Penetration Tests
02014. Seismic Exploration
02015.-02099. unassigned
02100. CLEARING
02101. Structure Moving
02102. Clearing and Grubbing
02103. Tree Pruning
02104. Shrub and Tree Relocation
02105.-02109. unassigned
02110. DEMOLITION
02111.-02199. unassigned
02200. EARTHWORK
02201.-02209. unassigned
02210. Site Grading
02211. Rock Removal
02212. Embankment
02213.-02219. unassigned
02220. Excavating and Backfilling
02221. Trenching
02222. Structure Excavation
02223. Roadway excavation
02224. Pipe Boring and Jacking
02225. Trench Backfill and
  Compaction
02226. Structure Backfill and
  Compaction
02227. Waste Material Disposal

02228.-02229. unassigned
02230. Soil Compaction control
02231.-02239. unassigned
02240. Soil Stabilization
02241.-02249. unassigned
02250. SOIL TREATMENT
02251. Termite Control
02252. Vegetation Control
02253.-02299. unassigned
02300. PILE FOUNDATIONS
02301.-02349. unassigned
02350. CAISSONS
02351. Drilled Caissons
02352. Excavated Caissons
02353.-02399. unassigned
02400 SHORING
02401.-02419. unassigned
02420. Underpinning
02421.-02499. unassigned
02500. SITE DRAINAGE
02501.-02549. unassigned
02550. SITE UTILITIES
02551.-02599. unassigned
02600. PAVING & SURFACING
02601.-02609. unassigned
02610. Paving
02611.-02619. unassigned
02620. Curbs and Gutters
02621.-02629. unassigned
02630. Walks
02631.-02639. unassigned
02640. Synthetic Surfacing

02641.-02699. unassigned
02700. SITE IMPROVEMENTS
02701.-02709. unassigned
02710. Fences and Gates
02711.-02719. unassigned
02720. Road and Parking
  Appurtenances
02721.-02729. unassigned
02730. Playing Fields
02731.-02739. unassigned
02740. Fountains
02741.-02749. unassigned
02750. Irrigation System
02751.-02759. unassigned
02760. Site Furnishings
02761.-02799. unassigned
02800. LANDSCAPING
02801.-02809. unassigned
02810. Soil Preparation
02811.-02819. unassigned
02820. Lawns
02821.-02829. unassigned
02830. Trees, Shrubs, and Ground
  Cover
02831.-02849. unassigned
02850. RAILROAD WORK
02851. Trackwork
02852. Ballasting
02853.-02899. unassigned
02900. MARINE WORK
02901.-02909. unassigned
02910. Docks

FIGURE 11–1B.

| | | |
|---|---|---|
| 02911.-02919. unassigned | 02933. Groins | 02951.-02959. unassigned |
| 02920. Boat Facilities | 02934. Jettys | 02960. Tunnel Excavation |
| 02921.-02929. unassigned | 02935.-02939. unassigned | 02961.-02969. unassigned |
| 02930. Protective Marine Structures | 02940. dredging | 02970. Tunnel Grouting |
| 02931. Fenders | 02941.-02949. unassigned | 02971.-02979 unassigned |
| 02932. Seawalls | 02950. TUNNELING | 02980. Support Systems |
| | | 02981.-02999. unassigned |

11–1B. (Continued)

The following are the actual cost figures and phasing strategy worked up by a site planning firm and presented to an owner interested in developing his land.

## Case Study: Cost Estimating and Project Phasing

Courtesy of Barta & Goforth, Inc., Planning Consultants, Memphis, Tennessee.

# INTRODUCTION

This information provides a financial analysis of the proposed development. Construction and development costs have been estimated and, with the exception of Sections J and K (Figure 11–3), are charged to the single-family lots. The only other section where uses other than single-family exist is Section A; construction necessary for the development of these lots will provide access and services to the townhouse parcels within this section. This phasing will, of course, provide less profit initially; however, it will make possible lower residential cost for the remaining parcels, providing greater development flexibility and profit.

Land values have been included in the development costs. Interest costs have not. Thus, the projections reflect a higher figure than will be realized. However, construction and development costs are based on market construction costs (1979) and thus do not reflect any savings that the developer may gain by doing portions of the work in-house. The profits from sales of the completed project are based on competitive market values in the subject county in 1978.

In studying the analysis, note that all the costs shown in the analysis are referenced to the sectional development plan (Figure 11–3).

**Wage rates, hours, and employer contributions for selected benefits: Selected cities - Southeast**

(Union building trades)

| City and job classification | July 2, 1979 Rate per hour¹ | July 1, 1980 Rate per hour¹ | Hours per week² | Insurance⁴ Dollars | Insurance⁴ Percent | Pension Dollars | Pension Percent | Vacation Dollars | Vacation Percent | Other⁵ Dollars | Other⁵ Percent |
|---|---|---|---|---|---|---|---|---|---|---|---|
| **ATLANTA, GA.** | | | | | | | | | | | |
| **Building construction** | | | | | | | | | | | |
| **Journeymen** | | | | | | | | | | | |
| Asbestos workers | $10.200 | $11.350 | 40.00 | $0.550 | – | $0.750 | – | ⁶ $0.500 | – | – | – |
| Boilermakers | 10.700 | 11.750 | 40.00 | 1.275 | – | 1.100 | – | – | – | – | – |
| Bricklayers | 9.200 | 10.550 | 40.00 | .750 | – | .570 | – | ⁶ .650 | – | $0.110 | – |
| Carpenters | 9.850 | 11.350 | 40.00 | .700 | – | .450 | – | – | – | – | – .- |
| Millwrights | 10.150 | 11.600 | 40.00 | .700 | – | .500 | – | – | – | – | – |
| Piledrivers | 10.000 | 11.500 | 40.00 | .700 | – | .450 | – | – | – | – | – |
| Cement finishers | 9.150 | 10.450 | 40.00 | .600 | – | .800 | – | – | – | – | – |
| Drywall tapers (finishers) | 9.650 | 11.100 | 40.00 | .650 | – | .900 | – | – | – | – | – |
| Electricans (inside wirers) | 11.150 | 12.050 | 40.00 | – | 8.00 | – | 12.00 | – | – | – | 1.00 |
| Elevator constructors | 10.030 | 10.700 | 40.00 | 1.045 | – | .820 | – | – | 6.00 | .035 | 2.69 |
| Engineers--Power equipment operators: | | | | | | | | | | | |
| Group A--Air compressors (365 cfm and over), cranes, derricks, draglines, hoists, shovels, trenching machines (over 6 ft. depth) | 10.000 | 10.900 | 40.00 | .630 | – | .750 | – | – | – | – | – |
| Group B--Trenching machines (to 6 ft.), scrapers, bulldozers, tractors, special equipment | 9.650 | 10.550 | 40.00 | .630 | – | .750 | – | – | – | – | – |
| Group C--Air compressors (600 cu. ft. or batteries of two, 300 cu. ft. and over) | 7.620 | 8.250 | 40.00 | .630 | – | .750 | – | – | – | – | – |
| Group D-2--Pumps (over 4 in., up to batteries of 4) | 7.020 | 7.500 | 40.00 | .630 | – | .750 | – | – | – | – | – |
| Group E--Mixers (skip type), except paving, rollers | 7.330 | 7.760 | 40.00 | .630 | – | .750 | – | – | – | – | – |
| Group F--Air compressors (up to and including 300 cu. ft.), pumps (4 in. or less) | 6.280 | 6.640 | 40.00 | .630 | – | .750 | – | – | – | – | 2.31 |
| Glaziers | 9.400 | 10.450 | 40.00 | .800 | – | .530 | – | ⁶ .950 | – | – | 2.31 |
| Lathers | 10.500 | 11.350 | 40.00 | .600 | – | .450 | – | – | – | – | – |
| Marble setters | 9.100 | 10.500 | 40.00 | .750 | – | .570 | – | ⁶ .700 | – | .100 | – |
| Mosaic and terrazzo workers | 9.100 | 10.500 | 40.00 | .750 | – | .570 | – | ⁶ .700 | – | .100 | – |
| Painters | 9.650 | 11.100 | 40.00 | .650 | – | .900 | – | – | – | – | – |
| Steel and swing stage | 10.150 | 11.600 | 40.00 | .650 | – | .900 | – | – | – | – | – |
| Spray | 10.650 | 12.100 | 40.00 | .650 | – | .900 | – | – | – | – | – |
| Paperhangers | 9.900 | 11.350 | 40.00 | .650 | – | .900 | – | – | – | – | – |
| Pipefitters | 10.650 | 11.400 | 40.00 | 1.000 | – | .850 | – | ⁶ .500 | – | .080 | – |
| Plasterers | 9.420 | 10.920 | 40.00 | .600 | – | .800 | – | – | – | .100 | – |
| Plumbers | 10.650 | 11.400 | 40.00 | 1.000 | – | .850 | – | ⁶ .500 | – | .080 | – |
| Reinforcing iron workers | 9.950 | 11.050 | 40.00 | .700 | – | .870 | – | ⁶ .500 | – | – | – |
| Roofers, composition | 7.450 | 8.400 | 40.00 | .350 | – | .200 | – | – | – | – | – |
| Roofers, slate and tile | 7.700 | 8.400 | 40.00 | .350 | – | .200 | – | – | – | – | – |
| Sheet-metal workers | 10.400 | 11.000 | 40.00 | .700 | – | .800 | – | ⁶ .500 | – | .100 | – |
| Stonemasons | 9.200 | 10.550 | 40.00 | .750 | – | .570 | – | ⁶ .650 | – | .110 | – |
| Structural iron workers | 9.950 | 11.050 | 40.00 | .700 | – | .870 | – | ⁶ .500 | – | – | – |
| Sheeters | 9.950 | 11.050 | 40.00 | .700 | – | .870 | – | ⁶ .500 | – | – | – |
| Tile layers | 9.100 | 10.500 | 40.00 | .750 | – | .570 | – | ⁶ .700 | – | .100 | – |

See footnotes at end of table.

FIGURE 11–2A. Wage rates and other data for various labor skills in the Atlanta area.

(Union building trades)

| City and job classification | July 2, 1979 Rate per hour[1] | July 1, 1980 Rate per hour[1] | Hours per week[2] | Employer contributions for selected benefits[3] | | | | | | | |
|---|---|---|---|---|---|---|---|---|---|---|---|
| | | | | Insurance[4] | | Pension | | Vacation | | Other[5] | |
| | | | | Dollars | Percent | Dollars | Percent | Dollars | Percent | Dollars | Percent |
| **ATLANTA, GA.** **—Continued** | | | | | | | | | | | |
| **Building construction** | | | | | | | | | | | |
| **Helpers and laborers** | | | | | | | | | | | |
| Bricklayers' tenders | $6.550 | $7.700 | 40.00 | $0.300 | – | $0.330 | – | – | – | $0.100 | – |
| Mortar mixers | 6.770 | 7.920 | 40.00 | .300 | – | .330 | – | – | – | .100 | – |
| Building laborers | 6.550 | 7.700 | 40.00 | .300 | – | .330 | – | – | – | .100 | – |
| Elevator constructors' helpers | 7.020 | 7.490 | 40.00 | 1.045 | – | .820 | – | – | 6.00 | .035 | 2.69 |
| Marble setters finishers | 7.000 | 8.200 | 40.00 | .350 | – | .100 | – | – | – | – | – |
| Plasterers' laborers | 6.550 | 7.700 | 40.00 | .300 | – | .330 | – | – | – | .100 | – |
| Plumbers' laborers | 6.550 | 7.700 | 40.00 | .300 | – | .330 | – | – | – | .100 | – |
| Terrazzo finishers and polishers | 7.200 | 8.300 | 40.00 | .350 | – | .100 | – | – | – | – | – |
| Tile layer finishers | 7.000 | 8.200 | 40.00 | .350 | – | .100 | – | – | – | – | – |
| Roofers' helpers | 5.420 | 5.640 | 40.00 | .350 | – | .200 | – | – | – | – | – |
| **Other heavy construction** | | | | | | | | | | | |
| **Journeymen** | | | | | | | | | | | |
| Engineers--Power equipment operators: | | | | | | | | | | | |
| Group A--Concrete pumps, cranes, piledrivers | 10.300 | 11.120 | 40.00 | .630 | – | .750 | – | – | – | – | 4.27 |
| Group B--Firemen (stationary or portable) | 9.360 | 10.040 | 40.00 | .630 | – | .750 | – | – | – | – | 4.27 |
| Group C--Air compressors, 600 cu. ft. and over | 7.980 | 8.320 | 40.00 | .630 | – | .750 | – | – | – | – | 4.27 |
| Group D--Oilers-truck and locomotive | 8.710 | 9.400 | 40.00 | .630 | – | .750 | – | – | – | – | 4.27 |
| Group E--Concrete pumps (boom type), water pumps (over 4 in. and battery of 4) | 7.460 | 7.840 | 40.00 | .630 | – | .750 | – | – | – | – | 4.27 |
| Group F--Air compressors (up to and including 300 cu. ft.), water pumps (4 in. or less), sand blasting machines | 6.720 | 6.980 | 40.00 | .630 | – | .750 | – | – | – | – | 4.27 |

[1] Basic (minimum) rates, excluding holiday, vacation, or other benefit payments made or regularly credited to the employee. Wage rates shown represent rates available and payable on July 1 of the survey year and do not include increases made later that are retroactive to July 1 or before.

[2] Hours are the same for both years unless otherwise indicated.

[3] Shown in terms of cents per hour or as a percent of rate; in actual practice, however, some employer payments are calculated on the basis of total hours or gross payroll. These variations in method of computation are not indicated in the above tabulation.

[4] Includes life insurance, hospitalization, and other types of health and welfare benefits; excludes payments into holiday, vacation, and unemployment funds when such programs have been negotiated.

[5] Includes all other nonlegally required employer contributions,

except those for apprenticeship fund payments, as indicated in individual agreements.

[6] Part of negotiated rate, not included in the basic rate shown. Amount may be included in computation of overtime and other premium rates.

[7] Includes a 5 percent contribution to savings fund. Part of negotiated rate; not included in the basic rate shown.

[8] Includes $1.00 contribution to savings fund. Part of negotiated rate; not included in the basic rate shown.

[R] Revision of data previously reported.

NOTE: Dash indicates no data, or no data reported. When referring to a rate per hour for a previous year, "-" indicates either a change in progression, or a new job or union not previously reported.

FIGURE 11–2B.

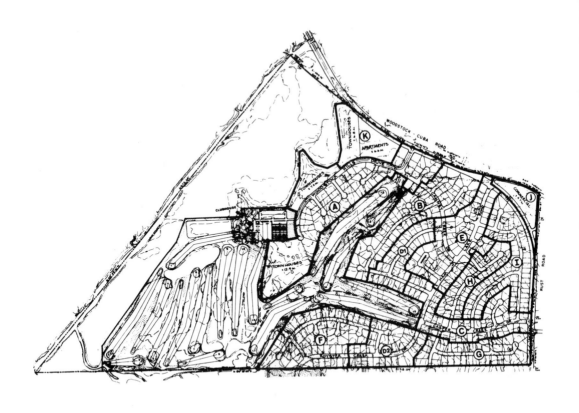

**LEGEND**

- - - - - PROPERTY LINE
■ EXISTING BUILDING
ROAD
GOLF COURSE
GOLF COURSE BOUNDARY
TREE MASSES
WATER AREA

**LOT SUMMARY**

| LAND USE | NUMBER of LOTS in SECTION | | | | | | | | | | | | TOTAL |
|---|---|---|---|---|---|---|---|---|---|---|---|---|---|
| | A | B | C | D1 D2 | E | F | G | H | I | J | K | |
| SINGLE FAMILY | 91 | 68 | 90 | 31 34 | 61 | 68 | 36 | 36 | 79 | | | 484 |
| TOWNHOUSE | 2 | | | | | | | | | | 1 | 3 |
| APARTMENT | | | | | | | | | | | 1 | 1 |
| COMMERCIAL | | | | | | | | | 1 | | | 1 |
| TOTAL | 93 | 68 | 90 | 31 34 | 61 | 68 | 36 | 36 | 79 | 1 | 2 | 499 |

# SECTIONAL DEVELOPMENT PLAN

FIGURE 11–3. The sectional development plan provides a key to project phasing. This project is made up of single family residences, townhouses, apartments, and commercial use, built in close proximity to a golf course. These major uses are shown in sections A through K.

Financial Analysis

| SEC-TION | NUM-BER LOTS | LOT SIZE | DEVELOPMENT COST PER LOT | DEVELOPMENT COST SECTION | SALES PER LOT | SALES SECTION | PROFIT (INTEREST EXCLUDED) PER LOT | PROFIT (INTEREST EXCLUDED) SECTION |
|---|---|---|---|---|---|---|---|---|
| A | 14 | 15,000 s.f. | | | $20,000 | | | |
| | 32 | 15,000 s.f. | | | 15,000 | | | |
| | 5 | 10,000 s.f. | $13,094 | $ 666,978 | 9,000 | $ 805,000 | $2,706 | $ 138,022 |
| B | 15 | 13,500 s.f. | | | 18,000 | | | |
| | 29 | 13,500 s.f. | | | 13,500 | | | |
| | 18 | 10,000 s.f. | 9,674 | 599,814 | 9,000 | 823,500 | 3,608 | 223,686 |
| C | 4 | 13,500 s.f. | | | 18,000 | | | |
| | 3 | 13,500 s.f. | | | 16,000 | | | |
| | 34 | 13,500 s.f. | | | 13,500 | | | |
| | 9 | 10,000 s.f. | 14,217 | 710,876 | 9,000 | 660,000 | −1,017 | −50,876 |
| D-1 | 7 | 13,500 s.f. | | | 18,000 | | | |
| | 24 | 13,500 s.f. | 8,316 | 257,824 | 13,500 | 450,000 | 6,199 | 192,176 |
| D-2 | 6 | 15,000 s.f. | | | 20,000 | 540,000 | 6,742 | 229,234 |
| | 28 | 15,000 s.f. | 9,140 | 310,766 | 15,000 | | | |
| E | 7 | 15,000 s.f. | | | 15,000 | | | |
| | 26 | 13,500 s.f. | | | 13,500 | | | |
| | 28 | 10,000 s.f. | 9,504 | 579,775 | 9,000 | 708,000 | 2,102 | 128,225 |
| F | 19 | 15,000 s.f. | | | 20,000 | | | |
| | 39 | 15,000 s.f. | 9,706 | 562,940 | 15,000 | 965,000 | 6,932 | 402,060 |
| G | 36 | 15,000 s.f. | 8,984 | 323,410 | 12,000 | 432,000 | 3,016 | 108,590 |
| H | 38 | 10,000 s.f. | 6,982 | 265,312 | 9,000 | 342,000 | 2,018 | 76,688 |
| I | 73 | 10,000 s.f. | 7,214 | 526,610 | 9,000 | 657,000 | 1,786 | 130,390 |
| Subtotal | 494 | | | $4,804,305 | | $6,382,500 | | $1,578,195 |

| SECTION | DESCRIPTION | ACREAGE | DEVELOPMENT COST | SALES PER ACRE | SALES TRACT[2] | PROJECTED PROFIT |
|---|---|---|---|---|---|---|
| A | Townhouses | 11.9 | [1] | $60,000 | $ 623,560 | $ 623,560 |
| | Townhouses | 7.0 | [1] | 20,000 | 103,600 | 103,600 |
| K | Townhouses | 6.8 | — | 20,000 | 100,640 | 100,640 |
| | Apartments | 6.6 | — | 20,000 | 97,680 | 97,680 |
| J | Commercial | 4.7 | $160,668 | 70,000 | 329,000 | 168,332 |
| Subtotal | | 37.0 | $160,668 | | $1,254,480 | $1,093,812 |

| | DEVELOPMENT COST | SALES | PROJECTED PROFIT |
|---|---|---|---|
| Subtotal (other) | $ 160,668 | $1,254,480 | $1,093,812 |
| Subtotal (lots) | 4,804,305 | 6,382,500 | 1,578,195 |
| Total | $4,964,973 | $7,636,980 | $2,672,007 |

[1]Development costs for these tracts have been absorbed by the single-family lots of the respective section.
[2]Excludes land value ($4,000/acre and sales commission, 6 percent sales price), Sections A and K.

# COST ANALYSIS

Each of the items listed were considered carefully in order to prepare the cost analysis. Unit costs reflect prices for the 1979 construction season.

| SITE WORK | UNIT COSTS |
|---|---|
| Clearing | $1,200.00/acre |
| Sodding | 1.75/s.y. |
| Seeding | .20/s.y. |
| Fill | 2.00/c.y. |

| SANITARY SEWERS | |
|---|---|
| Sanitary sewers | 10.65/l.f. (Average 9 feet deep) |
| 6-inch high-pressure sewer pipe | 6.00/l.f. |
| Standard manholes | 670.00 each |
| Manholes—sealed | 800.00 each |
| 6-inch house connections | 180.00 each |

| DRAINAGE | |
|---|---|
| Drainage (general) | 18.50 /l.f. of street |
| Reinforced concrete | 150.00/c.y. (drainage structures, headwalls, cut-off walls) |
| 60-inch concrete pipe | 70.00/l.f. |
| 48-inch concrete pipe | 50.00/l.f. |
| Drainage manholes | 670.00 each |

| STREET IMPROVEMENTS | |
|---|---|
| Excavation | 1.50/c.y. |
| Curbs and gutters, 6 inches | 4.75/l.f. |
| Curbs and gutters, 8 inches | 5.05/l.f. |
| Pavement (gravel), 6 inches | 1.85/s.y. |
| Pavement (gravel), 8 inches | 2.10/s.y. |
| Sidewalk, 4 inches × 5 feet (concrete) | 5.50/l.f. |
| Street name signs | 40.00 each |

## Average Lot Prices in the County

Listed next are average lot prices for various subdivisions in the county. Prices quoted are 1978 lot values. The values were utilized as comparables in determining prices for lots in the development.

| SUBDIVISION | AVERAGE LOT SIZE | AVERAGE PRICE |
|---|---|---|
| A | | $8,750 |
| B | 75 × 125 | $ 9,200–$10,000 |
| C | 80 × 125 | $ 8,500 |
| D | | $ 9,000 |
| D, Section 1 | | $11,500–$27,000 |
| D, Section 2 | | $11,000–$19,500 |
| E, Section 3 | 100 × 150 | $17,000–$18,500 |
| F | 75 × 125, 80 × 125 | $ 7,500 |
| G | 100 × 150 | $15,000 |
| H | 100 × 150 | $14,000–$15,000 |
| I, Section 3 | 100 × 150 | $14,000–$15,000 |
| J | 80 × 125 | $ 7,700 |
| K | | $ 7,000–$ 8,000 |
| L, Section 1 | | $18,500 |
| M, Section 1 | | $ 9,400–$10,300 |
| N, Section 1 | 100 × 140 | $14,125–$18,000 |
| O, Section 5 | 80 × 140 | $11,000–$19,500 |
| P, Section 20 | 100 × 140 | $17,500 |
| Q, Section 5 | | $10,000–$11,000 |
| R | | $15,200 |

# SECTION A

## Construction

51 lots

13.0-acre townhouse site

7.7-acre townhouse site

51.7-acres

Development will begin with this section. There is no unusual site work because the proposed roads follow ridge lines. The cost of sanitary sewers will be rather high for Section A. The high cost of sanitary sewers will, however, contribute to the lower cost of sanitary sewers for Section B. Also, the total cost of the sanitary sewer pressure line has been prorated to Section A on the basis of the total number of single-family lots in Section A to the total number of lots in Sections A, B, and C and the clubhouse. The pressure line cost was proportioned on the basis of effluent generated, being 89 percent for Sections A, B, and C and 11 percent for the clubhouse. In terms of street improvements, the 68-foot collector street to the country club must be constructed from Washington Road, and major street improvements will be required for 780 feet of Washington Road. Drainage improvements include the cost of storm sewers within the collector street, major street, and minor streets. By reviewing the sectional development plan, a clear picture of the actual cost of construction can be obtained.

| DESCRIPTION | COST | COST PER LOT |
|---|---|---|
| Site work | $ 16,200 | $ 318 |
| Sanitary sewers | 81,100 | 1,590 |
| Drainage | 105,700 | 2,100 |
| Street improvements | 151,240 | 3,000 |
| Extra (pressure line) | 8,300 | 160 |
| Total cost | $362,540 | $7,168 |

## DEVELOPMENT

| | | |
|---|---|---|
| Construction cost | | $362,540 |
| Planning and engineering ($186.50/lot) | | 9,511 |
| Electric service ($350/lot) | | 17,850 |
| Water service ($450/lot) | | 22,950 |
| Gas service ($200/lot) | | 10,200 |
| Sewer fee ($100/lot) | | 5,100 |
| Subdivision bond (1.5% construction cost) | | 5,438 |
| Advertising (2% sales price of lots) | | 16,100 |
| Contingency (10%) | | 44,989 |
| Sales commissions (6% sales price of lots) | | 48,300 |
| Land value ($4,000) 31.0 acres | | 124,000 |
| Total development cost (interest excluded) | | $666,978 |
| Proposed sales prices (lots) | | |
|     14 lots @ $20,000/lot (15,000 sq. ft./lot) | $280,000 | |
|     32 lots @ 15,000/lot (15,000 sq. ft./lot) | 480,000 | |
|     5 lots @ 9,000/lot (10,000 sq. ft./lot) | 45,000 | |
| Total sales price (lots) | | $805,000 |
| Projected profit (single-family lots, interest excluded) | | 138,022 |
|   Per lot | | 2,706 |
|   Per acre | | 4,452 |
| Proposed sales (other) | | |
|   Apartment      acres @ /acre | | * |
|   Townhouse   11.9 acres @ $60,000/acre | $714,000* | |
|           7.0 acres @ $20,000/acre | $140,000* | |
|   Commercial    acres @ /acre | | * |
|   School and park site   acres @ /acre | | * |

| | |
|---|---:|
| Total proposed sales (other) | $854,000 |
|   Less land value ($4,000/acre) | 75,600 |
|   Less sales commissions (6% sales price) | 51,240 |
| Total projected profit (other) | $727,160 |
| Total proposed profit (single-family lots and other) | $865,182 |

# SECTION B

## Construction

### 62 lots

### 29.8 acres

As stated in the preceding narrative on Section A, the cost of sanitary sewers in Section B is lower because this section ties into the main line serving Section A. The cost of the pressure line again has been prorated to Section B on the basis of the number of lots in Section B to the total number of lots in Section A, B, and C. Street improvements include construction of a segment of a 60-foot collector street and a segment of Washington Road, a major road. Drainage improvements include the cost of storm sewers within the collector street, major street, and minor streets.

| DESCRIPTION | COST | COST PER LOT |
|:---|---:|---:|
| Site work | $ 13,800 | $ 223 |
| Sanitary sewers | 64,400 | 1,039 |
| Drainage | 85,600 | 1,381 |
| Street improvements | 117,400 | 1,892 |
| Extra (pressure line) | 10,200 | 165 |
| Total cost | $291,400 | $4,700 |

| DEVELOPMENT | |
|:---|---:|
| Construction cost | $291,400 |
| Planning and engineering ($186.50/lot) | 11,563 |
| Electric service ($350/lot) | 21,700 |
| Water service ($450/lot) | 27,900 |
| Gas service ($200/lot) | 12,400 |
| Sewer fee ($100/lot) | 6,200 |
| Subdivision bond (1.5% construction cost) | 4,371 |

| | | |
|---|---|---:|
| Advertising (2% sales price of lots) | | 16,470 |
| Contingency (10%) | | 39,200 |
| Sales commissions (6% sales price of lots) | | 49,410 |
| Land value ($4,000) 29.8 acres | | 119,200 |
| Total development cost (interest excluded) | | $599,814 |
| Proposed sales prices (lots) | | |
| 15 lots @ $18,000/lot (13,500 sq. ft./lot) | $270,000 | |
| 79 lots @ 13,500/lot (13,500 sq. ft./lot) | 391,500 | |
| 18 lots @ 9,000/lot (10,000 sq. ft./lot) | 162,000 | |
| Total sales price (lots) | | $823,500 |
| Projected profit (single-family lots, interest excluded) | | 233,686 |
| Per lot | | 3,590 |
| Per acre | | 7,469 |

# SECTION C

## Construction

50 lots

23.4 acres

Section C is the only section within the development where drainage is a primary factor and which will require considerable expense in construction costs for subdivision development. A 4-foot by 8-foot box culvert is required underneath the 60-foot collector street for half the distance from the golf course to Rust Road. A 48- and 60-inch concrete pipe is required for the remaining distance underneath the 60-foot collector street to handle storm drainage that enters the development from the east side of Scott Road. Street improvements include construction of the collector street (60 feet wide) and a segment of Scott Road, a major road. The cost of the sanitary sewer pressure line has been prorated to Section C on the basis of the number of lots in Section C to the total number of lots in Sections A, B, and C. The high cost of sanitary sewers is attributed to the requirement of construction of a sewer line from the pumping station to the west edge of the golf course, then to the collector street, Lake Road. This line will provide service to remaining sections in the development, which will attribute to lower sanitary sewer costs in other adjacent sections.

| DESCRIPTION | COST | COST PER LOT |
|---|---|---|
| Site work | $ 22,000 | $  440 |
| Sanitary sewers | 53,300 | 1,066 |

| | | |
|---|---:|---:|
| Drainage | 34,200 | 684 |
| Street improvements | 121,720 | 2,434 |
| Extra: box culvert | 122,500 | 2,450 |
| concrete pipe | 79,000 | 1,580 |
| pressure line | 8,300 | 166 |
| Total cost | $441,020 | $8,820 |

## DEVELOPMENT

| | |
|---|---:|
| Construction cost | $441,020 |
| Planning and engineering ($186.50/lot) | 9,325 |
| Electric service ($350/lot) | 17,500 |
| Water service ($450/lot) | 22,500 |
| Gas service ($200/lot) | 10,000 |
| Sewer fee ($100/lot) | 5,000 |
| Subdivision bond (1.5% construction cost) | 6,615 |
| Advertising (2% sales price of lots) | 13,200 |
| Contingency (10%) | 52,516 |
| Sales commissions (6% sales price of lots) | 39,600 |
| Land value ($4,000) 23.4 acres | 93,600 |
| Total development cost (interest excluded) | $710,876 |

| Proposed sales prices (lots) | | |
|---|---:|---:|
| 4 lots @ $18,000/lot (13,500 sq. ft./lot) | $ 72,000 | |
| 3 lots @ 16,000/lot (13,500 sq. ft./lot) | 48,000 | |
| 34 lots @ 13,500/lot (13,500 sq. ft./lot) | 459,000 | |
| 9 lots @ 9,000/lot (10,000 sq. ft./lot) | 81,000 | |
| Total sales price (lots) | | $660,000 |
| Projected profit (single-family lots, interest excluded) | | − $ 50,876 |
| Per lot | | − 1,017 |
| Per acre | | − 2,174 |

# SECTION D–1

## Construction

### 31 lots

### 12.6 acres

Section D–1 will involve no high costs for development. Street improvements only involve minor streets, there is no unusual site work required, and no significant drainage is involved within the section. A sanitary sewer line will need to be constructed along the east edge of the golf course to a point in the sanitary sewer line serving Section A located in the proximity of the pumping station.

| DESCRIPTION | COST | COST PER LOT |
|---|---|---|
| Site work | $ 5,600 | $ 180 |
| Sanitary sewers | 30,800 | 993 |
| Drainage | 31,800 | 1,025 |
| Street improvements | 45,240 | 1,459 |
| Total cost | $113,440 | $3,657 |

| DEVELOPMENT | |
|---|---|
| Construction cost | $113,440 |
| Planning and engineering ($186.50/lot) | 5,781 |
| Electric service ($350/lot) | 10,850 |
| Water service ($450/lot) | 13,950 |
| Gas service ($200/lot) | 6,200 |
| Sewer fee ($100/lot) | 3,100 |
| Subdivision bond (1.5% construction cost) | 1,701 |
| Advertising (2% sales price of lots) | 9,000 |
| Contingency (10%) | 16,402 |
| Sales commissions (6% sales price of lots) | 27,000 |
| Land value ($4,000) 12.6 acres | 50,400 |
| Total development cost (interest excluded) | $257,824 |

| Proposed sales prices (lots) | | |
|---|---|---|
| 7 lots @ $18,000/lot (13,500 sq. ft./lot) | $126,000 | |
| 24 lots @ 13,500/lot (13,500 sq. ft./lot) | 324,000 | |
| Total sales price (lots) | | $450,000 |
| Projected profit (single-family lots, interest excluded) | | $192,176 |
| Per lot | | 6,199 |
| Per acre | | 15,252 |

# SECTION D-2

## Construction

34 lots

15.8 acres

This section has no unusual requirements. Site work will require some clearing of trees within road rights-of-way because this section is heavily wooded. Street improvements include construction of a 60-foot collector street, Lake Road, with remaining road construction involving only minor streets. Sanitary sewers will require minimal construction because sewers in this section will tie into the line along the west edge of the golf course, which was constructed to serve Section C.

| DESCRIPTION | COST | COST PER LOT |
|---|---|---|
| Site work | $ 14,200 | $ 418 |
| Sanitary sewers | 27,200 | 800 |
| Drainage | 38,600 | 1,135 |
| Street improvements | 58,980 | 1,735 |
| Total cost | $138,980 | $4,088 |

| DEVELOPMENT | |
|---|---|
| Construction cost | $138,980 |
| Planning and engineering ($186.50/lot) | 6,341 |
| Electric service ($350/lot) | 11,900 |
| Water service ($450/lot) | 15,300 |
| Gas service ($200/lot) | 6,800 |
| Sewer fee ($100/lot) | 3,400 |
| Subdivision bond (1.5% construction cost) | 2,085 |
| Advertising (2% sales price of lots) | 10,800 |
| Contingency (10%) | 19,560 |
| Sales commissions (6% sales price of lots) | 32,400 |
| Land value ($4,000) 15.8 acres | 63,200 |
| Total development cost (interest excluded) | $310,766 |

Proposed sales prices (lots)

| | | |
|---|---|---|
| 6 lots @ $20,000/lot (15,000 sq. ft./lot) | $120,000 | |
| 28 lots @ 15,000/lot (15,000 sq. ft./lot) | 420,000 | |
| Total sales price (lots) | | $540,000 |
| Projected profit (single-family lots, interest excluded) | | 229,234 |
| Per lot | | 6,742 |
| Per acre | | 14,508 |

# SECTION E

# Construction

### 61 lots

### 28.5 acres

This section requires draining and filling of an existing 7-acre lake. Street improvements include construction of a 60-foot collector street, Lake Road, and a segment of Washington Road, a major road.

| DESCRIPTION | COST | COST PER LOT |
|---|---|---|
| Site work | $ 15,600 | $ 256 |
| Sanitary sewers | 51,200 | 839 |
| Drainage | 80,900 | 1,326 |
| Street improvements | 218,160 | 2,101 |
| Extra (lake fill) | 12,000 | 197 |
| Total cost | $377,860 | $4,719 |

| DEVELOPMENT | | |
|---|---|---|
| Construction cost | | $287,860 |
| Planning and engineering ($186.50/lot) | | 11,376 |
| Electric service ($350/lot) | | 21,350 |
| Water service ($450/lot) | | 27,450 |
| Gas service ($200/lot) | | 12,200 |
| Sewer fee ($100/lot) | | 6,100 |
| Subdivision bond (1.5% construction cost) | | 4,318 |
| Advertising (2% sales price of lots) | | 14,160 |
| Contingency (10%) | | 38,481 |
| Sales commissions (6% sales price of lots) | | 42,480 |
| Land value ($4,000) 28.5 acres | | 114,000 |
| Total development cost (interest excluded) | | $579,775 |
| Proposed sales prices (lots) | | |
| 26 lots @ $13,500/lot (13,500 sq. ft./lot) | $351,000 | |
| 7 lots @ 15,000/lot (15,000 sq. ft./lot) | 105,000 | |
| 28 lots @ 9,000/lot (10,000 sq. ft./lot) | 252,000 | |
| Total sales price (lots) | | $708,000 |
| Projected profit (single-family lots, interest excluded) | | $128,225 |
| Per lot | | 2,102 |
| Per acre | | 4,499 |

# SECTION F

## Construction

### 58 lots

### 29.2 acres

Section F has no unusual requirements for development. Site work
will involve clearing of trees within road rights-of-way because this section
is heavily wooded. Street improvements include construction of a 60-foot
collector street. Sanitary sewers require minimal construction because sew-

ers in this section, like Section D–2, tie into the sewer line constructed for Section C along the west line of the golf course.

| DESCRIPTION | COST | COST PER LOT |
|---|---|---|
| Site work | $ 22,100 | $   381 |
| Sanitary sewers | 55,000 | 948 |
| Drainage | 70,900 | 1,222 |
| Street improvements | 107,200 | 1,848 |
| Total cost | $255,200 | $4,399 |

| DEVELOPMENT | |
|---|---|
| Construction cost | $255,200 |
| Planning and engineering ($186.50/lot) | 10,817 |
| Electric service ($350/lot) | 20,300 |
| Water service ($450/lot) | 26,100 |
| Gas service ($200/lot) | 11,600 |
| Sewer fee ($100/lot) | 5,800 |
| Subdivision bond (1.5% construction cost) | 3,828 |
| Advertising (2% sales price of lots) | 19,300 |
| Contingency (10%) | 35,295 |
| Sales commissions (6% sales price of lots) | 57,900 |
| Land value ($4,000) 29.2 acres | 116,800 |
| Total development cost (interest excluded) | $562,940 |

Proposed sales prices (lots)
19  lots @ $20,000/lot (15,000  sq. ft./lot)     $380,000
39  lots @   15,000/lot (15,000  sq. ft./lot)        585,000

| Total sales price (lots) | $965,000 |
|---|---|
| Projected profit (single-family lots, interest excluded) | $402,060 |
| Per lot | 6,932 |
| Per acre | 13,769 |

# SECTION G

# Construction

## 36 lots

## 18.0 acres

Site work in this section will require some clearing of trees within road rights-of-way because the majority of the section is wooded with rolling topography. Street improvements will require construction of a segment of a major road, Scott Road. Sanitary sewers will connect to the sewer line located in the collector street serving Section C.

| DESCRIPTION | COST | COST PER LOT |
|---|---|---|
| Site work | $ 12,600 | $ 350 |
| Sanitary sewers | 34,200 | 950 |
| Drainage | 50,600 | 1,406 |
| Street improvements | 66,380 | 1,843 |
| Total cost | $163,780 | $4,549 |

### DEVELOPMENT

| | |
|---|---|
| Construction cost | $163,870 |
| Planning and engineering ($186.50/lot) | 6,714 |
| Electric service ($350/lot) | 12,600 |
| Water service ($450/lot) | 16,200 |
| Gas service ($200/lot) | 7,200 |
| Sewer fee ($100/lot) | 3,600 |
| Subdivision bond (1.5% construction cost) | 2,457 |
| Advertising (2% sales price of lots) | 8,640 |
| Contingency (10%) | 20,499 |
| Sales commissions (6% sales price of lots) | 25,920 |
| Land value ($4,000) 18.0 acres | 72,000 |
| Total development cost (interest excluded) | $339,700 |

| | | |
|---|---|---|
| Proposed sales prices (lots) | | |
| 36 lots @ $12,000/lot (15,000 sq. ft./lot) | $432,000 | |
| Total sales price (lots) | | $432,000 |
| Projected profit (single-family lots, interest excluded) | | $108,590 |
| Per lot | | 3,016 |
| Per acre | | 6,032 |

# SECTION H

## Construction

### 38 lots

### 13.5 acres

This section requires no major development costs. Street improvements involve only minor streets. Site work is minimal with some minor clearing of trees in road rights-of-way because only a portion of this section is wooded. Sanitary sewers will connect to the sewer line located in the collector street, which was constructed in Section C.

| DESCRIPTION | COST | COST PER LOT |
|---|---|---|
| Site work | $ 9,900 | $ 261 |
| Sanitary sewers | 22,400 | 589 |
| Drainage | 35,000 | 921 |
| Street improvements | 48,680 | 1,281 |
| Total cost | $115,980 | $3,052 |

### DEVELOPMENT

| | |
|---|---|
| Construction cost | $115,980 |
| Planning and engineering ($186.50/lot) | 7,087 |
| Electric service ($350/lot) | 13,300 |
| Water service ($450/lot) | 17,100 |
| Gas service ($200/lot) | 7,600 |
| Sewer fee ($100/lot) | 3,800 |
| Subdivision bond (1.5% construction cost) | 1,740 |
| Advertising (2% sales price of lots) | 6,840 |
| Contingency (10%) | 17,345 |
| Sales commissions (6% sales price of lots) | 20,520 |
| Land value ($4,000) 13.5 acres | 54,000 |
| Total development cost (interest excluded) | $265,312 |
| Proposed sales prices (lots) | |
| 38 lots @ $ 9,000/lot (10,000 sq. ft./lot)  $342,000 | |
| Total sales price (lots) | $342,000 |
| Projected profit (single-family lots, interest excluded) | $ 76,688 |
| Per lot | 2,018 |
| Per acre | 5,681 |

# SECTION I

## Construction

### 73 lots

### 25.5 acres

This section will require substantial costs in street improvements, which involve the construction of a major road, Washington Road–Scott Road. No unusually high development costs are associated with site work, drainage, and sanitary sewers. Sanitary sewers for Section I will connect with lines located in the collector street, developed in Section C, and in Lake Road, developed in Section E.

| DESCRIPTION | COST | COST PER LOT |
|---|---|---|
| Site work | $ 12,100 | $ 166 |
| Sanitary sewers | 40,100 | 549 |
| Drainage | 90,800 | 1,244 |
| Street improvements | 131,020 | 1,795 |
| Total cost | $274,020 | $3,754 |

| DEVELOPMENT | |
|---|---|
| Construction cost | $274,020 |
| Planning and engineering ($186.50/lot) | 13,615 |
| Electric service ($350/lot) | 25,550 |
| Water service ($450/lot) | 32,852 |
| Gas service ($200/lot) | 14,600 |
| Sewer fee ($100/lot) | 7,300 |
| Subdivision bond (1.5% construction cost) | 4,110 |
| Advertising (2% sales price of lots) | 13,140 |
| Contingency (10%) | 38,519 |
| Sales commissions (6% sales price of lots) | 39,420 |
| Land value ($4,000) 25.5 acres | 102,000 |
| Total development cost (interest excluded) | $565,126 |
| Proposed sales prices (lots) | |
| 73 lots @ $ 9,000/lot (10,000 sq. ft./lot)       $657,000 | |
| Total sales price (lots) | $657,000 |
| Projected profit (single-family lots, interest excluded) | $130,390 |
| Per lot | 1,786 |
| Per acre | 5,113 |

# SECTION J

## Construction

### 4.7 commercial site

This section consists of 4.7 acres of commercial property. A small amount of site work will be required with substantial street improvements for construction of Washington Road, a major road, which offers frontage on the north side of the site. Street improvements will be required on the old alignment of Washington Road, east side of the site, and existing Scott

Road, south side of the site, to handle traffic flow into and out of the major road and around the neighborhood commercial center.

| DESCRIPTION | COST |
|---|---|
| Site work | $ 10,791 |
| Drainage | 49,025 |
| Street improvements | 50,045 |
| Total cost | $109,861 |

## DEVELOPMENT

| | |
|---|---|
| Construction cost | $109,861 |
| Planning and engineering ($186.50/lot) | 2,200 |
| Electric service ($350/lot) | |
| Water service ($450/lot) | |
| Gas service ($200/lot) | |
| Sewer fee ($100/lot) | |
| Subdivision bond (1.5% construction cost) | 1,648 |
| Advertising (2% sales price of lots) | 4,095 |
| Contingency (10%) | 11,780 |
| Sales commissions (6% sales price of lots) | 12,284 |
| Land value ($4,000) 4.7 acres | 18,800 |
| Total development cost (interest excluded) | $160,668 |

| Proposed sales (other) | | | | |
|---|---|---|---|---|
| Apartment | acres @ | /acre | * | |
| Townhouse | acres @ | /acre | * | |
| | acres @ | /acre | * | |
| Commercial | 4.7 acres @ $70,000/acre | | $329,000* | |
| School and park site | acres @ | /acre | * | |

| | |
|---|---|
| Total proposed sales (other) | |
| Less land value ($4,000/acre) | |
| Less sales commissions (6% sales price) | |
| Less total development cost | $160,688 |
| Total projected profit (other) | 168,332 |
| Projected profit/acre | $ 35,815 |

# SECTION K

## Construction

6.8-acre townhouse site

6.6-acre apartment site

This section consists of a 6.8-acre townhouse site and a 6.6-acre apartment site. Construction costs for this section would involve street improvements for widening Washington Road, a major road, which offers frontage on the east side of the sites. The 68-foot street, which is on the west side of the parcels, will already be improved as part of the development costs for Section A.

Construction costs for this section, estimated to be $47,663, have not been included in the cost-revenue projections. The buyer of these tracts will have the responsibility of the construction costs for Washington Road at the time these two parcels are developed for apartments and townhouses.

Proposed sales

| | |
|---|---:|
| 6.6 acres, apartments @ $20,000/acre | $132,000 |
| 6.8 acres, townhouses @ $20,000/acre | 136,000 |
| Total proposed sales | $268,000 |
| Less land value ($4,000/acre) | 53,600 |
| Less sales commissions (6% sales price) | 16,080 |
| Total projected profit | $198,320 |
| Projected profit/acre | $ 14,800 |

# INDEX